DEATH OF INNOCENCE

"A thoughtful examination... It raises serious questions, and it effectively demonstrates there are no inexpensive answers. A powerful book, it deserves reading by policy makers and the public."

—*Best Sellers*

"A solid crime story... though not for the squeamish ... Meyer handles the basic material capably and sensitively."

—*Kirkus Reviews*

"An important book... Meyer, an accomplished journalist, does a masterful job of presenting the details in this landmark case."

—*Topeka Capital-Journal*

"Raises disturbing questions about juvenile violence and its appropriate punishment."

—*Publishers Weekly*

DEATH OF INNOCENCE

"A clearly written account of the heartbreaking events: the gruesome crime, the detective work leading to the arrests, the revelations that a minor could not be punished for his part..."

—*Washington Post*

"Thorough and diligent... earnest and sympathetic."

—**Baltimore** *Sun*

"Meyer's book is a sensitive though gruesome account of the attack and a thought-provoking record of society's attitudes toward juvenile offenders. It is also a thorough interpretation of the way a criminal's mind works and how individuals can make a difference in their communities' laws..."

—*The State*
Columbia, South Carolina

"... brings the trauma back to life with a vivid retelling of the events."

—*Burlington Free Press*

DEATH OF INNOCENCE

"Grisly . . . stunning effectiveness . . . Meyer not only meticulously recounts the crime in all its horror, but he also furnishes a wealth of background on the victims, their assailants and key figures involved in the case."

—*San Diego Union*

"A briskly-told real-life thriller."

—*Herald-Dispatch*,
Huntington, West Virginia

"Journalist and author Peter Meyer has dealt with emotional issues in a no-nonsense way, presenting details of the crime without appearing sleazy and dealing with complex legal theories in a complete and understandable way."

—*Houston Post*

"Dramatic . . . thorough . . . vividly horrifying."

—*The Flint Journal*

DEATH of INNOCENCE

Berkley books by Peter Meyer

THE YALE MURDER
DEATH OF INNOCENCE

DEATH of INNOCENCE

A CASE OF MURDER IN VERMONT

Peter Meyer

BERKLEY BOOKS, NEW YORK

DEATH OF INNOCENCE:
A CASE OF MURDER IN VERMONT

A Berkley Book / published by arrangement with
G. P. Putnam's Sons

PRINTING HISTORY
G. P. Putnam's Sons edition / April 1985
Berkley edition / July 1986

ISBN: 0-425-10172-X

A BERKLEY BOOK ® TM 757,375
Berkley Books are published by The Berkley Publishing Group,
200 Madison Avenue, New York, NY 10016.
The name "BERKLEY" and the stylized "B" with design
are trademarks belonging to Berkley Publishing Corporation.

PRINTED IN THE UNITED STATES OF AMERICA

10   9   8   7   6   5   4   3

ACKNOWLEDGMENTS

I am indebted to many people for their contributions to the accuracy of this book.

Mark Keller and Susan Via, the Chittenden County States Attorney and his Deputy, gave freely of their time; as did Christopher Davis and Rusty Valsangiacomo, Louis Hamlin's defense attorneys.

Reconstructing the details of the massive manhunt for Meghan O'Rourke's and Melissa Walbridge's attackers would not have been possible without the assistance of numerous Vermont police officers, especially Robbie Yandow and Gary Taylor of the Essex Police Department, Nick Ruggiero and Robert Horton of the Vermont State Police, and Lee Graham of the South Burlington Police Department.

Hope Spencer and Carol Hathaway shared with me their experiences as leaders of the petition drive to change the state's juvenile law. Scores of other Vermont residents also offered their time, an invaluable aid in understanding the impact of this crime on the people and the institutions of the state.

In both Burlington and Essex Junction dozens of friends and neighbors, teachers, classmates, and relatives of Louis Hamlin and Jamie Savage cooperated with my research in the hope of making the description of the two teenagers' lives truthful and complete.

There are scores of other people who contributed their time and expertise to the making of this book—detectives, social workers, doctors, lawyers, psychiatrists, shopkeepers, law enforcement officers, politicians, librarians, and court officials. Without their help it would have been impossible to reconstruct the complexities of this case.

And I am especially grateful to those for whom the remembering meant only pain.

Finally, my thanks to Judy Cota for transcribing the many hours of tape-recorded interviews; to Belle Ballantyne for her administrative support; and to Martin L. Gross, my editor and friend.

TO THE MEMORY OF MELISSA WALBRIDGE
WHOSE LIFE WAS TOO SHORT

Contents

The Death of Innocence

The violence was brutal and youthful, and everywhere it struck—in the chest, the head, or the back, in the living room or bedroom or on the street corner, in Los Angeles or Long Island—there was blood that trailed off into some unanswerable question.

A 13-year-old boy shot his 42-year-old mother on Dec. 1 after a heated argument in the family's home on Long Island. The argument was said to have been over his refusal to go to school that day. . . . The boy told the court how he had gone to the attic and grabbed his father's .41 caliber revolver after the argument.

"Was the gun loaded?" asked the judge.

"No, I loaded it," the boy said. "Then I went downstairs. My mother was on the phone. I told her to get off. She didn't, and I shot her."

They were thirteen and fifteen and younger, and no one knew quite what to call them: "boys," "girls," "teenagers," "youth," "children." But the labels of mischievous innocence did not seem to fit any better than their parents' old clothes.

Their upper lips were often still fuzzy with adolescence, and yet they captured headlines for the razor blades, knives, or shotguns in their hands. Aphorisms about turning swords into plowshares were turned on their heads; and playthings, still in the hands of children, were turned into murder weapons.

A sixteen-year-old boy believed his fifteen-year-old girlfriend was pregnant with his child and beat her to death with a shovel and baseball bat. . . .

Ths maliciousness of their violence became all the more shocking as it violated the image of innocent childhood.

Authorities in a small California town had never seen such a case of bleak amorality and callousness. Last month, they report, a teenage boy bragged to friends about strangling his former girlfriend, and then invited them out to see the body. One onlooker tossed a stone at the corpse; another helped to hide it; for two days no one notified the authorities. . . .

In one year, 1982, more than 1,500 juveniles were charged with murder. Youngsters under eighteen now commit one-fourth of all the violent crimes in America. There was rape and robbery, kidnaping, hijacking, infanticide, patricide, and matricide. In Texas, the president of an oil and gas company and his wife were shot to death, not by a burglar, but by their sixteen-year-old son. The youngsters seemed to have little remorse or second thoughts about their adolescent behavior; the violent actions were self-indulgent, mindless, reckless, and in that they retained the vestiges of childishness.

They wore children's clothes and spoke with children's tongues and played children's games. They lived in the world of the immediate and fantastic, still ignorant of the concept of consequences, and unaware or unconcerned that murder is not a game, that death is forever.

They were children, but their acts were no longer the minor peccadilloes of the "good ole days," the days of "troublesome lads."

A 13-year-old girl who wandered into a park area where children were playing was raped for 40 minutes by two youths.... A group of youths crowded around and watched. People picnicking nearby ignored the girl's screams. A 17-year-old boy and a juvenile have been arrested in the incident.

In South Carolina, the United States Attorney, citing such adult conditions as "malice aforethought" and "intent to do bodily harm," charged a five-year-old boy with the murder of a five-year-old girl. Everywhere the record books were continuously being amended as the age of violent criminals descended, often below the limits of imagination.

When a pretty 12-year-old junior high school student walked tearfully out of a courtroom here this spring, she became the youngest person ever convicted of murder in New Mexico.

A twelve-year-old convicted of murder? Was there no longer a sensible line of separation between children and adults?

One young man was only fourteen when he fired a shotgun into the mouth of his foster mother. He was convicted of murder in an adult court, but before he was sentenced his attorney pleaded for leniency. "I would submit that society bears a great deal of responsibility for what this boy has done," he argued, "not directly, but there is only so much that we can expect from teenagers, especially one who has been shifted from foster home to foster home."

The boy was still just fifteen when sentenced to life in prison. "I have no alternative. I have to protect society," said the judge. "This young man has demonstrated qualities that a fifteen-year-old should not have. I consider him a danger to society."

With this violence has come the death of innocence, the

disappearance of an essential, mystical, fulfilling childhood, and the emergence of children who are no longer young yet not mature enough to have empathy or compassion. Childhood, it seems, has entered a state of profound confusion. Juvenile crime, particularly such serious offenses as rape and murder, is the horrific end product.

In this story of four young people in Vermont, two criminals and two victims, we will perhaps see what went wrong and what values there are left that can repair an injured society.

PETER MEYER
New York City
August 1984

DEATH of INNOCENCE

CHAPTER 1

"That Wouldn't Happen in Vermont"

BY THE TIME Melissa Walbridge and Meghan O'Rourke left the Lawton Middle School that Friday afternoon, most of their friends had gone home. Outside, the two sixth-graders met a chilled breeze blowing across the knoll on which the small school perched. Though the rain that had been falling intermittently all day had now stopped, the sky that stretched to the peak of nearby Mount Mansfield was still quilted with dense coffee-gray clouds.

Meghan and Melissa ignored the sodden ground and dreary sky as they moved across the slope of lawn in front of the school. Despite their wispy frames, the two twelve-year-olds were accustomed to the often granite-rough climate of their native Vermont, walking more than a mile and a half to and from school almost every day, even in blizzard-driven drifts of snow. Now that winter had completed its slow curve into spring, the walk was fun. By May the ragged stands of maple had

1

turned into a deep blanket of velvet green.

The two girls often walked home with a group of friends, but this Friday Meghan had to deliver a report to her music teacher. Too shy to intrude, she and Melissa had waited politely for twenty minutes in an adjoining room until the instructor was free. The dark sky had prompted the other students to hurry home before the rain struck again, and Meghan and Melissa were now alone as they reached the base of the grassy hill in front of the school.

Watching carefully for cars, the girls moved across the road and onto the asphalt path that led into Maple Street Park. On fair days the spacious recreation area was busy with activity. Today, because of the rain and the "mud season," as Vermonters refer to the long, wet weeks that follow the winter thaw, the park was deserted.

On their right the girls passed the tarpaulin-covered Olympic swimming pool, still a month away from its annual summer opening. A pair of joggers from the IBM plant, distant figures against the soupy sky, padded slowly around the running path on the far side of the park. No one was in the playground area farther down the path, or on the tennis courts near the woods. The school baseball games had been canceled and the two diamonds were empty.

Despite the dreary weather and the absence of other children, Melissa and Meghan chatted excitedly as they walked toward the playground. They were in no hurry; afterschool was a special time for the two girls. They savored walking home slowly, dawdling in the park, sharing stories about their teachers and families and boyfriends.

The two girls were inseparable, and classmates rarely saw one without the other. Besides their daily trips to school they talked on the phone at night, went to horror movies together, and slept at each other's homes on weekends.

Still three months from her thirteenth birthday, Melissa was less than five feet tall and weighed only seventy-five pounds— "a pint," as her mother called her. Meghan was several inches shorter and just as thin. Named Meghan April in honor of her April 1st birthday, she had just turned twelve. Precocious and outgoing, blue-eyed, blond-haired Meghan had a small but

husky voice that seemed incongruous in such a slight body.
Like her older sister, then studying drama in Boston, Meghan
wanted to be an actress.

Missy, as Melissa was affectionately known, was an honor
student at Lawton and a model of industriousness. Today, she
confided to Meghan, she had been reprimanded for working
on her baby-sitting business cards during social studies class.
Meghan laughed boisterously; her talents were not in business,
but in the arts.

Passing the nearest ball field, Meghan and Melissa went
directly to the playground near the edge of the woods. They
passed the merry-go-round—"the snail"—then jumped onto
the swings. No one was in sight, and there were no sounds
except their own soft voices and the brush of wind through the
large stand of trees in front of them. Rocking slowly, they
continued to talk, their feet scuffing across the well-worn ground.

Meghan and Melissa were growing up in an almost idyllic
land, in a community concerned, sometimes obsessively, with
the welfare of its children. There were no porn shops in the
village of Essex Junction, Vermont, no "adult" theaters, no
prostitutes, no night-stalking muggers. Children could walk to
school along safe streets in unpolluted air. Unlike some other
parts of the country, marriage and child rearing were still a
commonplace tradition, and one-fourth of the town's population
was, like Melissa and Meghan, under thirteen years of age.

Essex was a model town within a model state. "Eight years
ago," an immigrant to the state remarked, "my wife and I came
to Vermont to raise our children, much as people would go to
Kentucky to raise racehorses, or to California to raise their
consciousness."

In its long history Essex had rarely been the scene of violence. The town had not even bothered to build a jail until the
1870s, and the small building—two cells and a room upstairs
for the jailkeeper—collected more dust than prisoners over the
years. As late as 1927 the annual town report indicated the
paucity of crime: "4 arrests made: 2 vagrancies, 1 Chinaman,
1 smuggler." By 1938 the jail had been dismantled, never to
be replaced.

Even in 1980, with a population that had more than quad-rupled in fifty years, Essex maintained its aura of peace. When Bill and Dorothy Sole were robbed in December of that year, the Boston *Globe* sent a reporter to Essex to investigate. WHEN CITY TERROR HIT TOWN the paper headlined the ensuing story.

"This is a very quiet place," explained a local resident. "Nothing happens here. We have our drunks in town, a few vagrants, a couple of people on welfare who sometimes wander around, but never more than one or two."

Not the least of Essex's assets was its prosperity. A third of the town's families had annual incomes of $30,000 or more. From where they now stood in Maple Street Park, Melissa and Meghan could see one of the secrets to the small town's afflu-ence. Just across the railroad tracks, IBM had staked out a giant 8,000-employee industrial complex, its subdued smoke-stacks, parking lots, and landscaped grounds spreading almost invisibly over hundreds of acres through Essex Junction along the banks of the winding Winooski River.

Nestled in a valley in northwestern Vermont, between the great Lake Champlain to the west and a high ridge of mountains to the east, Essex was a civilized retreat in "a state," as poet Robert Frost once remarked, "in a very natural state." Vermont remained faithful to its French-given name, a land of *verts monts*, "green mountains," that stretched like a backbone from the Canadian border south to Massachusetts.

In 1981, Vermont still wore the title of the nation's "most rural" state. It was still a place of quiet havens for those seeking an escape from frantic urban life. Even in Burlington, the closest facsimile of a city—sitting along the banks of Lake Champlain—there were fewer than 40,000 people.

Essex (six miles from Burlington by way of the Winooski), with only 14,000 people, was the fourth largest town in Ver-mont. Even that label seems to exaggerate the size of the com-munity: With its silky web of sedate Victorian homes and wide, proper New England lawns, Essex was as quiet as a village.

From the town center it was only a five-minute drive to even more tranquil countryside, where narrow two-lane roads pitted by "frost heaves" twisted between low hills and grazing Herefords. The beaches and boat docks of Malletts Bay and

Lake Champlain were fifteen minutes to the north and west; winter skiing, a half hour to the east, by Adler Brook and South Hill into the mountains by Starbridge Ridge and Birnies Nose and Smugglers Notch; cross-country skiing no farther than the back door.

"The only things that normally disturb the peace of this old farming town," a Boston reporter once remarked, "are the sound of the Winooski River or the rumble of freight cars clattering along the Central Vermont."

As a slight drizzle now fell on the park, Meghan and Melissa debated which route to take home. They spoke about the short-cut through the woods, which would bring them to the railroad tracks and directly into town, cutting some five or ten minutes off their trip. School officials, fearing an accident in the dense and isolated vegetation, had told Lawton students not to use the woods, but the warning was universally ignored. Now that Maple Street was under construction and the alternate route to the village center even farther out of the way, teachers had relaxed their already loose enforcement of the rule.

No, Meghan said, suddenly serious, they should avoid the woods. Now it was Melissa's turn to laugh. She told Meghan not to worry. They had used the path through the trees many times, not only as a shortcut, but to add a touch of wilderness to their imagined adventures.

But Meghan persisted. She reminded Missy of the previous Wednesday when the two men had chased her. Out loud, Meghan now wondered whether they might not return.

Missy had not been with Meghan on Wednesday; she had to race home to get the cake ready for her mother's birthday party, leaving Meghan to walk home by herself. It had been a dreary, wet day—just like today. Not long after Meghan had started down the familiar path through the woods, she noticed two men standing in the bushes between the trees, facing each other but not speaking.

They made Meghan uneasy. One was tall, with kinky blond hair; the other was slightly smaller, dark-haired and bearded. Meghan thought the two, dressed in "messy, dirty clothes," looked "skuzzy." As she later recounted, "They looked like they'd been living in the woods or something."

Meghan quickened her pace, passing within a dozen yards of them. "I was too scared to look back."

She had heard a pop, what sounded like gravel or pellets hitting the trees beside her. The sixth-grader held her pace, walked a little farther, then turned a corner, running as fast as she could out of the woods onto the railroad tracks, where she dashed between two freight cars on a siding. "I was scared," she said later. "I just kept running for a while."

When she arrived home that Wednesday, Meghan called Melissa to tell her what had happened. A mutual friend, Heidi, who was at the Walbridges' at the time, heard the story on a phone extension, and all three girls talked excitedly about Meghan's exploit. "All she said was that they looked scary," remembered Heidi. "I didn't ask her, but I know what she meant. She meant they were frightening." Only a few other schoolmates knew of the incident; Meghan told neither her parents nor any other adult of the ominous strangers she had seen that day.

Now, on this misty Friday afternoon, at the edge of the same isolated woods, Melissa—who was aware of her friend's theatrical flair—tried to reassure Meghan. But as they talked, the two twelve-year-olds considered the possible implications of the event and innocently began to speak of crime and violence, rape and kidnaping.

Those who knew Melissa were aware that the serious little girl reacted strongly against violence. At home she would walk away from the television set if mayhem was being depicted on a show. "There was one thing she would always become angry about," her father recalled, "and that was rape. It made her very angry that a man would do that to someone. She couldn't fathom it."

In English class the week before, Melissa had surprised her classmates with an unexpected burst of verbosity. "For some reason we started talking about crime and violence and rape and molesting, stuff like that," a friend recollected. "Usually, Melissa didn't talk much in class. But when we got on that subject, suddenly she was very outgoing. She said that rape was the worst thing that could happen to anyone. She really,

really hated it. She couldn't see how a person could be that sick to do such a thing and it really bothered her. We always talked about it after that. She said that if it ever happened to her she would scream and kick and pound on them."

But, her friends also recalled, Missy had little fear of such violence in Essex Junction. She read the newspapers, watched television news, and talked with her parents. "She knew what happened in the big cities," remembered a classmate, "and she didn't think there was anyone that sick around here."

It was now almost four o'clock. The rain, finally coming down in earnest, convinced the girls to take the quick route home. Jumping off the swings, they pushed aside their fears and walked toward the woods, which by the middle of May were as much a densely woven hideaway as a shortcut.

A few hundred feet away, in the parking lot of Maple Street, two young friends of Meghan and Melissa were climbing into a car when they noticed the two girls on the swings in the distance. They considered calling to offer them a ride, but as they did, Meghan and Melissa disappeared into the trees.

The rain was falling in heavy sheets, but the canopy of limbs overhead offered Meghan and Melissa some protection as they started down the narrow path that laced through the underbrush. On their right the ground dropped steeply into a small ravine; along the muddy bottom a curving creek flowed rapidly with the spring rains. At their left was a thick warren of brush and scrub oak that discouraged entry.

For Meghan, since Wednesday, the woods had taken on a sinister sheen. Again she told Missy she was worried that the two men would come back.

As the rain trickled through the leaves, Meghan's clogs slipped across the ground. She held close to Missy, watching the branches heave, the shadows bend around one another, trifling with her fears.

"But what if they're there and they kidnap us and rape us," Meghan said.

Missy looked confidently at her friend. "No, Meghan. That wouldn't happen in Vermont."

CHAPTER 2

Blood on the Tracks

As RAILROAD FLAGMAN Alton Bruso surveyed the long line of freight cars strung along the Central Vermont tracks, he thought it odd that a little girl would be wearing a red bathing suit in the rain on this chilly May day.

He was not surprised to see a child near the train; many students from nearby Lawton Middle School in Essex Junction used the tracks as a shortcut home. The girl was on the path that ran next to the tracks, a few hundred feet from where Bruso stood, and seemed to be coming his way. But the train-man was preoccupied, his hand resting impatiently on the cross-over switch, anxious for the long caravan of cars to pull off the passenger track so he could get on with the trip home.

Bruso looked at his watch. It was 4:40 and getting late. He and the other members of the crew of Train 555 had started their day at eight that morning in White River Junction, almost a hundred miles to the south and east of Essex Junction, and it was still another thirty miles north to St. Albans, their terminus.

Bruso looked toward the train's engine, now pulling around the bend, and back to the caboose clattering slowly by the perimeter of Maple Street Park. In front of him, he could see the girl, now only fifty feet away. But this time Bruso held his gaze as he realized something was wrong. The tiny figure stumbling toward him was not wearing a bathing suit. The red he saw was not clothing, but blood. It seemed to cover her entire nude body.

Bruso immediately dropped his hand from the switch and bounded toward her, shouting "Stop the train!" into his walkie-talkie as he ran.

Ten feet away, Bruso heard the staggering girl whimper, "Please help me, sir. I've been raped," as she collapsed at his feet.

"Call the base!" Bruso screamed into his radio. "Tell them to get the police over here. There's a girl hurt." Looking down at the motionless body sprawled on the muddy path, Bruso added, "Send an ambulance, too. There's blood all over." In the center of her chest bubbles of bloodied air gurgled upward from a gaping hole.

The burly flagman bent and scooped the girl into his arms. As he tried to cradle her in a comfortable position, she moaned. Bruso lay one of her limp arms on his broad shoulder, and let the other curl around his neck. The blood from her chest wound was spilling onto the trainman in gushes, soaking first through his shirt, then his undershirt. Bruso started down the tracks, pressing the girl to his chest in a desperate attempt to control the flow of blood streaming from the hole. "I thought it would at least clot the blood," he recalled. "She was bleeding bad. She was bleeding very, very bad."

Howard Constantine, the brakeman working near the train's engine, had run toward Bruso as soon as he heard the radio call, while Alfred Laidman, the engineer, uncertain about what was going on, had immediately stopped the train. "I didn't know what was happening back there," Laidman said afterward. "I still hadn't seen them."

By this time Bruso had run the hundred yards to the engine

with the girl in his arms. Out of breath, he shouted up at Laidman, "Back the train up and maybe we can get her on." Laidman called back down to Constantine to pull the headpin on the locomotive and release it so that he would not have to pull the whole train with him as he backed up.

As Bruso aligned himself with the engine's cab, Laidman peered down from his perch, six feet up a vertical ladder, at the girl in Bruso's arms, but was unable to offer any help. The three men simultaneously came to the same conclusion: It would be impossible to get the injured girl into the cab. "The bars were straight up," Constantine pointed out. "We grab them to hold on, but when you got somebody in your arms, there ain't no way to get up."

Bruso, who was almost sixty, was exhausted from running with the near-lifeless weight. When he realized that the nearest open area accessible to an ambulance was still a hundred yards from the tracks, Constantine took the limp girl from Bruso and started running.

"She was off and on, you know what I mean," Constantine recalled. "She was conscious, but she had no clothes on and was covered with blood from head to feet. I kept her squeezed against me so the blood wouldn't come out of the cut in her chest. All I could think of was a dolphin hole. It opened and closed every time she'd breathe."

As the men crossed the last remnant of open ground and stepped onto the parking lot of the United Maple Products company, they could hear the girl struggling to talk, moaning the same phrase over and over.

"My friend," she whispered. "My friend."

Bruso leaned closer. "You mean another little girl?"

"My friend," she repeated hoarsely. "My friend is still in the woods."

Alton Bruso's walkie-talkie distress message unnerved the quiet Vermont town, more accustomed to stability than to the frenzy of crisis. In Essex Junction's six-room police station, the dispatcher, who had just logged a report about a missing white Siberian husky, quickly alerted the village's small emergency rescue network, which was mobilized within minutes.

Police Chief John Terry hurried into the squad room, where four officers—almost one-fourth the town's entire police force—were lounging around a battered table. Although unsure of the urgency of the distress call, Terry dispatched all four to the United Maple Products lot, only a few hundred yards from the station house.

Volunteer rescue captain Wayne Eells, then in the squad's new garage off Main Street, ran to his car. Judy Stafford, who was both a nurse and a rescue squad crew captain, had just picked up her son and his friends at the Lawton School because rain had forced the cancellation of the baseball game. Driving down Maple Street, she heard her dashboard radio squawk. "They said there was a girl on the railroad tracks covered with blood. I knew it was critical. But in this community, you think that probably someone tripped and fell."

Robbie Yandow was confused when he heard the emergency call. Driving home, the new lieutenant of the Essex police was trying to decide whether to wear his foul-weather suit to jog in. The garbled radio account did not initially seem urgent. "They said there was a kid who'd been seriously assaulted," Yandow recalled. "I thought someone had the bejesus kicked out of him by another kid and that maybe they needed me to take pictures because I had the color camera with me."

But as radio reports provided more details, Yandow pushed the cruiser faster. In the next few minutes, the force of the tragedy became clear. The emergency vehicles raced onto Elm Street, brakes scattering gravel and mud, lights assaulting the mist. Residents came out of their Victorian frame homes and stood in their front yards in the drizzle, questioning expressions on their faces as the cars raced by. Carol Hathaway asked a neighbor if she knew what was happening. "No, but I'll check my scanner," the other woman responded.

Carrying an emergency jump kit, Wayne Eells arrived just as Bruso and Constantine approached the lot with the frail young body. The police officers in their squad cars skidded to a stop behind Eells, Judy Stafford pulling in moments later. Everyone was soon running toward the men, who had the bleeding girl between them, their arms intertwined in a fireman's carry.

The exhausted railroad men softly laid the semiconscious girl down on a blanket. Eells took a quick look at the victim and surmised that she had been badly burned, but Judy Stafford, now bent close to the girl, realized that the injury was more sinister. Without looking up, she told Police Chief Terry, "This child has a knife wound." Stafford worked fervently on the girl, immediately triaging the wound to control the bleeding.

In shock, the girl offered little sign that she knew what was going on about her. Her eyes were large, dry, and completely red. She was not crying and did not appear to be reacting at all to her wound.

"She was in real rough shape," remembered Michael Bolduc, one of the four police officers dispatched to the emergency. "She was very pale, real pale."

The girl was lifted into the ambulance, which had just arrived with a half dozen volunteers. Radioing Code 3—serious emergency—the driver raced to the Medical Center Hospital of Vermont in Burlington. Though moaning with pain, the young girl was conscious during the ten-minute ride. Eells leaned close and asked her name. "Meghan O'Rourke," she answered, almost inaudibly. In a labored breath, she asked if they had found her friend.

"Who is your friend?" asked Eells.

"Melissa Walbridge."

The assault suddenly hit home for Judy Stafford. Missy Walbridge was one of her daughter's best friends. Up until that moment, Stafford was unaware that the injured girl was even a classmate of her daughter's. "She was so battered, so covered with blood, her hair so matted down, that I couldn't have said who it was," Stafford later explained.

Eells told Meghan that the police were having difficulty finding Melissa. Meghan grimaced, then, in a painful whisper, said they had taken the path through the woods to the railroad tracks.

"Do you know the person that attacked you?" Eells prodded gently.

"No," Meghan responded.

"Was it a man—an adult—that did this to you?"

"Yes."

Eells hoped for more information, but Meghan could not continue. "Could you wait and ask me questions later?" the child whispered.

"She was exceptionally together," remembered the rescue crew chief. "It was amazing she could talk at all."

Eells radioed the Essex police, deciding to risk broadcasting Melissa's name. "We normally don't like to do that before the relatives are notified," Judy Stafford explained. "This is Scannerville, U.S.A. Every Mr. and Mrs. John Q. Public has one of those scanners. But we had to radio it in because Missy could have been out there in the woods wandering around in shock."

The police dispatcher had logged the message in at 4:56 P.M., only eleven minutes after the first call had come from the railroad station. "Confirmed second victim," noted the dispatcher, "name is Melissa Walbridge; assailant was adult male."

Marie Walbridge jumped at the phone, hoping it was Melissa. She and her husband, Eric, had been concerned about their daughter since four o'clock. It was not like her to be a full hour late in coming home. The rain had been steady for the past half hour, and the Walbridges thought it unlikely their daughter would still be out playing.

Mrs. Walbridge assumed that Melissa was at Meghan's house. "She didn't mention that they were going to Meghan's after school," Mrs. Walbridge explained. "But I figured that was because she had gone out with Meghan early and they didn't have a chance to tell me."

Now some eight hours later, the phone rang just as the worried Walbridges were considering what to do. It was Heidi, one of Melissa's friends, with some unsettling news. "She said her brother had heard on the scanner about two girls attacked on the railroad tracks," Mrs. Walbridge recalled.

"I know it's Meghan and Melissa," Heidi said nervously.

But Marie Walbridge, aware that twelve-year-olds could be overly dramatic, tried to calm the little girl. "Now, Heidi," she said, "that's a very terrible thing, but I'm sure it's not them."

Heidi continued excitedly, saying that it could have been Meghan and Melissa because that was the route they always took. Mrs. Walbridge grew more concerned, but consoled Heidi. She was sure that Melissa had gone to the O'Rourkes'. "I'll call you back," she told Heidi. "I'll get in touch with Melissa and Meghan at Meghan's house and I'll call you back and tell you they're okay."

Less than a mile away, Essex Police Officers Michael Bolduc and Gary Taylor were racing down the rain-slicked railroad tracks toward Maple Street Park in search of the second girl. With only sketchy information to guide them, they hurriedly glanced over the brush and into the trees on both sides of the track as they moved on. When they reached the woods at the edge of the park, the two men split up. Bolduc searched the path that ran along the ravine to the left, through the middle of the woods; Taylor took the wider path, running parallel to the first, along the outside of the woods.

Bolduc had gone only a couple of hundred feet when he encountered a man walking in the opposite direction. The policeman gave the stranger, dressed in a three-piece suit and carrying an umbrella and attaché case, a quick glance and assumed that he worked at the nearby IBM plant. He asked the man if he had seen anyone coming out of the woods. No, the man responded, but pointed out a smaller path that led deeper into the woods, telling the officer that kids often played in there on their way home from school. The policeman plunged into the brush.

About twenty feet along this path, Bolduc came to a small clearing whose ground, he noticed, was freshly scuffed. The leaves, which should have been peacefully rotting into mulch, were torn. It was obvious there had been a struggle here recently. To one side Bolduc saw a small clog, caked with fresh mud.

A few yards farther, through the branches of brush, Bolduc could see what appeared to be another small clearing. The spindly wet twigs slapped at his face as he moved toward it, the leaves loosening cold drops of water over his shoulders. His pants were now soaked from the wetness of the thick brush. As he ducked under the last limbs protecting the perimeter of the small opening, Bolduc knew that he had found the spot.

Two wet and mildewed foam-rubber mattresses were on the ground. Beer cans, liquor bottles, shreds of old notebook paper, and cigarette butts were scattered around. The mattress on the far edge of the clearing bulged in the middle, as if someone had crawled out from under it. Almost at Bolduc's feet was a second mattress. He felt an instantaneous flutter in his chest. Protruding from under one edge of the soggy material was a tiny arm and the top of a little girl's head.

"I found her!" Bolduc screamed as he leaned toward the figure. His voice hammered against the web of silent vegetation. "I found her!" he shouted again.

Patrolman Taylor froze in place. He was standing only two dozen yards from Bolduc, but he could not see him through the thickness of the trees. Taylor hesitated momentarily before pushing directly through the wet brush toward the shouting voice. In a few moments he found the clearing. Bolduc was on one knee holding up a corner of the mattress.

"She's over here," Bolduc said without looking up. "She's dead."

Taylor started toward him, but stopped as soon as he saw the child. "It was very hard for me to believe what I was looking at," recalled Taylor, who was born and raised in Vermont. "It was something that you read about in New York City. But it was here in Essex Junction, Vermont. And after seeing the first victim in the parking lot, and now with Bolduc kneeling down beside this girl, I was having a real problem dealing with the feeling 'It is happening here.'"

Taylor crouched beside Bolduc, who had lifted the mattress and was checking the girl's wrist and neck for signs of life. "She was naked and lying face down," Taylor continued. "Her head was kind of at rest against a tree that had toppled across the path. She had grubs and worms and dirt all over her back from being covered by the mattress. There was a knee sock tied through her mouth and knotted in the back of her head, actually tied into her hair. She was gagged so tightly that her face had become distorted.

"Her hands were tied behind her back and her fingers were in a distorted position as if she had grasped to try to untie herself. There was a BB just beneath the surface of the skin on her back. And she had a horrid wound to her chest, like she had been hacked. Whoever did it—it was like you'd use a hacksaw, like they just kept pushing it in and cutting it at the same time. And there were X's carved on her chest, between her breasts."

Taylor knelt down and put his face close to the little girl's, an act of desperation, to see if he could detect any sign of breathing. "I looked at her face," he said, "and saw that her eye was just running all over. She had been shot through the eye."

In an instant, Taylor knew he had seen too much. The young policeman felt a rush of nausea, rose quickly, walked a few paces into the trees, and gagged.

A half dozen miles away, at her district courthouse office in downtown Burlington, Chief Deputy State's Attorney Susan Via was finishing a few items of business as she prepared to go home for the weekend. Down the hall Harold "Duke" Eaton, another deputy state's attorney, leaned back into his chair and scanned the low gray city skyline outside his window. It had been an uneventful week for the Chittenden County prosecutors. Like Via, Eaton had only routine paperwork to complete before leaving. Everyone else on the third floor of the modern courthouse had left.

A few minutes before five, two phone lines lit at once. Via and Eaton both reached for their phones and by chance hit separate buttons. For a few moments Eaton spoke with a policeman from the nearby town of Milton who wanted advice on an assault investigation. The attorney offered to do some checking and get back to him on Monday.

In her office Susan Via was shouting into the phone, "Whoah! Slow down," as she scribbled rapid notes on a scrap of paper. A distraught voice had identified himself as an Essex police officer, but he was speaking so fast and erratically that Via could not understand what he was trying to say.

She had heard the officer mention little children, but immediately thought the report was exaggerated. "I was thinking five-year-olds. You know, maybe a little girl said something had happened and it had been magnified over time and it wasn't a sexual assault. Maybe it was that somebody scared them with a knife."

But when Via finally slowed the policeman, she realized it was serious. Two girls attacked in Essex . . . one sexual assault . . . one girl was on her way to the Medical Center Hospital; the other, the policeman thought, might be dead.

"Get your coat, Duke," Via shouted as she ran out of her office. The two attorneys rushed to the elevator, into Via's car, and up the hill to the hospital. When they arrived, the Essex rescue squad ambulance was still parked, lights flashing, under the canopy outside the emergency room entrance.

A few miles from the courthouse, State's Attorney Mark Keller and two of his assistants were walking through the front door at the Channel 22 television studios to tape a show on bad checks. As Keller looked around for someone at the reception desk, he was startled by a voice from an intercom speaker. "Mark Keller, pick up two," it said. The young prosecutor reached for the receiver on the receptionist's desk.

A high-pitched voice excitedly identified the speaker as an Essex police officer. "We have a murder out here!" the policeman bellowed. He pressed on, explaining that a girl had been killed. Another girl, in serious condition in the hospital, had been raped.

Keller hung up. "Now, ladies and gentlemen," he announced to his colleagues, "we're going to see Bob Simpson performing all by himself." Simpson, a soft-spoken young deputy state's attorney, protested, but Keller quickly explained that there had been a murder. He was already signaling to his other deputy, Jim Crucitti, and hurrying toward the door.

The two rushed outside into a driving rainstorm and leaped into Keller's ragged '74 Buick Apollo, the vehicle Keller was proud of not having washed since he bought it. He pressed the flasher button and dashed up Shelburne Road, through Burlington's five o'clock traffic. For Keller, who often described his office as a "mixture of *Barney Miller* and *Hill Street Blues*, but mostly *Barney Miller*," this was the most exciting part of his job, the rush to the scene, the only time that he could legally speed along the quiet Vermont streets.

Untimely deaths were uncommon even for Vermont's busiest state's attorney's office, but murders were even rarer. In Essex Junction, where he could not remember a single murder ever having been committed, Keller knew the public outcry would be violent. Besides, Keller himself lived in the town.

His adrenaline coursing, Keller pressed his foot on the accelerator. He sped around cars, onto the interstate highway, off at the St. Mike's College exit. As he drove, Keller traded grim jokes about other murders with Crucitti, interspersing the defensive joviality with instructions: Make sure Susan Via was at the hospital; get Nancy Sheahan, another young deputy state's attorney, to come to the scene; tell Simpson to come out; contact Steve Miller, the office's investigator.

The rain was still coming down hard as they sped along Pearl Street into the center of Essex at Five Corners, where the traffic was blocked with end-of-the-day congestion. Keller, with his flashers on and hand against the horn, maneuvered through the cars, in the wrong lane, against the lights, up Maple Street, around the construction, and into Maple Street Park. He stopped, with brakes screeching, but nobody was there.

"The damn sons of bitches! Where are they?" The police radio on Keller's dashboard had not been operative for a week. The frustrated prosecutor spun the car around and raced down Maple Street again, to the Essex Police Department, where he was told he had been at the right spot. Keller drove through Five Corners again, astonished that he hadn't been killed, and back to the park.

This time he saw a policeman in a yellow slicker pointing in the direction of the playground. Instead of parking, the attorney bumped his old car over the curb, onto the asphalt walkway, into the mud at the edge of the baseball diamond, and slid to a stop near the outside path along the woods. Wearing only a light cream-colored shirt and tie, Keller was soaked by the pelting rain as he got out.

A policeman led the two prosecutors down the outside path to the woods, and the men pushed their way through the wet brush. At the clearing, Keller walked toward the soggy mattresses as another policeman lifted the edge of one to reveal the mutilated body of Melissa Walbridge. "This is where we found her," the policeman murmured. Keller looked intently at the little girl, and for the first time in his career, his professional detachment disappeared.

"It wasn't so much the injuries," Keller recalled. "It was the pitiful look in her eyes. It was very clear from her wounds that she had been tortured, had been begging, and had suffered a great deal. Her eyes seemed to say all that, like, 'Somebody, please help me.' It just made you feel rotten."

Keller gave a sigh of disgust. "Oh, fuck!" he growled, turning to Crucitti. "When the people in this town find out that two little girls got attacked leaving school, everyone's going to go crazy."

Susan Via waited anxiously just outside the hospital emergency room, aware that perhaps the only witness to the killing was barely alive herself. Across the room Judy Stafford, finally relieved of her duties as a nurse, was, through her sobs, telling Via who the girls were, their ages, and where they went to school.

From behind half-drawn white curtains off the emergency room corridor, Via could see the hospital staff clustered around a bed and hear the painful cries of Meghan O'Rourke.

The prosecutor stopped one of the medical residents as he scurried by and asked about Meghan's condition. "Pretty rough shape," the doctor answered, rushing off.

The emergency room was part of the Medical Center Hospital, the state's largest, most prestigious medical facility. The room had been ready for the ambulance the moment it arrived at the hospital entrance a few minutes before. "There was a full trauma crew waiting," remembered Wayne Eells, "including three or four thoracic surgeons, already scrubbed and in their gloves. They were prepared with some eight or ten people, ready to do major surgery on her immediately."

Meghan was brought into the emergency room surrounded by a contingent of purposeful medical personnel. Intravenous injections were started as pediatric surgeon Richard Mellish began to examine the extent of her injuries. At once he determined that her chest wound was "life-threatening."

The stab wound, a V-shaped incision almost an inch wide, had opened a hole in the upper left side of Meghan's chest, ominously close to her heart. The knife had also punctured her left lung, which meant that the area between the lung and the chest wall was filling with blood and air.

Meghan's other injuries offered further evidence that her attackers had been brutal. There was a circular puncture wound in the right side of her neck; Mellish concluded that it was made by a pellet or BB shot at close range. Another puncture wound, less severe than the one in her chest, was on her lower left back. The scratch marks across her neck seemed to Mellish to have been caused by pressure from a blunt-edged object. Both Meghan's cheeks and her eyes were crimson red; blood vessels had broken, the doctor believed, when Meghan was strangled.

Susan Via paced. Because the attack had sexual connotations, the case became the responsibility of the Columbia Law School graduate. In the small Burlington prosecutor's office, that was her department. Via had become the expert on sexual assaults, a specialization new to Chittenden County and unique in Vermont, but one that Keller and Via had decided needed attention. "Mark had talked about my taking on the sexual assault cases when he first hired me," Via recalled. "He wanted to make it a priority, something that the prosecutor's office hadn't really done in the past." The specialty suited her: she was tough, brassy, and bright, but sensitive to the pain of victims.

As another doctor hurried by, Via stopped him, explaining that Meghan might be the only witness to the attack. Since time was crucial, she asked permission to speak to Meghan as soon as possible—as long as it did not endanger the girl's life. The physician assured her he would do what he could. "We had a zillion police officers that were ready to do practically anything to get these guys," Via later commented. "But they didn't know who to look for."

The scene in the operating room overwhelmed the prosecutor. "It seemed like every square inch of the bed had a body around it," Via recollected. Meghan, still in critical condition, was conscious. Rubber tubes were jutting from her chest and an oxygen mask covered her mouth. Mud from the wet forest caked her body.

"She had been really dirtied up. Every portion of her not covered by the sheet or bandage was covered with dirt. I mean, dirt and little bits of leaves, brown clods, leaves in her hair. Both her eyes were very badly hemorrhaged. She barely could open them, but when she did, they were totally red, like they had been painted. She was in terrible pain. You could see her grimacing and wincing. The staff was extremely kind and solicitous; they realized that they had a little girl in there. A doctor was holding her hand, talking to her, patting her hair, you know, just kind of soothing and caressing her."

The slim, dark-haired attorney moved cautiously to Meghan's side. "I know you are really hurting right now, sweetie, but I need to ask you just a couple of questions." Meghan's blood-red eyes looked up, as if to acknowledge the attorney's request.

Via devised a plan to ease Meghan's discomfort at being questioned so soon after her attack. A woman doctor was to pass her questions on to Meghan, while Essex patrolman Robin Hollwedel wrote the child's answers on a pad. The doctor told Meghan just to nod "yes" or "no" or raise her fingers in answer to the queries if she could not talk.

When the female physician asked if she knew who attacked her, Meghan rocked her head slightly back and forth. No. Were they in a car? Again, no. Did she remember what they looked like? This time, Meghan nodded affirmatively. The doctor carefully removed the oxygen mask and put her ear to Meghan's mouth. One of them was blond-haired, Meghan whispered in a frail voice. The other was dark-haired and had a beard. Meghan had seen the two men in the park two days before and they had chased her, she related.

It seemed that Meghan could go no further, but in her small, raspy voice she struggled to ask, "Where is Missy?" No one responded. The physician patted the young girl gently on the head and told her to rest.

"God bless her," Via later remarked. "She is a very courageous little girl. She provided us with useful information while they were still working on her wounds."

Via emerged from the short interview flushed. In her three years as a prosecutor in Burlington, she had seen bloody crime and accident scenes, but had never become inured to people's suffering. It touched her more than seeing the face of death, however brutal. "As unpleasant as death is, I have a harder time dealing with the pain of living people—even more than seeing someone who has been decapitated. Whether you are religious or not, you have a sense that they are lifeless in death. But in dealing with people who are alive and in pain, I feel very impotent—that there is nothing I can do to help them.

"I remember having to interview somebody who was dying after having been rear-ended in a car on North Avenue. The man was in the hospital with third-degree burns over ninety percent of his body. He had no skin left. He was shivering and he kept telling me he was cold. I asked if they could get a blood sample for his blood alcohol content, and they said there wasn't enough fluid left in his body. This poor man was suffering and he was going to die, and there was nothing I could do for him. I had those same feelings with Meghan O'Rourke. Oh God, this poor child, and there is nothing that I can do."

But Meghan's ordeal was far from over and Via's own work was just beginning. At 5:50 that afternoon, Meghan's information prompted a BOL (Be on the Lookout), which was flashed to all state law-enforcement agencies. "Two men involved," it relayed. "One is tall, dark hair and beard, straight hair. Other is younger, tall, curly short blond hair. Both white."

State's Attorney Mark Keller had by this time returned to the Essex Police Department, where a call from Via gave him reason to be hopeful. "Mark, if this little girl pulls through, and I think she will, she is going to be able to give us a decent description. She saw them just a couple of days ago." As a precaution, Via asked Officer Hollwedel to stay with the girl at all times. If the attackers discovered that one of their victims survived to identify them, Via believed, they might try to finish their bloody work.

Via was leaving the hospital to drive to Maple Street Park when she spied a nurse at the reception desk holding a telephone, waving frantically at her. With her hand cupped over the mouthpiece, the nurse looked desperate. "I've got Mrs. Walbridge on the phone!" she explained in a loud whisper. "What do I tell her?"

An angered Via could not understand why no one had been sent to the Walbridge house. At first, she wondered how much Mrs. Walbridge knew, then concluded that if she were aware of the tragedy, she would not be calling the hospital. Via paused a moment, then picked up the phone and identified herself.

"How's Meghan?" The woman's voice on the other end of the line was high-pitched, edged with strain.

"She's okay, Mrs. Walbridge," said Via. "She'll be all right."

Then, the question that Via hoped would never be asked. "How's my daughter? Where is she? The police won't tell me anything!"

Via held the phone receiver tight. "Mrs. Walbridge, are you alone?"

"Yes. My husband is out looking for Melissa."

"Let me send a police officer over to you?" Via was bartering for time.

"No. No." The woman's voice rose, almost in panic. "I'm coming down to the hospital."

"Mrs. Walbridge," the attorney said slowly, "I am so sorry, but Missy has been killed."

The silence seemed endless. When Mrs. Walbridge finally spoke, her voice quavered.

"Oh. Oh, my God," it finally came. Then, so softly that Via could hardly hear, "Well—well, I know you're very busy. I'm sorry to bother you. I'll just go now."

Via was still talking, pleading with Mrs. Walbridge to let her send a police officer to the house when the phone went dead.

CHAPTER 3

Outrage

THE RAIN NOW came in spurts, soaking the somber men gathered in the small clearing in the woods of Maple Street Park. Police hovering over the mattresses were silent. Unprepared for the rain but indifferent to their drenched clothing, they stood immobile before the sight of the tiny body in the mud. Each of the law enforcement officers, in his turn, felt the same slice of anguish pierce his professional armor.

Duke Eaton, arriving from the hospital, his hair matted from the rain, took in the cameo of death, then looked away, seeking refuge. "The one eye I could see was open, but I remember her hands more than anything; more than the gunshots or her hair being all wet or her eyes. Her hands being tied was particularly troubling to me. It just showed how desperately she must have resisted. Her fingers—they seemed to be grasping. It was really sickening."

At Eaton's side, Susan Via lost her avowed preference for

the deceased over the dying. As she looked at Melissa's corpse
in the shadows of the thick stand of trees, not even the fading
light lessened the starkness of the image. "It was just horrible,"
she recalled.

The evidence of brutality pelted the investigators' senses.
One gaze at the little body was enough to touch nerves of
nausea, dread, empathy, and, finally, anger. It was obvious that
Melissa Walbridge had been tortured and had died suffering.
"You could tell she had not had an easy death," said Via. "It
was not like seeing somebody who had been shot in the back
of the head and died quickly. There was a tremendous amount
of blood around, but you don't bleed after you are dead. The
wounds had to be delivered while she was alive."

It was Melissa's vulnerability that most frustrated those who
now viewed her. "She was so very tiny and frail-looking," Via
continued. "I was struck with the feeling that 'This is just a
baby.' They were both so little. They probably hadn't the
vaguest idea of what these men had on their minds. Nobody
should be subjected to that kind of attack, but *certainly not
children*. When I saw her lying there, she looked younger than
twelve. Just a tiny, bony kid, that age before girls really have
any sort of gender, when they are like little colts. I remember
feeling a kind of nausea thinking that anyone would attack
somebody that looked like a baby."

The male officers yielded to an unprofessional desire for
vengeance. Patrolman Gary Taylor, normally easygoing, had
learned the police maxim: "Nothing is personal." But the tortured body of Melissa Walbridge changed that. Recalling that
night in the woods, the policeman's voice quavered with emotion. "There are certain rules between cops and criminals," he
said. "One is that nothing is personal. I make a good collar
and the guy hires a good lawyer and the state's attorney tosses
the charge out and he walks. I don't get hung up on that. A
man shoots at me, I don't take that personally.

"But if he shoots at somebody in my family, that's personal.
Another rule is that kids don't become victims. But now, I saw
one of my own children. It suddenly became personal!"

It was the same for every investigator who saw Melissa's
innocence lying lifeless in the mud. "This was something most

people had never dealt with," remembered Robbie Yandow. "It was now very clear that this was the most vicious crime that had ever been committed in Vermont."

Keller and Yandow made sure that the woods were sealed off and, as daylight disappeared, the Essex Fire Department and the State Police Crime Lab fired their generators and dragged wires and lights through the trees.

Curious about the commotion, residents of the neighborhood had gravitated to the park, but tight-lipped police stood at barricades and kept them from entering as they ushered a stream of law enforcement vehicles in and out. Bernard Lemieux straddled his bicycle, watching. "I heard about it when I went home after golfing," he told a local reporter. "My wife had the door locked even though she never locked it before. When I got in the house she said there had been a murder down here."

Newsmen, used to an almost comradely rapport with police, were now ordered to stay back. Mike Donoghue, a brazen Burlington *Free Press* reporter, eluded the barrier at the park entrance and headed toward the woods. But Mark Keller was in no mood for his characteristic banter with the press.

"Get him outta here!" Keller shouted to the policeman at his side.

Donoghue was surprised by Keller's impatient order. "I'll stand right here," he shot back.

"Either move him or arrest the son of a bitch," the prosecutor swore. "But I want him outta here!"

The two men, the policeman and the reporter, looked at each other quizzically and decided that Keller meant what he said. There would be no rule bending tonight, no pleasantries.

The rain continued to drench the investigators as they plodded through the underbrush that Friday evening. Some of the men wore raincoats brought to the scene from the police department; most worked in the slacks and sport shirts they had been wearing when they first received the duty call. The fire department generator droned, its powerful electric lights projecting shadows through the dark night.

Melissa Walbridge dominated the scene. Camera strobes

ricocheted off the trees as police photographers worked to preserve the grotesque image of death. They flashed harshly against the little body, from the left, from the right, on the head, on the feet, then were gone.

"I remember at one point seeing a mosquito walking across the girl's face, walking over her eyes," recalled Mark Keller. "It bothered me a great deal. It took all of the strength I had in me not to order the cops to keep the bugs off her, but I knew if I did, they'd think I was off my rocker. I had to turn and walk away." Keller, who had worked in the state's attorney's office almost since graduating from Notre Dame Law School in 1976, was known for his gallows humor, his ability to eat a hamburger while watching an autopsy. But tonight, for the state's attorney as for everyone else, things were different.

"I have been with Mark to many grisly scenes before and I'd never seen a crime hit him like that," Duke Eaton later said. "One of the things that we do in this business in order to deal with it is to make light of death. You know, tell jokes and say things like, 'Well, he sure made a mess of himself,' you know, that kind of thing. But now it was all dead serious. Stone-cold, sober."

The men went about their business in silence, their senses alerted by the sordid spectacle, exaggerating every detail. "I remember looking over at Mark as he was staring at her," Duke Eaton continued. "And I don't know why I have this recollection, but I do. I remember a drop of water coming down and staying on the end of his nose for a minute. It was water from the branches. And it stayed on his nose. Then it dropped off."

At ten o'clock that evening State Health Commissioner Dr. Lloyd Novick, who had come in place of the out-of-state medical examiner, allowed the body to be removed. The heavy hearse from the Corbin and Palmer mortuary backed over the slippery ground to the very edge of the woods, and an aluminum-wheeled coffin stretcher was half-dragged, half-carried to the site. Delicately, as if the little corpse still carried life, the police slipped Melissa's body in a cold rubber and canvas bag and laid it on the stretcher.

The crime lab specialists and policemen stopped their work and watched in silence as Keller, Yandow, a mortician, and a

state trooper grabbed the silver rails on the sides of the stretcher.
It seemed heavier than it should have. The men tried to drag
the stretcher along on its wheels, but it bogged down in the
mud. As they lifted it and started to walk, their feet slipped
across the saturated ground.

It started to pour again. The rain trickled down the men's
heads and necks, and under their already soggy shirts. With
the mud up to their ankles, they had to stop for a few moments.
Keller's old shoes were coming apart, his soles flapping loose
and filling with mud as he helped move the stretcher along.
Finally the four men reached the hearse, lifted the stretcher
and pushed it in, their faces etched with the expressions of the
long night of horror.

Thousands of Vermonters turned on their television sets that
Friday night at eleven o'clock for the news. On Channel 3,
Vermont's largest state-based station, the drumbeat introduction
was cut short. The camera focused on the announcer, and as
he intoned the usual "Good evening," the wall behind was
illuminated with a red, pink, and blue target, across the center
of which a black silhouetted stick figure sprawled. "A small
army of law enforcement officers are searching for two men
tonight in connection with an attack on two young girls in
Essex this afternoon," he began somberly. "One girl is dead.
One is hospitalized. Details are few at this hour."

The news of the killing shattered the equanimity of the state.
For much of that evening Duke Eaton, who had once been a
radio disc jockey, sat by a telephone at the Essex Police Department, answering a deluge of questions from the press and
pleading for cooperation in disseminating the descriptions of
the suspects. The media needed little prompting. Phone calls
from the region's newspapers, radio and television stations, the
Associated Press and United Press International wire services
streamed in. Eaton fielded calls from New Hampshire, New
York, Boston, Maine. "The word spread like crazy," he remembered.

Those members of the press who did not call Eaton were
contacted by him. He gave them Meghan's brief descriptions
of the men and asked them to broadcast the details. He even

called stations in New York State, including his former station, WGFB in Plattsburgh, across Lake Champlain, and went on the air live with his request that the public be on the lookout.

Later that night, Chief John Terry, Keller, Yandow, Vermont State Police investigator Nick Ruggiero, and a dozen other municipal, county, and state law enforcement officials, wet and exhausted, dragged themselves into the Essex Police Department squad room. They had abandoned their search in the woods and stationed a guard at the scene. It was now almost midnight and most of the men had been on their jobs since early that morning.

They munched on hamburgers and french fries as they planned their strategy. There was virtually no new information except what they had learned from Meghan through Susan Via. The consensus was that the killers were not local men. No one could recall a crime so brutal, and in the chauvinistic spirit of decent Vermonters, it seemed obvious that the killers were from out of state, a couple of "flatlanders," drifters. Bob Simpson of the state's attorney's office remembered that there was a traveling carnival in South Burlington; he suggested that the "carnies" be checked out immediately.

"The cops thought about the sleaziest, scummiest people they had ever dealt with," Susan Via recollected, "but they still couldn't come up with anyone they thought was capable of this."

The investigators divided up responsibilities for tracking leads and decided on a meeting for early the next morning. Every possible source of manpower would be tapped, including police from other parts of the state. Local criminal files would be searched, state agencies would be put on alert, the lookout would be broadcast through all New England via NESPAC, the New England State Police Administrators Compact.

Mark Keller did not return home until after one in the morning. He grabbed a beer from the refrigerator, gulped it, and, ignoring his wife's entreaties to tell her what had happened, collapsed into bed.

When Bob Simpson finally walked through his front door early that morning, he made an uncharacteristically somber vow to his wife. "I'm going to work on this one until I'm no good anymore," he said. "Then I'm going to sleep. Then I'm going to work on it till I'm no good anymore. Then sleep. And I'm going to keep doing it until we catch these sons-a-bitches."

CHAPTER 4

Mountain Peace

THAT FRIDAY MORNING had begun with the promise of another tranquil Vermont day. Meghan O'Rourke was awake unusually early. Outside the window of her bedroom the sun glistened over the tops of the trees on the other side of the road. It was only a little after 6:30, but the end of a school week was always cause for happy anticipation. With the weekend ahead, there was a birthday party to look forward to; and that night Melissa's father was taking Meghan and Melissa to a drive-in movie.

Meghan put on a pair of jeans, her white turtleneck sweater with the multicolored stars, and her clogs. As she ate her breakfast, her parents were preparing for their hour-long drive along Interstate 89 through the mountains to their jobs in Montpelier, the state capital, where Meghan's father served as deputy commissioner of social welfare. With her parents working, and both her older sister Jennifer and older brother Timothy away at school much of the time, Meghan nourished her independent spirit.

Stephanie O'Rourke was a small woman, soft-spoken but strong-willed. After raising three children, she had returned to work. James O'Rourke, with his longish, sandy-brown hair, button-down shirts, and Ivy League ties, was a liberal, articulate, well-educated man in the Kennedy mold. He could speak as intelligently about local politics as about a recent article in the *New Yorker*, and despite the daily headlines of crime and war, was still an optimist. Jim O'Rourke steadfastly believed in the redeemability of man. "One thing we found," he would say, speaking of his first job as a social worker ministering to the poor of Burlington, "was that given a little help and encouragement, those people who were thought of as lazy and shiftless really wanted to improve their lot and work."

O'Rourke refused to give in to those who found in rising crime statistics reason to criticize the state's welfare system. "The increase in crime, in family problems, in juvenile delinquency," he stated with conviction, "is not attributable to the welfare state. My feeling is that without these programs there would be far more juvenile crime, delinquency, and twice as many jails. And if we cut the programs, we'll end up with many more serious problems."

Though only a few minutes from the center of Essex Junction, the O'Rourkes' modest home on Cascade Street was on the last road on the village's southern boundary, overlooking pastures and forests that ran to the banks of the Winooski River.

As Meghan left her house this Friday morning the peace was evident; little was stirring. A few birds flitted through the early air as she headed away from the Winooski and toward town, slowly making her way across fields, vacant lots, and winding streets that took her to Indian Acres, the residential area where the Walbridges lived. The local place-names spoke of North American Indian tribes. There was Hiawatha grade school, and in rapid succession Huron, Mohawk, Seneca, Abnaki, Cree, Oneida, Onondaga, Algonquin, and Cherokee avenues.

Meghan usually met Melissa on the corner of South Summit Street, but having arrived early this morning, the young girl continued on to her friend's house. The Walbridges' new cream-colored, ranch-style home rested among large pines and maple trees near the end of Iroquois, a half mile from the village center. Behind the house the grass had been worn thin by play, much of it with the Walbridges' German shepherd. The trees and tall grass at the back fronted on the railroad tracks that moved west to Burlington and east through the village. A small dirt road running near the tracks was used as a shortcut when Melissa and her younger brother, Judd, both went to Hiawatha Grade School.

Melissa had been up since six, her usual hour of rising. By the time Meghan arrived, she was already dressed, her long brown hair swept to one side of her freckled face. She had put on her "Le Team" shirt and laced up her new high-top boots, and over her shoulder she slung her blue knapsack. Melissa loved the morning hours, reserving her late sleeping for weekends. The alarm clock beside her bed, which she had bought with her baby-sitting money, woke her in time to beat her mother to the shower in the morning.

In a jar on the kitchen table, enterprising Melissa kept a list of seasonal work opportunities that included shoveling snow in the winter, raking leaves in the fall, and washing cars in the summer. For her baby-sitting, a venture begun only that winter, Missy had produced her handmade business cards with construction paper and Magic Markers.

Her salesmanship had proven profitable. Melissa had accumulated $200 in her own bank account and had promised to treat her mother to a Caribbean vacation. "I never doubted for a minute that she would do it," Marie Walbridge told friends. "She was sort of like myself. When it was time to work or settle down, she did it. And when she was doing anything in recreation, she did that. She had a wonderful sense of humor, she could be a terrific tease, but she took care of business first."

Marie Walbridge, the third of ten children of the local Bessette family, had her own painting and wallpapering business which she operated out of the family garage. Marie, who knew how rough it was to compete with seven sisters for clothes, made sure that her work would spare Melissa and Judd any such hardships.

A small, dark-haired woman, Melissa's mother was endowed with immense energy and a storehouse of New England independence. Marie Walbridge had just celebrated her thirty-second birthday two days before, and for the second year in a row Melissa had organized the party. "When she was just eleven," Mrs. Walbridge remembered, "Melissa came up to me and said, 'You always make such a nice to-do about our birthdays, who gives you a party?' And I said, 'Nobody.' And she said, 'But that's awful! That just isn't right.' And she gave me a super surprise birthday party. And she did the same thing again when she was twelve."

"Melissa was a little business lady emulating her mother," added Eric Walbridge, a native Vermonter and the son of a well-known University of Vermont physicist. Eric had eschewed his father's time-consuming professionalism for the assembly line at the local General Electric plant, where he was a "seek-and-find" specialist, and preferred to devote his free time to his family. He joked that his family was his number one priority, his job number five.

The parents' concern for family unity rubbed off on the children, creating a sense of openness. "It wouldn't have occurred to Melissa or Judd not to share with Eric and myself all of their experiences," Marie Walbridge explained. After her first sleepover at Meghan's, Melissa confided in her mother. "Missy came home and said, 'Guess what we did? We experimented with cigarettes.' I said I didn't like that, but I understood. The next time that Melissa went over there, Meghan fixed her a drink. Meghan was upset when she realized that Melissa had told us about these pranks. But Missy told her, 'Don't worry, my parents are cool.' I very much liked that— the children's honesty and the fact that they trusted us." That trust was mutual and well placed. No sooner had Marie Walbridge become concerned than the pranks stopped.

That morning, at 7:45, Melissa ran to the door and let her friend in. "Mom," she shouted, "Meghan's here. I'm going." Mrs. Walbridge, running late, had just stepped into the shower.

She usually would have been up in time to chat with Melissa in the sunny breakfast room off the kitchen, but now she had no chance to speak with her daughter. Hearing Melissa call her good-byes, Mrs. Walbridge moved her head outside the bathroom door. "You look nice, honey," she yelled to Melissa. "I love you, have a good day. We'll see you after school." Melissa closed the house door behind her and was gone.

Melissa and Meghan cut across the front yard of the Walbridge house and turned left down Iroquois. The neighborhood was so familiar that Melissa had mapped it in her head. The girls made the round trip on foot almost every day, but occasionally they would vary their route. They might pass through the center of the village at Five Corners and amble up Maple Street, or cut through the parking lot of the Lincoln Inn, a popular restaurant-hotel, then pick up the straight line of railroad track that ran behind the Maple Street Park woods.

This morning their route took them through the Indian Acres development, down Park Street, and into the center of the old village. Except for the early-morning traffic at the Five Corners intersection, it was much as it had been for the last hundred years. Old two-story red brick buildings on Main Street housed some of the same stores and offices that Missy's mother had frequented when she was a child. When Melissa went into Phil's clothing store to buy pajamas for her grandfather, Phil knew exactly what size Gilbert Bessette needed.

A wood and brick structure that in 1819 served as the village tavern covered one side of the Five Corners intersection. Municipal offices and police headquarters now occupied the colonial building. The girls passed in front of the sprawling Lincoln Inn, situated on still another corner of the intersection, on their way to the Lawton School a half mile up Maple Street.

Except for a gas station in back of the Lincoln Inn, the building looked much as it did when Job Bates built it as a home for his wife and eleven children in the late 1800s. The mansion was converted to an inn and restaurant in 1914 and had been the hearth of the village ever since. Marie Walbridge had worked there as a waitress, as had two of her sisters, and Meghan and Melissa often ate there with their families.

As they continued on to school, Meghan and Melissa passed within a hundred yards of Gaines Court, the closest thing to a slum in Essex. Little more than a forgotten alley behind the railroad tracks in the center of the village, it was only a few blocks from the Lincoln Inn, the police station, and Maple Street. The small gravel road, rutted with holes and banked by weeds, a vacant lot, and deteriorating wood-framed houses, represented a face of Vermont absent from the idealized postcards sold to urban visitors. It was an inconspicuous sore tucked away in the affluent Green Mountain village, and few people had ever paid it much attention.

Less than twenty minutes later, the girls were at school, where classes passed quickly. At 3:15, when the school bell sounded and students rushed to go home, Maple Street custodians Kevin Plant and Joseph Barber were sitting in their pickup truck on the edge of one of the two baseball fields deciding whether to line the diamond with lime. "It was cloudy and it looked like it was about ready to pour any second," Plant recalled.

Plant and Barber noticed two young men walking along a path at the far edge of Little League Field A about forty feet away. They were moving off toward the railroad tracks on the far side of the woods. One was short and stocky, dark-haired, with a half-grown beard. The other was taller, skinny, and had a red baseball cap covering his curly blond hair. They seemed to be talking to each other, but Plant and Barber could not hear what was being said. Over the years, the custodians had learned to recognize the many faces of the kids and IBM workers who used the park. But they didn't know the two men they saw this Friday.

"I wasn't really thinking about them," Plant recalled. "I was thinking about the field. I just looked over and saw these two guys walking by; and I can remember looking to see if they'd nod hello or something. But they didn't, and I didn't think anything of it."

In a few moments the two strangers had turned onto the path by the tracks and disappeared into the woods.

CHAPTER 5

Mountain Shadows

AT TEN O'CLOCK that same Friday morning, fifteen-year-old
Jamie Savage and sixteen-year-old Louie Hamlin made their
way up Elmwood Avenue in Burlington, where the tired, once
proud Victorian and Italianate homes lined the street like rows
of battered shoe boxes. As on most weekday mornings, the
streets running through the bedraggled Old North End neighborhood of Burlington were all but deserted. Adults were either
at work, if they had jobs, or inside one of the many dilapidated
houses, pestering over babies, flicking the television selector,
or sleeping the listless sleep of the unemployed, food-stamped
and welfare class.

Under the gray Vermont sky, the neighborhood looked more
depressed than usual. Jamie and Louie passed the whitewashed
Free Methodist Church and the sprawling graveyard on their
right, the bar on their left, and crossed North Street, the neighborhood's central artery. It was now a decaying line of bars,

struggling small grocery stores, boarded-up businesses, and two-story wood-framed tenements.

In the tough North End Louie was known as the Hulk, a boy who was eerily quiet and violently explosive. His physique was the North End equivalent of a Harvard MBA, earning him the respect of the intimidated. From his high-school weight training and wrestling, Louie's neck had thickened to become almost indistinguishable from the beginnings of his head.

Though only sixteen, Louie looked ten years older. Well muscled, short but solid, his five-foot seven-inch frame looked angular enough to square a house by, strong enough to raise one. Louie already had a menacing appearance: His straight black hair fell almost to his collar line, his face was covered with a scraggly beard and mustache, and his dark brooding eyes were protected by a solid broad line of bushy eyebrow. Louie walked with his arms swinging straight by his side, his legs unbending and rigid. Always quiet and sulky, he barely spoke to his friend Jamie as they marched toward Hamlin's house.

The two teenagers were an odd couple save for their similar origins. Jamie, his light-complected skin pitted by acne scars, was called Crater Face. He was as tall and lanky as Louie was squat and burly. Though four months away from his sixteenth birthday and eleven months younger than his friend, Jamie was already over six feet, a head taller than Louie. His head was topped by a jungle twist of sandy-blond hair.

Jamie was content just to be at Louie's side. In the last few years Jamie had taken his older brother's place as Louie's constant companion. "They're like brothers," said Jamie's brother Rene. "They just hang around each other."

Together the two teenagers regularly roamed the streets of Burlington's North End. His shirt sleeves rolled above his bony elbows, Jamie strutted like a nervous pelican over the broken sidewalks of Elmwood, while beside him Louie seemed to roll like a Vermont boulder. With knives, pellet and BB guns they preyed upon the seagulls at the city dump or squirrels in the woods; they hitchhiked to Malletts Bay for rollerskating, shoplifted soda and cigarettes.

Jamie and Louie's vagabondage was never hurried. This

morning, as they walked toward Louie's house, they moved at a pace that seemed without destination. There were those who felt that Louie was a negative influence on Jamie. "It was just like a light switch," said teenager Patricia Colby, who occasionally worked with Jamie at the Lincoln Inn in Essex Junction. "When Jamie was by himself, he was friendly. He could sit down and hold a normal conversation with you. But when he was with Louie, you couldn't even talk to him. They would look at me and they might snicker or something but neither one of them would come up and say anything to me." Added Patricia's mother, Betty Colby, "Louie was like Fonzie to him."

Doubts about Louie did not influence Jamie, who felt he had finally found true comradeship in his brooding partner. He even preferred Louie's companionship to that of his girlfriend, Theresa Robair, who had broken up with Jamie earlier that week. Theresa and Jamie had been friends since the Savages' Spring Street days in Burlington, and Jamie—who now lived in Essex Junction—was angered by the rift because Theresa, though only twelve, was his "steady."

They played tag together and, occasionally, "catch and kiss." Jamie gave Theresa trinkets that he stole from Woolworth's or Mall Drug downtown, and treated her to sodas. "Jamie was always really nice to me," recollected Theresa, a petite, dark-haired girl with braces. "He always used to have money and would buy me things. I guess he stole it. I don't know. Sometimes, I just used him for his money, but then we got really close and I cared more about him than I did about his money. If I wanted a quart of soda, he'd buy me it. RC and Seven-Up. And we used to sit around on the tree stump by his house and drink soda and eat."

But when Louie became Jamie's near-constant companion, Theresa was shunted aside. "Jamie was different when he was around Louie," Theresa recalled. "He always used to wait for me when I got out of school. But when he's around Louie, he doesn't even care about me. He was always talking about shootin' things, and I didn't really like it 'cuz I love animals. One day him and Louie were talking about how they killed this squirrel and sliced it all up. They were laughing about it. It was fun for them."

Theresa, too, was concerned about Louie's influence on Jamie. "Louie's the one that's crazy," she would later say. "They were shootin' knives at each other and Louie tried to hit me in the foot with a knife. When I was startin' to go out with Jamie and I got really close, I told Jamie that I didn't want him hangin' around with Louie. That's when he moved up to Essex. Then we broke up, and he started hangin' around with Louie again."

Theresa had now given Jamie an ultimatum. If he wanted to hang out with Louie, he would have to do without her. "He called and we talked for a little while and he wanted me to come over, but I told him no. And he got all mad at me."

Jamie followed Louie across the grass to the Hamlins' front porch. The home, like many of the North End residences, was a worn, two-story house in need of repair. A once pleasant and sturdy Greek Revival structure, it had gone for a generation without maintenance. It was as if the olive-green paint had always been peeling, the six slender white columns on the porch always spotted with mud, the balustrades always cracked, the front lawn always unmowed. The weeds mingled with wild shrubs and a few children's toys before curling their way up the banister and over the porch stairs.

Louie pushed a small bicycle away with his foot and swung open the tattered screen door. The stale air from inside rushed by him. "Ma, look what Jamie got for me." Louie saw his mother on the other side of the living room and stopped inside the front door, by the lone plant stand. He was pulling a box from under his arm.

Mary Hamlin had not seen Louie since Thursday morning, when he had grabbed a change of clothes and left. Before that, the last time Louie had been home was Tuesday, the day he was suspended from school. Louie had come home angry, telling his mother that the suspension was not justified. He claimed he had sold his BB gun to a classmate, who had refused to pay. When the classmate accused Louie of stealing his bicycle, Louie came at him. Shouting his intention to go to Jamie's for a while, Louie gathered up some clothes and left.

He had now returned, but Mary Hamlin had long since

stopped worrying about Louie's whereabouts. She only glanced blankly at her son from the overstuffed, shabby chair where she cradled a squirming child in her flabby arms. Above her head, dancing nervously in the morning light, a tiny bird chirped around its cage. The room was disheveled. The few pieces of furniture looked tired, as did Mary Hamlin.

At thirty-four, Mary was a small, dark-haired, fair-complected woman who stood not much over five feet tall and whose obesity belied her pixieish face. Her once comely figure had succumbed to the strain of a chaotic household; she now weighed over two hundred pounds. Mary Hamlin had her first child, Louie's older brother John, when she was only fifteen. Now, with five children in all, she was showing the emotional scars that almost twenty years of hard mothering had inflicted.

Her husband, Butch, worked long hours for little pay at the Koffee Kup Bakery, and spent considerable time at home secreted away in his basement photo lab. Her oldest child, seventeen-year-old John, had been in and out of foster homes as a juvenile delinquent. Louie, seven months past his sixteenth birthday, was on probation after being convicted of assaulting a college coed with a knife. Lisa and Carol, fifteen and ten, were having trouble in school. And Mark, the youngest child, who was not yet two, was sick.

Mary's dark eyes looked sleepy. She had been up most of the night with Mark and was beginning to feel sick herself. The child moved feverishly in her arms as Mary tried to calm him.

"See what Jamie got me," Louie repeated, now opening the small cardboard carton. "It's a pellet gun." From the box Louie extracted a sleek, gleaming pistol, tossing the package into a corner of the entry hall.

Mary had seen pistols before, but never like the one Louie was now waving from across the room. "It was a big one," she later recalled, "bigger than anything I'd seen before." But Mary did not have the energy to pay much attention to her son's newest exploit. She pulled Mark closer to her bosom and sighed, barely noticing as Louie and Jamie crossed the room and disappeared down the short hallway.

In the kitchen Louie reached for the wall phone and dialed

~~the number for the Chittenden County Office of Probation and~~
Parole. Sine April, when he had been given a suspended sentence on the assault charge, Louie had submitted grudgingly to supervision, his resentment of authority etched hard on his prematurely grizzled face. Louie saw his court-imposed sessions with a psychiatrist at North Country Counseling as only a good excuse for skipping school.

"Nothing I told him was true," Louie would later declare. "He wanted me to get more into what happened at school and that kind of stuff, but I wouldn't tell him. He would ask me how my family life was. I would get around that question and tell him it was fine. I really never got into any discussion of any problems that I might've had because I didn't trust the guy, and I didn't like him and I didn't want anyone to bother me. I don't like people trying to help me like that. I figure that if I had a problem, there was only one person to take care of it and that was me."

Louie slammed the phone down and swore. He had asked his probation officer if he could skip their appointment today, offering as an excuse the need to stay by the phone so he could receive a call about a job. The officer had said no.

"Jamie, let's go," he shouted to his friend.

"Yah. Okay," Louie's lanky compatriot called back from a tiny bedroom just off the kitchen where he was sitting on a narrow bed rumpled with dirty clothes, turning dials on a cheap stereo, tapping his sneaker on the floor to the beat of incandescent static.

"Come on!" Louie shouted, thrusting his head into the room. The door to Louie's bedroom had long since fallen off its hinges, and a tall sheet of plywood, now leaning against the outside wall, was shoved across the opening when Louie wanted privacy. Louie reached across Jamie and grabbed a handful of cassette music tapes, and from his dresser drawer he pulled some clothes and his buck knife. "Come on," he repeated.

"All right. All right." Jamie punched the power button on the machine and followed Louie back to the living room.

"Well, where are you going now?" Mary Hamlin had to shout to make herself heard above the cries of the baby.

As Louie turned to face his mother, Jamie slid through the

front door and onto the porch. "I'm goin' to Jamie's, so what!"
His voice, though still slightly inflected with the high pitch of
adolescence, cut savagely through the room.

Mary Hamlin was used to it. "I don't want you hanging
around with those bad friends of yours," she continued. It had
been Mary's constant complaint. She was not aware of all of
Louie's criminal activities, but she knew about his frequent
school suspensions, one of his car thefts, and his violent temper.
She had long since given up trying to control her son directly.
A few years before, when she tried to paddle him, the fight
had ended up with her own back against the wall.

Instead she had taken to berating Louie, when she had the
energy, for the company he kept. Like Jamie Savage, most of
Louie's few companions in the North End were light-fingered
delinquents. "You're always gettin' into trouble when you're
around with those people," she carped, her voice filled less
with authority than with desperation.

"I can pick my own friends!" Louie hissed and stormed out
the door.

In retracing their steps back down Elmwood Avenue, Jamie
and Louie were following a route familiar to many Old North
Enders. They turned right on Pearl Street, the dividing line
between Burlington's downtown commercial district and its
poorest residential neighborhood, and walked toward Lake
Champlain. Many Old North Enders traveled to Pearl Street to
stand at a government window: to pick up their social security
checks, their food stamps, their welfare payments, their unemployment compensation, or, as Louie was doing, to answer
for their crimes.

From the Old North End came Burlington's most disadvan-
taged. Some 10,000 people, almost a third of the town's total
population, lived in the half-square-mile residential area
squeezed between downtown to the south, the city dump to the
north, the waterfront to the west, and "the Hill" to the east.
Once the town's most prosperous commercial and residential
district, the flesh of the original North End had all but rotted
away.

In the nineteenth century the area around North Street had

sprouted with sturdy homes for a busy labor force working in
Burlington's then booming waterfront lumber trade. Prominent
citizens such as Ephraim Mills, publisher of Burlington's first
successful newspaper, had lived in the North End. By the turn
of the century North Street had become a bustling avenue lined
with tobacco and barber shops, drugstores, fruit and meat mar-
kets, a creamery, and carriage house.

But the 1950s and 1960s had been an era of precipitous
decline for the North End, a time when buildings burned and
were never replaced. The nearby waterfront lumber industry
had died and its laborers went elsewhere to look for work.
When IBM moved into the Burlington area, it located in the
suburbs, as did new immigrants from out of state. With them
came the mammoth shopping centers that began to appear in
South Burlington, in Essex Junction, and other once rural areas.

Others, drawn from the hinterland to the city by the promise
of jobs, could not find work. But the unskilled blue-collar
workers arrived in numbers greater than the promise and took
their unfulfilled dreams and empty pocketbooks to the cheapest
area in town, hastening the decline of the North End.

By the time Louie Hamlin and Jamie Savage were born into
the neighborhood, it had become the Old North End, tired and
delapidated. There were no drugstores, no banks, no barber-
shops. Mazel's shoe store was boarded up, a constant reminder
of former days.

Unlike most city ghettos, the streets of the Old North End
were lined with once elegant houses on ample lots shaded by
trees, but the suburban nature of the streets only masked the
severity of the blight. The houses sagged, their paint peeled,
and if not for the solidity of the original construction, they
would long since have fallen into heaps of lumber.

"Do the touring shutterbugs who snap pictures of scenic
Vermont vistas ever wonder who lives in the trailers and all
the shacky houses they don't record on film?" mused the editor
of the magazine *Vermont Life*. "Do they notice the sad and
ugly towns they drive through to get to the pristine villages
which outsiders have restored?"

Few tourists got close enough even to wonder. From the
Hill, where many of Burlington's upper class shared space with

a prosperous university community, the Old North End was all but invisible. The sightline passed over the treetops and the graceful church spires of the town to the vast expanse of the silver-gray waters of Lake Champlain and the dark silhouette of the mountains on the western horizon. Under the trees and out of view, the Old North Enders crowded into their old homes or federal housing projects.

"I look out my window," exclaimed a young mother living in the Old North End, "and see people pissin' in the yard, young kids goin' in the bar to drag their mother or father home. Sure, I'm concerned. What's my little girl gonna do when she's old enough to see all this? And we can't move. There just isn't the money."

As they walked down Pearl Street in Burlington, Louie and Jamie first passed a small brown row of broken-down wooden row houses, then the state unemployment office outside of which a few men and women always loitered. They entered the district court and office building through a side entrance and passed the door to the state's social welfare department. Waiting for the elevator, they could peer inside the open double doors where a flaxen-faced crowd of men in faded jeans, work boots, and baseball caps and rotund women in bright polyester pants sat around on hard molded plastic chairs puffing on cigarettes or holding pallid infants.

On the third and top floor, the typical height of downtown Burlington buildings, Jamie and Louie emerged from the elevator in front of the state's attorney's office. Through those doors some 4,000 criminal cases passed each year, many from the Old North End.

From his large corner office, State's Attorney Mark Keller commanded a view of both sides of the Vermont postcard: the picturesque portrait on the front and the dirty message scrawled on the rear. To the west was the new six-story Senior Citizens Center, the modern swept-wing Episcopal Cathedral, the Lakefront Radisson Hotel (the city's most expensive), acres of grass and parkland, the lake, and the mountains. It was a view not unlike the one from the Hill.

But Keller also had another view. Turning in his chair, he

could also look north and east, across the street, into the bowels
of the North End. Many of the crime scenes he had to inspect
were visible from his office, as were the homes of the suspects
he would prosecute. "That's where we found Ronnie Bevins,"
he would say, pointing down North Champlain Street as it
headed into the heart of the North End. From a bookshelf he
would take a box of color slides showing a man's dead-white
face distorted by bloody blue and red splotches. "He got hit
fourteen times with a hammer," Keller continued. "And the
guys that did it," he said, now pointing to the right, "lived
right over there, just a few blocks away. I could see the whole
case from my office window."

Louie and Jamie walked away from Keller's office and down
the corridor to the office of probation and parole. After Louie
presented himself to the secretary in his monosyllabic grunts,
he was asked to take a seat. Jamie had already sat down in one
of the folding metal chairs against the wall, lit a cigarette, and
leaned back as if to say he knew the terrain. He had often
accompanied Louie when his friend came to see his probation
officer. The two now sat patiently against the wall talking
quietly, smoking Jamie's cigarettes.

Louie, on a suspended sentence for a "simple assault," had
been lucky. The label attached to the crime represented only a
thin, but significant, line between what was assault and what
easily could have been murder.

It took almost ten minutes before Niel Christiansen, a nine-
year parole and probation veteran in Chittenden County, emerged
from his office and summoned Louie Hamlin to follow. It was
to Christiansen that Louie reported each week during his probation "sentence." They walked ahead, leaving Jamie behind
to smoke his cigarettes.

"There was nothing different about Louie that day than any
other day," Christiansen recalled. But the fact that Louie was
no different that Friday was of little consolation to the probation
officer. Christiansen, a soft-spoken, slim man in his early thir-
ties, saw something in young Louie that was alarming.

When they first met, Christiansen could not decide about
the young criminal. "In many respects," he later explained,
"Louie was not different from other kids his age. He was a

young person, just sixteen. And that's a volatile age group. There is a lot of stuff going on in their lives, and it is not real even-keeled even for the people that can handle it well."

But as he came to know Louie, Christiansen found something in the shy, uncommunicative teenager that was especially troubling. "Talking with Louie and with the family, you knew something didn't quite fit together. It's like when you know you are being conned, you have this feeling, but you can't quite figure out what it's all about."

Louie Hamlin's routine meeting with Christiansen that morning, May 15th, lasted only a half hour, during which Louie sat with his arms crossed over his chest, his head down. "His aspect in general is very monotonish and flat," reported Christiansen, "and that fit his mood on Friday morning." Louie told Christiansen about his school suspension, about his plans to get a job, stating that he might be working at the Lincoln Inn in Essex that afternoon. But Louie typically opened no doors to his hidden life.

He emerged from Christiansen's office a little after the noon hour, telling the parole officer he was going somewhere to be near a phone; he had to wait for the call to work. In the waiting room Louie nodded knowingly at Jamie and the two teenagers strolled out of the office together.

In downtown Burlington, Jamie and Louie jumped on an Essex-bound bus, and within a half hour they disembarked on Lincoln Street in the small village. Having started at Jamie's house in Essex that morning, they had traveled the few miles to the Hamlin home on Elmwood in the Old North End of Burlington, then to the probation office for Louie's regular stone-faced session, then back to Essex, where they stopped at Henry's Market on Main Street, bought soda and cigarettes, and returned to Jamie's house on Gaines Court.

Inside the paint-chipped house at the end of the isolated street, the wakeup call that Friday morning had come, as it usually did, hard and early. A little after six, Janet Lefebvre roused her son Jamie from sleep and reminded him to get the younger kids off to school. She passed by the burly figure of Louie Hamlin curled up on the living room sofa as she walked out the side door onto the landing. The screen slammed shut as the slight, nervous-looking, short-haired woman stepped down the squeaky wooden stairs into the dawn chill, climbed into a dusty blue station wagon, and drove off to work.

Jamie couldn't wait to get his younger brothers and sister up, even though they did not have to be at school until 8:30. Once awakened by his mother, Jamie almost immediately began to rouse Jesse and Julie from their beds. In the hubbub that ensued, his other brother, John, and Cathy Bailey, the upstairs boarder, were also awakened.

Jamie shouted to John, shouted to Jesse, shouted to Julie. He walked grouchily into the kitchen, poured cereal into cracked bowls, grabbed a gallon jug of milk and spilled it over the dry flakes of hydrogenated wheat. The tall, gangly, half-dressed teenager peered up the dimly lit stairway. "Damn it, Julie, get the fuck up, will ya!"

Jamie screamed again, this time in another direction. From a room to his right a boy's voice shouted back at him. "Screw you, Jamie!" Jamie stepped to the closed door and banged on it. "I said to get up, Jesse!" He opened the door, marched inside, and cuffed his younger brother on the side of the head. "Hurry up!"

In the still dark living room, Louie squirmed on the sofa, trying to sleep. Suspended from high school that Tuesday, Louie had been staying with Jamie almost all week. But this would be his last day at the house. Jamie's stepfather, Bernie, would be returning from National Guard camp that evening; he did not like Louie and had ordered him to stay away.

There was more screaming and crying as Jamie terrorized his siblings. "As soon as Jamie gets up I know he is up because he starts yelling," remembered Cathy Bailey, who rented a second-floor bedroom in the house. Since the family had only one car, Janet and Bernie usually left at the same time each morning, Bernie to his job as a garbage collector with the Gauthier trucking company and Janet to her cleaning duties at the Medical Center Hospital in Burlington.

Jamie's morning temper occasionally erupted into violence. "Once Jamie was yelling for Julie to hurry up because her cereal was soggy or something," Bailey recounted. "She wasn't fully dressed yet. And he came upstairs and he had her by the hair, literally, and he just pulled her down the stairs. Suddenly I heard a clunk-clunk-clunk and wondered what it was. So I came out of my bedroom and there was Jamie pulling her down the stairs."

There were eight in the family. Jodie, Rene, and Jamie were Savages, children of Janet Lefebvre's first marriage. Jodie, the eighteen-year-old eldest, had often been in and out of juvenile homes and earlier that year had moved out of the Gaines Court house in order to live with his natural father upstate and join the National Guard.

Rene Jr., a short, wiry sixteen-year-old, was a roamer who had often escaped from juvenile homes and used the Gaines Court house only as a temporary resting place. "Put it this way," Rene would say. "Every time I go to my parents' house, I'm not welcome. There! Flat out!" Rene hung out on street corners in Burlington, stayed with friends all over the county, and often stopped in at the Essex Police Station to ingratiate himself with the police by providing them with tips about crimes.

Jamie, the youngest Savage, still lived at home. Like his older brothers, he was a high-school dropout, once diagnosed as "borderline" retarded. Jamie had quit school in the ninth grade, not long after the family moved from Burlington to Essex in 1979. He had found a job as a dishwasher at the Lincoln Inn, but did not work on a regular basis, taking advantage of the restaurant's constant need for kitchen help.

To Jamie's stepfather, Louie Hamlin seemed to be the cause of Jamie's laziness. "I always thought Louie was a good kid until I moved to Essex and he got kicked out of school," Bernie Lefebvre asserted. "Jamie wouldn't go to school or work when Louie was around. He would call in sick and then they'd take off somewhere."

That week the two teenagers had divided their time between Jamie's home in Essex Junction and wandering around Essex, Burlington, and Winooski. Jamie worked a few hours at the Lincoln Inn, but spent most of his time with Louie. They cleaned the Lefebvre garage one afternoon, scraped the living room walls to prepare them for new paint, watched television, sipped cheap brandy, listened to music in Jamie's room, and cleaned their BB guns.

They were in Jamie's room one afternoon trying to hang curtains for Mrs. Lefebvre when Rene Savage barged in demanding to know what happened to his pellet pistol. The two brothers had been arguing all week over each other's belongings. "He was usin' my stuff," complained Rene. "My stereo; strobe lights. Wearin' my clothes."

"What the hell you doin' here?" Jamie growled at his brother.

"He was in a bitchy mood," Rene remembered. "He says that to me all the time. My father asks me the same thing. 'What the hell are you doin' here?'" For the past few weeks Rene had been living with a friend and only came by the Gaines Court house to check for mail, pick up clothes, and eat an occasional meal. He had left his new pellet pistol, which he obtained from a friend in exchange for a 760 BB rifle, with his mother for safekeeping. "When I first got it, the cops thought it was as big as a .357 except for when I took the cartridge off," Rene recalled. He had looked for the gun in his mother's room but could not find it.

"Where's my gun, Jamie?" he said as he walked into Jamie's downstairs bedroom, convinced that his brother had taken it.

"How should I know where your fuckin' gun is?" Jamie shot back.

"'Cuz you knew it was up there," Rene yelled. "Ma showed it to you and I know you said you liked it."

Jamie was getting angrier. He shouted back at Rene, "Every time there's somethin' missin' you come back at me, Rene. I don't know where your fuckin' gun is!"

Louie stood by as the two brothers screamed at one another, moving closer to blows until Janet finally interceded. Rene stormed out, swearing at Jamie. He would never see his gun again.

Before Essex Junction, the Savage/Lefebvre clan lived on the second floor of a sagging two-story stick-framed structure on the corner of Spring Street and Intervale Avenue in Burlington in the midst of a deteriorating neighborhood. Below

them the food market went through several name changes—
Nelson's Market, Reno's Market, the S and P Market, then
Lovely's Market—a symbol of flux in the Old North End,
where only the poverty was constant.

The rickety staircase leading to the family's apartment clung
to the outside of the old building. The steps were icy in winter,
slippery in the spring rains, squeaky in the hot summer nights.
To the right, down a half-enclosed balcony walkway, was the
Savage/Lefebvre front door. All eight of them lived in the four
small rooms they had called home for more than eleven years.

The air circulated slowly inside because it had no place to
go—especially in the winter, when the windows had to be
closed. The refrigerator was in one corner of the kitchen; in
the other was the clothes dryer, into which little Julie would
sometimes crawl. Next to the kitchen was a small bedroom
where three of the boys slept in a triple bunk bed, stacked up
to the ceiling.

It was a make-do life on the fringes of poverty. Janet and
Bernie obtained some privacy by mounting a thick, solid wood
door on their bedroom, locked with a dead-bolt. When Julie
got older, a room was whittled out of the living room using
pieces of paneling.

It had all begun on June 23, 1962, when Janet Grant, twenty,
and already five months pregnant, married Rene Carl Savage.
Janet had only an eighth-grade education and her husband,
Rene, was just seventeen and a laborer. Both native Vermonters, Janet and Rene lived on the rough, working-class fringes
of the Green Mountain state.

Though many people would call the third boy James, he
was officially born Jamie, on September 20, 1965. His father
picked up odd jobs, but there was never enough. Anger filled
their lives, and the marriage was soon over. "I came home one
day and found my bags packed," remembered Rene Savage,
Sr. "She told me to get out."

Jamie was only two when his parents' marriage disinte-
grated, but before long he and his brothers had a new provider,
Bernie Lefebvre. Neighbors worried little that Bernie and Janet
did not have a marriage license. Most of the residents of the
neighborhood were nominally Catholic, but the ethos of their

marginal class held more influence than the Church. Vermont tradition—the Puritan, disciplined ethic of the old Yankees—was not the tradition of the Old North End, where families were often made and unmade as needs dictated. But even without the license, Bernie was a loyal family man; he stayed, year after year, contending with the chaos of the growing family and their small apartment.

Collectively, the three young Savages grew up to become community terrors. "They were always getting into trouble," recalled Bobby Changon, who lived nearby. "Breakin' windows, ripping off stuff, pickin' fights all the time." The boys would sometimes dare one another to sprawl out in the middle of a street for ten minutes without moving. Cars came to an abrupt halt as a Savage boy creased the pavement with his immobile form while youngsters shouted insults and encouragement from the sidewalk.

Even the family dog suffered at their hands. From the time it was a puppy, it grew to hate children, not knowing that there was a difference between the little Savages who threw rocks at it and other children. "They'd do anything to that poor dog just to be mean," recounted Mrs. Lane, mother of Scott Lane, Jamie's boyhood friend. "They'd actually take a hammer to that dog and just beat on it."

As they got older their mischief grew bolder. "We were walking to school once," Scott Lane remembered, "and you know how the curb sometimes breaks off into big hunks of cement. Well, Rene picks up a piece and walks into the middle of the road and this tiny old guy drives by and he flings it right through the window. They all used to do stuff like that. They'd go out at night and maybe bust thirty or forty windows."

Jamie Savage was not to be trifled with. "He wasn't very strong," Bobby Changon later remarked, "but if he had something in his hands, he could do some damage." Changon recalled passing in front of the big yellow house on Decatur Street where Barbara Grant, Janet Lefebvre's sister, lived with her mother. "Jamie, Theresa, Dede, and Louie were all standing there," he later recounted. "And Jamie comes over to me and he's got this knife with a big blade. It must have been seven inches. And he goes, 'Here, stab me.' I says, 'I ain't goin' to stab you.' So Jamie takes the knife back and he goes, 'Okay, I'll stab you then,' and he starts chasing me down the street. He was crazy, man!''

Police were often at the Savage door inquiring after the boys, but they generally got no farther than a brief encounter with Janet. "The Savage kids figured they always had their mom to back them up," Mrs. Lane later commented.

If there was a robbery in the neighborhood, Jamie was often an immediate suspect. Theresa Robair, Jamie's girlfriend who lived across the street, observed such an episode. "Down the street from my house, there's a house that used to be blue. These college guys was living there. And Jamie took a lot of money out of the house. So the college guys asked me if I knew anything about the money. And I go, 'No.' And they go, 'You have any idea that it could be the Savages?' I said, 'I don't know.' Well, Jamie, of course, had a lot of money that day and he bought everybody everything. Everything they wanted.''

Janet and Bernie married in 1979, but that did not help them exercise control over Jamie, who had now taken to stealing his parents' car. Jamie was only thirteen when he took the car for a joyride, but the consequences were slight. "My mom just pulled me by the hair and threw me out of the car," he said.

Kevin Mongeon, a neighbor, remembered that "Jamie was always wise-mouthed. He had a really negative attitude. You'd try to talk sense to him and he'd say, 'Yeah, yeah, yeah. Get bent.' They were basically street kids, out till twelve, one, or two at night." They were often seen in the neighborhood driving around in someone else's missing car. "They'd steal cars left and right," according to Michael Sweeney, a classmate of Jamie's in junior high. "They'd come by in a car and the police would be after them. Then they'd disappear for a few days."

When the Savage youngsters were caught by police, they merely entered the revolving door of the juvenile justice system. With the Weeks School closed since 1977, Vermont had no locked juvenile detention center. The Waterbury Detention Center, an annex of the state mental hospital, had only ten beds and was reserved for the most serious of juvenile offenses. Few delinquents feared a stay at Waterbury, for the facility was prohibited from holding any youngster for more than forty-eight hours without a special court order. Even then, youngsters could be held for only a relatively short period. The only "punishment" available for youthful criminals was a system of foster homes and one camp in the woods run by the state's Social and Rehabilitation Services Department.

"One of the biggest problems is that there is no bottom line for juveniles," commented Corporal Larry Soutiere, the Burlington Police Department's juvenile officer. "And by the time you work your way to the bottom line, an adult prison, you are already a hardened criminal. Right now a kid gets picked up by the police, he goes to juvenile court, and if he gets placed in SRS [Social and Rehabilitation Services] custody, he will probably be sent back home. SRS will then try to work with the family.

"This process may take anywhere from one to two months while the court is processing the case. During that period the juvenile will go out and commit two more crimes and go back to court. And SRS can't do anything with him because he's still in court. So after he gets done with the two other crimes and he is through with the court system, he is turned over to the SRS as a delinquent. They place him in a group home. He doesn't like it, and starts acting up. They throw him out and put him in another home, where he acts up again. It goes on like that until they get tired of him and send him back home. And the majority of them, because they are street-wise, know just what the system is going to do."

Rene Savage, picked up for theft, was sent to the Benson Wilderness Camp in southern Vermont, where there were no bars and no fences. He escaped, was returned, and escaped again. "Benson is a joke," Scott Lane said candidly. "You can walk out of there anytime you want to. So it's no big deal to get sent there. It was more like status, like a vacation. There was no place they could send you that worried anybody too much."

The young Savages knew the ineffectual juvenile system intimately. "I learned how to drive and watched other people drive, so we stole cars and we'd get in trouble for it," Jodie Savage would later remark. "We were too young so we couldn't go to jail or nothing. We'd get on probation or custody of our parents and stuff like that. I told everybody, 'Well, we ain't going to get in any trouble—don't worry about it, we're juveniles.'"

But in the fall of 1979, Jodie came to realize that becoming sixteen had turned his juvenile pranks into serious business. Jodie, Jamie, and Louie Hamlin drove into Rene Savage Sr.'s driveway in Enosburg Falls, a village fifty miles north of Burlington, to show off the car they claimed to have bought. Jodie and Jamie had not lived with their natural father for almost twelve years, but Rene Sr. knew enough about his sons to ask them to produce the bill of sale. When they could not, he ordered them to leave.

Later that day, police officer James King of Colchester spotted the stolen Chevy Impala on the Interstate highway and forced it to pull over. When King learned that Jodie, who was driving, did not have a driver's license, he took the three teenagers to the stationhouse. This time Jodie spent thirty days in the Chittenden Community Correctional Center before being given a four-to-six-month suspended sentence and released in his father's custody. Louie and Jamie, both under sixteen, went free, just as if they had never been apprehended.

By his own estimate, Jamie lied most of the time—to everyone from parents to teachers—but his forte was thievery. He would sneak into his parents' room and steal money from his stepfather's wallet or his mother's purse. Forty dollars. Fifty dollars. "I only got caught once," he boasted.

Jamie also victimized local stores in Burlington, stealing two and three times a week from the age of ten on. He took rings from Penney's; candy and cigarettes from the Mall Drug on Church Street; pants and boots from Woolworth's. A manager caught him a few times, but nothing happened. "He just said put it back and get out," Jamie recalled. A week later Jamie was back. He didn't think stealing was wrong. "I figured they couldn't do anything about it."

By the time he was picked up on the Interstate, Jamie was fourteen and had just entered Burlington High School as a freshman, already on the threshold of permanent truancy. Though he graduated from Edmunds Junior High unable to read beyond the first-grade level, Jamie always pretended that he had no problems in school. "I did all right," he would say. "I never stayed back." His mother saw life through the same Pollyannaish glasses. "I thought he did, you know, pretty good for himself," she would say later. "He was going to school. Was goin' to join the Air Force.... When he got out of school, he wanted to be a pilot or something."

It was a grandiose dream. Jamie had always been in special programs, where his answers to teachers were limited to "Yup" and "Nope." The only reason he was not held back was because teachers had no hope that Jamie could ever master more than the rudiments of the ABCs. In class he was given to occasional angry outbursts; in the lunchroom he sometimes threw food around. His suspensions from school were frequent, but he was never expelled. One of his teachers saw in Jamie "a quiet kind of anger. He would blow up and walk out of class in response to class structure. He, like a lot of kids, had trouble with structure and self-control."

The school psychologist offered little hope for improvement. "Academic progress is likely to remain very limited." On IQ tests Jamie's scores ranged from "below 45" in vocabulary to a surprisingly good 106 in "coding," with an overall average of 78, a figure that put him in the "borderline retarded" category.

After less than two months at Burlington High, Jamie had already been absent twenty-five times, and by the beginning of December he had dropped out altogether. When the family moved to Essex Junction, Jamie's transcripts were forwarded, but he never appeared at school. Instead, though still only fourteen, he was at the Lincoln Inn applying for a job, telling the manager that he was sixteen.

"We never heard from him at all," an Essex High assistant principal reported. "If a parent wants to take a child out of school, the child can fall through the cracks. There are so many loopholes." Jamie's parents did not actually take him out of school, but they offered few objections to his leaving. "Jamie tried going back to school and they told him, I guess, that it wouldn't do him any good unless he was in a training program," maintained Janet Lefebvre. "Then he got this job at the Lincoln Inn."

With his younger brothers and sister off to school that Friday morning, Jamie got dressed. Louie was still not fully awake when Jamie ambled out of the Gaines Court alley, his red baseball cap perched like a neon wart atop his shaggy head, his faded blue jeans ripped below the right knee, and headed for the Lincoln Inn.

He crossed the village center railroad tracks, and within a few minutes walked through the Inn's coffee shop entrance. Jamie had not come to work that morning. An unreliable part-time dishwasher, he was paid the minimum wage of $3.35 an hour when he worked. On a good week, he made over $100, but half of his pay went to his mother, the other half Jamie spent on movies, roller-skating, and occasional presents for his youngest brother and sister. He once opened a savings account at the bank with a $10 deposit, but never added anything to it.

This week, because of Louie, he had not worked more than a few hours, and he asked his co-workers in the kitchen if he could borrow $10. Refused the loan, Jamie met Arthur Kourkoulis, the Inn manager, and asked to borrow the money, saying his mother needed it. "Sometimes they needed money for fuel, sometimes for groceries," explained the soft-spoken, Greek-born restaurateur. Kourkoulis gave Jamie the money, expecting that he would, as usual, pay him back from his next paycheck.

Outside, the traffic was still snarled at Five Corners as crossing guards were ushering the last of the children bound for the Lawton School through the maze. Jamie glanced briefly at the youngsters, shrugged, tugged at the brim of his cap, and walked back toward home. Louie was already dressed when Jamie arrived; he was stuffing some clothes in the knapsack. After Louie finished packing, the two left for the bus stop behind the railroad station and boarded a bus for nearby Burlington to visit Louie's probation officer.

The day had been like any other the two spent together—wandering, concocting makeshift plans as they went, led by the moment and the accumulation of impulses. Now, a little before 2:00 P.M., back at Jamie's house in Gaines Court, they listened to the radio and watched television. The time passed rapidly, and Jamie and Louie decided to go to Maple Street Park and hunt squirrels. Jamie grabbed his paring knife, the one he used at the Lincoln Inn for cutting vegetables, and a pellet pistol that he always kept in his room. Louie took the pistol that Jamie had given him earlier in the day. Stuffing the guns into the front of their pants under their shirts, they walked out the front door.

On the porch Cathy Bailey was settling down to write a couple of letters. The young boarder kept to herself except when she helped Janet clean the house or baby-sit for the younger children. Louie and Jamie mumbled a quick "Hi" as they strode down the front steps and wandered off down Gaines Court. At Railroad Street Jamie said, "Let's take the tracks. It's shorter." Louie nodded his assent and the boys followed the railroad right-of-way that ran through the center of the village.

Behind the Lincoln Inn, Louie and Jamie walked along the slow curve of track. To the left of the high bed was a small, wooded residential neighborhood; to the right were the sprawling grounds of IBM. It was only a few hundred more yards to the edge of Maple Street Park. As Louie and Jamie were skittering down the railroad embankment toward the thick woods behind the park, they pulled their pistols from their pants.

"So, ya still wanna get a couple of girls?" Louie called to his trailing companion.

"Yah. Sure," Jamie called back as he followed Louie onto the path that led into the trees.

Although Louie and Jamie had been talking about "getting some girls" for the last few weeks, they had no specific plans, did not know exactly what they would do or where. They had followed women on a number of occasions looking for an opening to rape. They had even walked around downtown Burlington in search of victims, but had failed to find a place secluded enough to carry out their half-formed plans.

What Jamie and Louie knew about sex came from the streets of their working-class neighborhood. It was literal, guttural, primitive. "I was out with a friend one night, walking down the street, when Louie hollered some pretty raunchy things at us," recalled one Essex girl. "He was standing by Jamie's house with Rene and we were walking by the gas station and he hollered. 'Why don't you come over here and give us a little lip-lock,' and other stuff like that."

Janet Lefebvre remembered Louie talking about girls quite a bit, and concluded that his view of women was crude. "Sometimes he would say dirty things about them. Like they're only good for one thing or they're no good and things like that. I don't think he cared too much for girls."

Jamie Savage knew nothing about sex unless it was expressed in four-letter words. When he talked about sex, he spoke only of "fucking" and "giving head." He did not know the meaning of "orgasm" or "ejaculation," had neither taken a sex education course nor spoken to his parents about the subject. To the word "intercourse," he drew a blank; he only understood "getting laid." Jamie had never heard of an "erection," but he was familiar with the term "hard-on." He had no true concept of anal and oral sex, but he talked about "fucking a girl in the ass and making her suck on my dong." When asked where he learned these things, Jamie responded, "I just learned it. You pick 'em up word by word and you can put 'em together."

Both teenagers were quite familiar with the woods next to Maple Street Park, where they had hunted squirrels and scouted possible sites for their rape plans. That week, the two went to the park almost every day. On Monday they took their friends, Jeanie and Barbara Parker, with them, and as the quartet walked through the woods, Jamie and Louie fired their guns at animals. On Wednesday, by themselves, they found a couple of musty old mattresses in the underbrush. When a young girl wandered down the narrow path through the woods, they frightened her with their pellets and laughed as she ran.

The next day, Thursday, seventh-grader Kelley Krauter-Nelson left school about five o'clock; fortunately, she was with four other school friends as she started through the woods. "Two men passed by us," the girl recalled. "And they looked kind of scummy. We all noticed them and one of my friends went, 'Oh, he has a gun.' I turned around and saw one of them with a gun in his hand." Kelley remembered both men vividly. "There was a shorter one, kind of husky, and he had black hair, and he had a small triangle between his two eyebrows like one big eyebrow. The other was taller and thinner, and he had blond hair." The children walked quickly away, unaware of the intentions of the intruders.

By now Jamie and Louie were familiar with the Lawton School schedule and knew when the children—Jamie's brother John being one of them—went home for the day. Their plan this Friday was as rudimentary as it had always been. "We were just looking around there to find some squirrels and look for girls," Jamie later recounted. "If there were no girls, we was going to get squirrels."

They wandered up the path as if there were no distinction between the two activities. Emerging from the woods next to the tennis courts, they again shoved their guns into their pants and walked by the playground, the baseball diamond, and the swimming pool, up to Maple Street.

Across the street, up a slight incline of well-manicured grass, they could see the children in the distance beginning to spill out of Albert D. Lawton Middle School. An afternoon wind drifted across the hill carrying a spring chill in its wake. It had been raining most of the day, and heavy clouds still floated by, promising more showers. The schoolchildren began fanning out across the spongy-wet grass, parading down the hill.

Louie and Jamie stayed on the sidewalk only a few moments before turning around to retrace their steps back into the woods, to wait.

CHAPTER 6

The Attack

As IT STARTED to rain in the park, Jamie impatiently yelled to Louie that it was time to start for home. The two were already wet from their walk through the woods and the new downpour was sure to soak them. But just as Jamie signaled his desire to leave, he saw Louie motioning for him to hide. "Get over here," Louie said in a brusque whisper.

Following Louie's gaze through the branches, Jamie could see two small girls approaching the woods from the playground.

"Should we get 'em?" Jamie asked as he came up to Louie, who was already hiding behind a big elm.

"Why not," said Louie under his breath. "What the hell. My mom don't give a shit. I ain't got nothin' to lose."

As Missy Walbridge and Meghan O'Rourke started into the woods, talking about Meghan's frightening encounter two days before, they had no idea they were being watched from the shadows at the edge of the tennis court. Savage and Hamlin waited until the girls had started down the narrow path toward the railroad tracks and were a few dozen yards in front of them. Quietly, they emerged from their hiding place. "You take the blond," Louie whispered to Jamie. Softly, walking on the balls of their feet, they began to follow the girls.

The rain was now falling steadily and the ground was mushy. Meghan and Melissa were intent on their conversation as the boys closed in on them without being heard. The boys glanced at each other, gripping their pistols tighter. When they were just a few feet away, Louie struck, and Jamie moved at almost the same instant.

In the middle of a sentence, Melissa felt a large hand clamp over her mouth, muffling her scream of terror. At the same instant, Meghan's face was covered by another forceful hand. Instinctively, both girls tried to pull away, but the hands over their mouths only tightened. Meghan and Melissa were dragged backward roughly, pressed between arms and bodies. Suddenly, they felt the muzzles of guns in their backs.

"This is a .45. Don't try to yell or I'll shoot you," Jamie hissed at Meghan.

Louie pushed his own gun against Melissa's throat, and quickly, as if to prevent himself from losing heart, dragged the little girl off the path into the brush. Melissa struggled vainly to squirm free, but the grip of the 160-pound teenager held her firmly. Jamie, now dragging Meghan, followed Louie into the bushes. The vegetation scratched against the girls as their attackers propelled them farther into the woods.

A few yards off the main path they came to a slight clearing where Louie and Jamie stopped. They released their hands from the girls' mouths, but still held them firmly.

"Why are you doing this?" Meghan blurted.

Jamie pushed the gun to her head. "Shut up or I'll shoot you!"

"Take your clothes off," Louie commanded, his dark eyes moving from one horrified girl to the other. Louie felt his anger ease the words from his mouth.

Meghan hesitated. Jamie still had the gun pointed at her head. He towered a foot over the tiny girl, his eyes glassy, drops of water running down his acne-pitted face. Too frightened of the gun and the hulking teenager to resist, Meghan slowly began to take off her clothes.

A few feet away Louie was holding his gun at Melissa's head repeating his command to disrobe. "No, no," Melissa cried. "You can't do this. I'm only twelve years old."

Her defiance enraged Hamlin. Persistently, Melissa tried to talk rationally to Louie, asking him why he was doing this. But her questioning only fueled his anger. His lifelong sense of powerlessness was threatened once again, this time by a twelve-year-old girl. He clasped his hands around her neck and began choking Melissa, his wrath pulsing through his arms. Melissa was gasping for breath. Then with a brutal stroke Hamlin pushed her to the ground and began ripping her clothes off.

When Jamie Savage saw his friend choking Melissa, he reached out and grabbed Meghan by the neck. As he squeezed, Meghan's pain became unbearable. She was sure she was going to die.

But almost as quickly as he had clenched her neck Jamie released his grip. "Take the rest of your clothes off!" he ordered. When the girl had done what he asked, Savage forced Meghan down on her knees in the mud.

He fumbled with the zipper of his jeans.

"Now suck on my dong!"

"But what for?" Meghan sobbed, tears drenching her cheeks.

"Because I want you to!" the teenager exclaimed.

After Savage was finished, he pushed Meghan to Hamlin, who had just raped Melissa. Hamlin then tried to have vaginal, then rectal, intercourse with Meghan. For the next ten minutes Hamlin and Savage continued their rape.

Melissa struggled against her attackers, telling Meghan she was sorry for not having taken her fears more seriously. At one point, when Melissa noticed that Hamlin had loosened his grip on her, she lunged to the side, desperately trying to flee.

Missy did not have the experience to counter her attacker. She was a fighter, but she was no match for the teenager. Hamlin raced after Melissa, grabbed her, and brought the struggling girl back.

He then spoke to Meghan, who now knew these were the

same two young men who had chased her on Wednesday.

"What do you think we ought to do with you, lady?" he said.

"I think you ought to leave us here and just run away," Meghan said, her voice a bare squeak.

"I don't do that," Hamlin said. He aimed, then shot Meghan in the side of her neck with his BB gun.

Forcing the two girls to lie flat on their stomachs, Hamlin and Savage tied their hands behind their backs with the girls' own pants and gagged them with their knee socks. Meghan, sobbing with fear, looked over to her friend. Melissa was lying naked on her stomach on the moldy leaves and the prickly wet twigs. The dark-haired youth was now standing over her, pointing his pistol at her back.

"Now you're gonna know what it's like to be shot five times and killed and slaughtered like a pig," Hamlin cried out maniacally, pulling the trigger on his pistol. Melissa winced as the high-powered pellets struck her in the back. Meghan then saw Louie bring one of his black combat boots down hard on Melissa. Melissa's gagged and contorted face twisted with pain, but she refused to cry.

Hamlin and Savage bent over the girls, grabbed them under their arms, and jerked them to their feet, pushing them deeper into the woods. As they did, Meghan and Melissa fell on their knees, were picked up, and forced to duck under branches that slapped against their faces. Melissa was still kicking and twisting, desperately hoping to get away.

At another slight clearing, fifteen feet from the spot where the girls were raped and some thirty feet from the main path, Hamlin and Savage threw their victims on the ground beside the two soggy foam mattresses they had found on Wednesday. Hamlin raised his BB pistol again and shot Melissa in the eye, destroying its sight.

He then disappeared for a few moments and returned with a stick. Throwing Meghan on her back on one of the mattresses, he bent over her and dragged the rough wood hard across her throat, cutting it. Meanwhile, Savage was bending over a prostrate Melissa, looping another piece of clothing around her neck. As he pulled on it with all his might, Melissa's face turned blue.

"You look, and I'll blow your head off," Savage warned Meghan, who was now on her stomach a few feet away.

"Gimme the knife," Hamlin suddenly ordered Savage.

The command stopped Savage from his choking of Melissa. He reached into his back pocket and gave the shiny paring knife with a six-inch blade to Hamlin.

"We gotta get rid of 'em," Louie said. "We don't want no witnesses." Jamie nodded in agreement.

Meghan turned her head slightly and saw the blond-haired youth handing the other the knife. Hamlin bent over Melissa and started slashing at the child's body, stabbing her in the neck, then her chest, opening the chest cavity with ragged cuts as each time he removed the knife at an angle different from its entry. He stabbed the bleeding child several times, at least once directly through the heart. Between her breasts, he teased the knife into a crisscross design of torture.

When he finished with Melissa, Hamlin walked over to Meghan and stabbed her in the back. Meghan passed out from the wound, but Hamlin continued his bloody orgy. He sat on Meghan's legs and grabbed her by the hair. Pulling her limp, unconscious body up toward him, he took the knife and thrust it into her chest. As he pulled it out, it left a gaping hole, which started to bleed profusely.

Louie Hamlin stood up and flung the blood-stained knife into the trees. It dropped into the underbrush, where it became mixed with moist dead leaves and barnacles of wood that suffused the air with a wet, earthen smell. With the steel blade's last whoosh, the woods fell to eerie silence. The rain had now stopped. Only the intermittent patter of drops brooked the quiet. There were no more little girls' cries. Their whimperings had been stilled.

In the slivers of light filtering into the small clearing Hamlin and Savage hovered a moment over the two naked bodies sprawled in the mud. As far as they knew, their victims were now dead. They waited for a sounding from their instincts, a change in the wind to tell them the next step to survival. "Let's get the fuck outta here," Jamie said, his voice a high-pitched whine. He started to leave, but the sight of the mutilated body of Melissa suddenly affected him. He threw up at the feet of the lifeless child.

"Get the stuff," Louie ordered.

Jamie hurried off to the place where they had stripped and raped the girls, frantically retrieving the knapsacks and clothes. The momentum of the attack, fired by increasing bursts of rage against the defenseless girls, had carried Hamlin and Savage, step by step, from senseless assault to violent murder. The teenagers now struggled to cover their tracks.

"C'mon, man!" Jamie's call carried anxiously through the trees. In his arms the gangly teenager already cradled the girls' wet belongings. "Let's get outta here before somebody comes."

Because she had been lying on her stomach, Meghan's slight breathing was imperceptible to Hamlin, who thought both girls were dead. Louie quickly grabbed the edge of a soggy mattress and flung it over Meghan. Jamie's continuing cries to hurry increased Louie's mounting anxiety. Hesitating, Louie reached for the second mattress, threw it hastily over Melissa, and stumbled off through the brush to meet his friend.

"We gotta get rid of this shit," Louie muttered as he passed by Jamie, crossed the main path, and began descending the steep embankment toward the creek. The two slipped their way down the short incline and leaped over the shallow waters.

Just a few yards above them, on the top of the embankment, were stacks of two-by-fours, yellow Caterpillar tractors, and the foundation work of a new apartment building. Had the weather been good, the construction site would have been buzzing with a half-dozen workers. But the woods, usually well traveled by IBM employees and schoolchildren, had been empty throughout the attack. Because of the rain, the builders had left early.

On the other side of the little gully, Hamlin and Savage kicked furiously at a patch of ground. They threw the clothes and bags into the hole in the earth and covered it with leaves. Walking another twenty feet along the hill, the teenagers found a rock, turned it over, and carefully placed their guns beneath it. They walked back down the creek and washed their bloodied hands in the clear waters.

Their fortunes held as they emerged from the woods and started down the railroad tracks toward the village at a slow trot. A crew that had been working on the electrical lines along the tracks that week had quit early. The Central Vermont freight had not arrived yet. They saw no one.

"I hope we don't get caught," said Jamie, breaking a long period of silence.

Louie looked straight ahead. "Don't worry about it," he told his friend.

As they passed behind the Lincoln Inn and crossed Maple Street, the evening traffic at Five Corners was beginning to pick up with homeward-bound IBM employees. The congestion boosted the teenagers' confidence. The world was as it always was. They slackened their pace.

"Let's get a soda," suggested Savage. The memory of the attack was drifting off to an unused corner of Jamie's mind. He was thirsty and needed a cigarette.

Louie zipped up his plaid hunting jacket to hide the spot of blood on his white shirt, and the two passed through the squeaky wood-framed glass door of Henry's Market as if nothing had happened.

CHAPTER 7

Legacy of Hate

IT WAS IN THE fall of 1979 that Louie Hamlin's perverted passions—the impulse that would lead him almost two years later to stalk young girls in Maple Street Park—became evident. All the demons of self-hate, anger, and boredom, all the distortions within the Hamlin family unit converged.

Two days before his fifteenth birthday, on October 27th, Louie's own mother reported him to Burlington police for attempting to rape his sister. When Mary Hamlin returned home from teaching catechism classes at church that Saturday morning her thirteen-year-old daughter, Lisa, told her that Louie had raped her. Mrs. Hamlin called the Burlington police, who assigned the case to Detective Stephanie Schoggen, the department's specialist in sexual assault. Lisa told the officer that her brother had put his "thing" inside her twice "in the front" and once "in the back," and said he would kill her if she told anyone what had happened.

Because it was Hamlin's mother who had turned in her son, the complaint was taken seriously. At the pediatrics ward of the hospital, where Lisa had been taken for an examination, Detective Schoggen met Susan Via, her counterpart from the state's attorney's office; Mrs. Hamlin; Sister Aline Paris, a nun and friend of Mary Hamlin's from St. Joseph's Catholic Church; a number of doctors; and David Martin, the Hamlin family caseworker from the SRS, the state's juvenile department.

The medical examination, performed by a gynecologist and a pediatrician, proved inconclusive. "The doctors questioned whether penetration had occurred," Schoggen noted in her report, "stating that the victim had said that she had not been in pain during the incident, but that the exam had caused her pain; that there was no injury or trauma whatsoever to the genitalia or rectum; that the victim had very little understanding of her anatomy."

If Lisa had little understanding of her anatomy, how could she have invented such a story? Perhaps what technically constituted rape, which to officials meant penetration, meant something else to a thirteen-year-old girl. When Schoggen finally spoke with Lisa, her account seemed too detailed to be a complete fabrication.

The policewoman coaxed Lisa into writing down her account of the episode. In a shaky, little-girl scrawl, with big circles above all the *i*'s, Lisa wrote: "It was between 9:00 and 9:30, I think. I had my baby brother in my arms and I was sitting in a chair when my brother came in and picked up the baby and put him in his crib. I said, 'I'm going to tell Mama on you.' And I had dialed the telephone and was waiting for a voice to talk on the other end when my brother pushed down the metal piece and dragged me in his room and got me undressed and he got undressed and he started fucking me. He had my hands and feet down on the ground. I was crying and then he picked me up and carried me to his bed and started fucking me again for a few minutes. Then he turned me over. Then he started it again for a few minutes then he stopped and I grabbed my clothes and ran upstairs and locked myself in the bathroom and he followed me and I didn't let him in and then he left and I came down and fed the baby."

After the interview with Lisa, Schoggen asked Mrs. Hamlin to talk to her daughter again about what had happened, explaining that the doctors did not think that sexual intercourse had actually occurred. Mary Hamlin returned from the hospital, where Lisa stayed that night, with a fuller account of her son's sexual assault on Lisa. "Her daughter had indicated that she and her brother were both nude during the incident," Schoggen later noted, "and that her brother had lain on top of her such that his penis touched the area between her legs and between her buttocks but that there had not been penetration."

No official charge was lodged against Louie and the teenager would later brusquely dismiss the question of whether he actually raped his sister. "Let me make this clear! I was accused of raping her; nothing was proved," he would retort. "I ain't sayin' I did, and I ain't sayin' I didn't. They checked her out, and they couldn't find anything to prove that I did it."

But residents in the Old North End accepted the essentials of the story. "His sister spread it all around," Theresa Robair claimed. "And Louie admitted it."

Louie was sent to a foster home under a "voluntary care" agreement with SRS, and family caseworker David Martin arranged for family counseling at the Howard Mental Health Center. Both experiences, however, proved unproductive. Less than a week after his arrival at the foster home, Louie, Jodie, and Jamie stole the car for which they were arrested on November 6th. Since he was already in the juvenile system's equivalent of "jail," there was no more "punishment" that Louie could receive.

Louie was taking full advantage of the discretion allowed him under the Vermont juvenile law. After the arrest for the auto theft, he stayed less and less at the loosely structured juvenile facility, and gradually came there only to sleep, spending more time at his own home, less than a mile away. Eventually, Louie simply moved out of the foster home, and the SRS, its hands tied, terminated its "care" agreement with the Hamlin family.

The counseling sessions went awry the same way. The Hamlin family had initially given David Martin hope that the sessions might succeed as Louie, his mother, and his father dutifully traveled to the clinic every week. Butch Hamlin was positive, telling the caseworker that both Louie and John were doing well in school, and that Louie was interested in computers. He said he was going to get Louie an Apple.

But in less than a month the experiment in rehabilitation was all over. Butch Hamlin had changed his attitude. "He became more and more rigid," Martin later explained. "He was demanding that both John and Louie be removed from his home, saying that they were bad boys. He couldn't deal with them anymore, and had to protect his daughters."

Louie Hamlin had inherited almost everything from his father but his bulky build. Butch Hamlin was a loner, a quiet, mysterious man who lived in a world that outsiders could not penetrate. He was dark-haired like his son, but unlike Louie, Butch was short and skinny. "He was a little guy," an acquaintance would later comment. "About five feet four or something like that."

As small as he was, Butch, the third child of Francis and Delphine Hamlin, grew up to raise hell around his native Burlington. Born into the Old North End, he would raise his own family there. His delinquent behavior as an adolescent landed him in the Weeks School for two years; but not long after his release he married, at age seventeen, a neighborhood girl.

Mary Safford was just fifteen at the time. She had met Butch in high school and fell madly in love. In large part, her adolescent love was an attempt to escape a tempestuous home life. She was the first child of Walter and Theresa Safford, themselves only nineteen when she was born.

Their marriage dissolved when Mary was seven. Her mother kept the six children. As Mary remembered, her mother was always overworked, authoritarian, and unable to offer much affection. "If you don't have love," she would later remark ruefully, "how can you give it?" The first signs of affection shown to Mary came from young Butch Hamlin, into whose arms she rushed. Mary quickly became pregnant.

The first three children came in rapid succession, all within four years. The family was soon beset by serious problems. Soon after Lisa was born, it was discovered that she had a life-

threatening congenital heart lesion. At the same time, Louie—
barely two years old—developed fulminating bronchopneu-
monia and had to be rushed to the hospital. "My mother said
she found me in my crib and I was all blue," Louie later
recalled. "She took me to the hospital and they had to do an
emergency tracheotomy and there's a possibility—but nobody
knows—that there was some brain damage done."

Through the medical crises, which strained Mary's energies,
Butch worked at the Koffee Kup Bakery, oddly detached from
the family's problems. Ten to twelve hours a day he stood on
the loading dock at Koffee Kup, shepherding shipments of
bread and doughnuts on and off the big semis. Normally he
worked the graveyard shift, from 7:00 P.M. to 8:00 A.M. Butch
seldom took time off, almost never had a vacation, often worked
weekends.

Though a loyal employee, Butch struck some of his co-
workers as strange. "He was always talkin' camera stuff, Butch
was," said Randall Colby, a truck driver at Koffee Kup and
husband of Betty Colby, who worked with Jamie at the Lincoln
Inn. "You know, 'I went downstreet and bought a big camera
today' and 'I went down and got parts for my camera,' and 'I
got a dark room downstairs' and 'I am taking pictures of this
and that' and 'I am developing this.' He would come in in the
morning and say, 'I took some weird pictures,' that he was
developing pictures of girls. But I never had any faith in any
of it."

Butch Hamlin had few friends, and even refused to take
Mary out because of his fear of crowds, preferring to stay for
hours in the little photo lab in the basement of their Elmwood
Avenue house. No one was quite sure what went on in that
room; Butch kept the room sealed with a lock and key.

Mary, meanwhile, began to show the strain of a life that
was beyond her control. Lisa's heart condition demanded most
of her time for years, and Mary could not give much attention
to the two eldest, John and Louie. Frustrated, she ate inces-
santly, and her obesity only aggravated Butch's repressed anger,
sending him farther into his isolated world.

To Mary it seemed that her husband had "two personalities."
He could be affectionate with her, but he also had a violent

temper. He would not strike Mary, but his rage would result in his smashing dishes or throwing furniture around the house. The children looked on, but Butch rarely struck them during these episodes. He was an inconsistent disciplinarian, meting out absurd punishments, then relenting.

Amid the turmoil of the Hamlin family, Louie became a brooding, sullen child, given to bouts of intense anger and passionate silence. Extremely shy, he seemed to be without emotion except for wildly violent outbursts. Physically, he grew up faster than all his peers, and felt uneasy about his appearance. His thick, bushy eyebrows were a constant source of embarrassment. His attitude toward himself was reflected in his dress, which, as a friend remarked, was "on the downer side," replete with dark and heavy flannel shirts, jeans, and tennis shoes or hiking boots.

His peers tended to leave Louie behind because he was unsociable, even unattractive, and Louie soon developed the habits of a loner. Television, to which he was soon addicted, became his source of solace. "If there was nothing else on but garbage, I'd just watch something that I'd like just a little better than the rest," Louie recounted. "I watched it until my mother said that I had to go to bed."

Television did not calm Louie's tempestuousness. Even as a young child, he had frequent tantrums. "When Louie was only two, he would throw himself on the floor, hit his head on the wall," remembered his aunt, Joyce Hoffman. "Whenever he was in bed, he would rock back and forth all the time. He completely destroyed a crib." When Mary Hamlin took little Louie out with her, she placed him in a harness to prevent him from rushing into the street. Mary knew that there was something wrong with Louie, but felt powerless against whatever was making him unruly.

At H. O. Wheeler Grade School, Louie's explosive personality became more exaggerated as he vacillated between silence and rage. He was a chronic troublemaker, stealing pens from teachers' desks, bullying the younger children. The Hamlins were periodically called to school to discuss their son's temper. Beating up on other kids gave him some relief from his frustrations, but if Louie dared his schoolmates, he also felt picked on. Because he was larger than most, he became self-conscious about his size, viewing it as the cause of his problems. "I was a little big for my age and guys would just pick fights with me and beat me up," he claimed.

Louie constantly searched for signs that his sense of persecution was real. His mother didn't understand him; his father either ignored or berated him; John and Lisa teased him. It bothered Louie that his father sometimes showed a preference toward Lisa, feeling that in any dispute his father "stuck up for" his sister. Louie's hostility toward his sister grew as he saw her capturing their father's favors. He suspected that something sexual was going on, but never had any proof of it.

"He wanted the boys thrown out in order to save the girls," Louie later said. "Lisa always gets what she wants from him." Unable to get affection from his father, Louie would approach his mother, who would try to listen, but found it too much for her burdened mind. To Louie it seemed that she never understood, and increasingly over the years he felt that she lost her temper with him too often, criticized him for his choice of friends, and scolded him for his difficulties at school.

Louie was not unintelligent; he even struck some teachers as being bright, but he had problems with math and reading and always required extensive remedial help. He felt the need to advance slowly in school and begged his parents to let him stay behind a year, but they refused.

"John and Lisa had a thing where they tried to get me mad and lose my temper," Louie recollected. "I don't know why. My mother told me, 'They're deliberately trying to get you mad.'" They usually succeeded. Maturing physically more rapidly than his older brother, Louie once tried to choke John. "Verbal, fist, you name it," said Louie. "I stabbed him three times. He just got me mad. After I calm down, I don't even remember what the fight was over. One time we had an argument and we were on the front porch and I don't even know how I got the jackknife in my hand. But I just lunged at him and it went into his side. I stabbed him with a screwdriver once. And he's got the scars to prove it."

In another burst of rage, Louie once came after John with

an ax. He chased his brother upstairs and just as John scurried into his room and slammed the door, Louie crashed the blade through it. Splinters flew, as the crunching thwacks and Louie's screams echoed through the house. In panic, Mary Hamlin called the police.

"He had a very short fucking temper," recalled his constant grade-school companion Steve Galyean, from a Vermont prison. "He got mad pretty easy. Louie and John got into a lot of fuckin' fistfights, you know. They got right down to the fuckin' bloody nose and puffed-up eye and stuff. It was really weird."

Louie's angry outbursts were not limited to his family. There were moments when he erupted against friends, including Jamie's brother, Jodie Savage, who once thought Louie was going to kill him. "He pulled a knife on me, put it to my throat, and I was scared. Like, I didn't know what to do, that was the first time I ever got a knife pulled on me. From a friend, a best friend I grew up with."

Louie was not sure what was happening, or why; he only knew that if he had a bad day at school, had been bothered by someone, he was likely to blow up. Whenever his mother harped at him he would storm out of the house and walk for hours without a destination, fuming with anger. A Catholic nun, a friend of Mary Hamlin's who watched Louie at the catechism classes at St. Joseph's, consulted a colleague about Louie's behavior. "I was afraid that Louie was going to kill somebody sometime," she later said.

"I had a reputation in grade school and junior high for not taking no shit from nobody," Louie would later boast. "It helped a lot. People weren't bothering me as much." But the reputation that protected him isolated him as well. The world was out to get him, Louie believed. He fought back, and as he fought, the world left him alone.

Louie walked alone with his devils. Quiet and suspicious around peers and adults, he gravitated toward animals or unthreatening individuals. He could not get along with John and Lisa, but he did enjoy his other sister and younger brother. "Mark and Carol, neither of them don't bother me," said Louie. "Me and Carol are pretty close. I'd always take her out or something, or buy her something or give her money. And when Mark came along, he just sort of took to me. He would always be in my room listening to my stereo or just come right in."

But "best friends" for Louie were a cat and a dog. The cat was "the only thing I really loved," he said. His mother got rid of it when he was thirteen, and King, a large, rangy, jovial black mutt, took its place. "King was a better friend than the people I knew. After I got home from school, we would run around in the backyard for a while or down in the fields. On weekends, I would take him to the river and we would run around in the woods down there."

Louie felt close to nature, which, like him, had its own primal, uncontrollable impulses. Mean and harsh, soft and serene. It had no conscience, no empathies or sympathies, only instincts, urges, and reactions.

To Louie, the world of people was "strange." At school he felt out of place because of his early physical maturity, which forced him to shave before most of his male classmates did. "People would make fun of my beard or the eyebrows that met on the bridge of my nose," Louie would complain. "I always thought that people hated me."

Louie felt pressured from all sides, and that his problems were legion. The only accomplishment he recalls being proud of at school was swimming the length of a pool underwater. "My mother and father, teachers, everybody—they all wanted me to be something I wasn't. I've always looked older than what I was so people have always treated me older, and that didn't help at all. They wanted me to act the way they thought I should act. Like, with my schoolwork. They always gave me harder schoolwork. I'm a slow learner. It's a possibility I had brain damage when I had that tracheotomy. That could be one of the reasons."

In Edmunds Junior High, Louie had his first opportunity to break out of the crippling cycle of poverty, family chaos, and hostility. He was accepted into the Paradise Project, an innovative program that gave the pupils special attention in classes separate from the rest of the school. The project recruited a cross section of students from the Hill—the sons and daughters of doctors and lawyers—as well as the offspring of the working and welfare classes from the North End.

It was then, by happenstance, that Louie had a possibility of channeling his rage. A project teacher, Eric Mortensen, noticed that Louie had expressed an interest in poetry and offered him the opportunity to write poems as a way of improving his poor grades. Susan Craighead, a student who was starting a Project newspaper, was intrigued. A talented young girl from the Hill who would go on to Princeton University, she was taken by the incongruity of Louie Hamlin writing poetry.

"He has a rough manner—at least on the surface—and isn't your typical poet," she explained. Susan met Louie one afternoon in study hall. "I understand that you write poetry," she said.

"Yeah," said Louie timidly. "A little."

"You don't suppose I could see some of it?" Susan asked gingerly. "It's for the magazine that we're starting."

Louie didn't respond at first. "Well," he finally offered, "it really ain't no good."

Louie would never admit that his poetry was anything but "dabbling," as if aware how inconsistent it was for the Hulk to be serious about poetry. But Susan pursued Louie. "It took me several sessions to get him to bring it to me. And when he finally did, he was very shy about it. He didn't know what I was going to say, but was sure that it couldn't be anything complimentary."

Louie gave Susan a few sheets of lined paper with his tight scrawl covering the page. The spelling was atrocious, the grammar bad, and punctuation almost nonexistent. The poems were written in prose format rather than in poetic stanzas and meter. But with Susan's patient help, Louie turned his writing into readable verse.

When the first issue of *The Noun* was published, even Louie Hamlin could not disguise his satisfaction. Though he would later claim that these poems "were just something to do when I was bored," Susan Craighead knew he was feigning. "I remember when he saw it for the first time in print. He had a smile on his face and actually looked satisfied with himself, which is something you didn't see too often from Louie."

For an eighth-grader, especially one who had spent most of his school years in remedial reading classes, the poems were remarkable. In Louie's uncoordinated verse, a yearning for tranquillity stood in contrast to the chaos of his daily life. There was also a subtle opening to his deepest fears, to the violence that lurked within him.

Night

Night is dark, night is cold,
Night is quiet and so nice. . . .
We take time to enjoy
All of the things in life . . .
Like the owl, wolf, panther, mountain lion.
I just hope we let things live
Instead of die.

Louie was at war with himself, in a struggle between living and dying—even killing—and there were few areas of neutrality.

Live

There is only one life to live
And one lover to love . . .
You kill and kill but don't say sorry
Or so long,
You only say die!

Anger had already become the central theme of Louie's existence. At some level of his untutored consciousness, he knew what demons were at his gate.

Anger

. . . It is out of my nature to kill, therefore
I will not kill if provoked.
But some people can kill just out of anger!

It was a bizarre friendship. Susan from the Hill, daughter of a Vermont doctor, rich, articulate, Ivy League-bound. Louie— from the Old North End, son of a warehouseman, bound for a life of crime. Susan gave Louie constant affirmation and Louie reciprocated with a yeoman's deference. "He was particularly polite to me," said Susan. "He made me feel like someone out of a Victorian novel; like he was the servant who was always polite, someone who had been in the family for years. And it always made me feel comfortable because I didn't feel like I was 'Miss Susan.'"

At school, Louie found company not only with local ruffians but with misfits of a different ilk, among them John O'Halloran, son of a well-to-do furniture retailer. Socially insecure, O'Halloran was as meek as Louie was violent. "Louie was one of the few people in school who didn't taunt me or try to make me lose my temper," O'Halloran recollected. "I liked him."

To O'Halloran, Louie was a different kind of "tough guy," one who was self-possessed. "Most of the other kids were trying to prove something. But Louie didn't need to do anything like that. All he had to do was prove it to himself. To the people he didn't know, Louie generally acted like a thug. He'd either ignore them or intimidate them if they caused him any trouble. If you got him riled up, you were in trouble. He didn't fight all that much because he made it very plain that fights with him were not a joking matter and he was going to win. And it wouldn't be just wrestling around on the ground."

O'Halloran believed Louie had a rudimentary code of conduct better suited to the Middle Ages than to twentieth-century Vermont. "He had his own honor system and he stuck by that. He didn't really think it was a crime to steal; the crime was being caught. Vermont is a very calm place. I got the feeling that he would fit better in New York City or maybe back in the past as a knight, when his violence would have been more acceptable and be put to better use."

In the Paradise Project, Louie had an opportunity to break out, but once again he failed. As Louie described it: "I don't like talking before the class. And whenever we would go on a trip, you would have to keep a journal. I wasn't no good in that. Then when you got back you had to write a report on it, and I ain't no good in writing reports."

What Louie was good at was walking the other side of the law. He started stealing when he was six. At first he took small things from school: books from the library, pens from teachers. Occasionally a teacher would catch him, but the scolding did nothing to curb his penchant. When he was only ten, and still living on Vermont Park next to the Koffee Kup Bakery, he jimmied his way into a car and pocketed some money.

Over the next five years Louie became a proficient "second-story man." Always working alone, the youngster canvassed the upper-class neighborhoods of Burlington making mental notes about which houses were unoccupied or unprotected. He returned at night and quickly moved to the rear of the house to test the doors. If they were locked, he tried the ground-level windows. If he still could not gain entry, Louie found a way to climb to the roof, where he usually located an open or unlocked second-story window.

Louie would set out on his breaking-and-entering escapades not only for gain but to fight off boredom. He did not break into houses when he was angry, he said, only when he felt "blue." The success buoyed him. He was proud of his skill, the speed of his entry, the fact that he had not been caught. If stopped—which happened on occasion—he was proud of his ability to escape punishment.

A psychiatrist once asked Louie, "Is there anything wrong about breaking in?"

Louie responded, "All depends. If you do it for a reason, like if you need the thing you're going after, I can see, you know, breaking and entering." That psychiatrist would later call Louie Hamlin a "moral imbecile." Louie, he said, functioned at "a level of moral development normally seen at ages nine or ten."

Three times in 1978, while he was only a fourteen-year-old freshman at Burlington High, police picked Louie up on theft charges. The arrests would have seemed dire to Louie, except for two factors. First, Louie was a juvenile and could not be prosecuted. The police did not even bother to press an investigation. Second, the few times that Louie was stopped for his "suspicious" activity represented only a fraction of his criminal behavior. By his own estimate, before he reached sixteen, Louie had broken into more than twenty homes and stolen more than a hundred cars.

It was classmate Steve Galyean who introduced Louie to car theft. They were bored, and cared about nothing except breaking the boredom. "We went downtown and seen a coupla cars with keys in them and said, this is it," Galyean later explained. "We are goin' for a drive. It was right there on Church Street, and we took it down to the Intervale. Of course, I knew how to drive anyways and I took Louie down there. He didn't fuckin' know how to drive but he wanted to try it out. I guess he liked it and just started stealing a lot more."

Louie would claim that every one of the cars that he stole during his youthful crime spree had keys in them. For Louie, with his primitive sense of morality, that meant, "Take me." "There ain't nothin' wrong with it if people are dumb enough to leave their keys inside," Louie would rationalize.

Occasionally Steve and Louie would strip the stolen cars and try to pawn the goods. After he learned the effects of apricot brandy at age fourteen, Louie would sometimes engage in simple destruction. "Coupla times we went out breakin' into cars," recalled Galyean. "He'd be drinking his brandy and I'd be smokin' my joints. He was pretty crazy. He seemed like he was King Kong. He would jump onto a car and he'd start stomping on it. Run right up on top of the car and fuckin' start stompin' on the hood, saying 'Aaaaheee.'"

During these episodes Louie and Steve were detached from any reality save the one that excited them. Galyean: "We just thought it was pretty funny. Just to have somethin' to do. We didn't really care about nothin'. It was like we didn't give a shit what happened. We were still young. Nobody did no disciplinary fuckin' thing to us, ya know what I'm sayin'.

"If I thought I'd get thrown in jail for stealin' cars, there's no way I'd do it," Galyean later said. "You are under that age there and you can go in and there is nothin' that anybody can do about you 'cept for to call up your parents." That he uttered those words from an adult prison while serving a sentence for robbery was a bitter irony.

Louie found that he was virtually immune from the law. In addition to his arrest for car theft in the fall of 1979, his brief stay in the foster home and the aborted counseling sessions after the rape charge involving his sister were the only disciplinary consequences he endured.

But Louie still kept a cautious eye on the calendar. He knew that until he was sixteen, he could roam the streets of delinquency with relative impunity, and that afterward they would be the avenues of crime, vulnerable to arrest and prison. Even though part of him believed in his willpower—the ability to curb his appetite for antisocial behavior—other malignant forces were hard at work.

One such force was Louie's uncomfortable relationship with girls. In the ethos of the North End, sex was an early sign of manhood and womanhood. As Louie saw things, "If I can't make it with a girl, who am I?"

"He usually don't go out with too many girls," Rene Savage explained. "Like, I've set him up a couple of times when I go skatin' 'cuz I know quite a few girls. And I set him up with one girl and he just stays with her, you know, he hardly kissed her or nothin'."

From an early age, Louie knew what sex was, but his knowledge was crude. From the time he was fourteen, he tried, as he said, to "get in bed with a girl," but without success. Watching his brother with girlfriends, Louie began to dress like John in the hope that girls would like him too. But he couldn't escape the hateful image in his mirror.

"I went out with girls for a few years, but just for a couple weeks," Louie said. "My brother fixed me up with one girl, but I didn't really care for her. I got in bed with her once, but I was smokin' pot and drinkin' and it was no great success. I ain't so great with girls. I just don't like to make a fool of myself."

The girl that Louie finally "made it with," at the age of sixteen, was someone with a loose reputation. "She probably conned Louie into thinkin' that she was his real girlfriend or somethin' like that," hypothesized Steve Galyean. "She was what you call a town slut, ya know what I'm sayin'? She was over to my house three or four months before she went out with Louie. And there was a bunch of us over there. It was like a gang bang. I guess Louie just ended up pickin' her up or somethin'."

Louie's feelings of hostility, his anger toward his sister and his mother, and his ethos of machismo were a dangerous combination. Louie began to see women as objects of rape. By the time he was sixteen, he was seriously following women, a diversion he had begun in junior high. It was usually after an argument with his mother that he would storm out of the house and find himself stalking women, trying to get up the courage to rape them.

It was after one such violent session at home on a Sunday afternoon in January 1981 that Louie slammed the front door as hard as he could, grabbed his coat and his buck knife, and left the house. Though the snow was still stacked along the streets and the air crisp, the sun was out and the thermometer had risen to a mild thirty degrees.

Louie was not thinking; the fierce argument with his mother had triggered reflex behavior. Hands stuffed in his coat pockets, head cocked rigidly ahead, he barreled along the sidewalk in a simmering rage. He headed up Elmwood, past his old grade school, toward Manhattan Drive.

Passing through the familiar opening in the cyclone fence on the ridge above the dump, he skittered on the icy ground and made a quick descent of Deadman's Trail. At the bottom, the Intervale spread in front of him like a flat, unbroken white sheet. Crossing the railroad tracks, Louie struck out across the field, crunching through the ice-crusted snow with his heavy black combat boots.

He held the same angry pace all the way to the river. On the bank Louie stopped for a moment, looking across the thick, motionless ice shards crowding the Winooski. He turned around, paced back through the snow to the railroad tracks, and marched along the ties toward the lake. On an unused siding, Louie climbed atop a row of abandoned boxcars and walked to the end, sure-footed as he leaped from one snow-covered car to the next.

A few moments later he found himself walking down to the lake. Suddenly, Louie spotted a young woman climbing up the steep escarpment of Rock Point. She looked like she was having trouble.

"You need some help?" Louie yelled.

"No." An athletic college junior at the University of Vermont, Candy Hackett was in no trouble. She had decided to take a walk that afternoon and had wandered along the banks of Lake Champlain, a few minutes from her Old North End apartment. Hackett enjoyed watching ice skaters glide across the frozen waters and found the climb up Rock Point invigorating. But despite her assurances that she was all right, Hackett saw that the bearded young man was starting up the rocks toward her.

"And in seconds he was up there beside me," she later recalled. "He just swung up the trees like a monkey."

Louie pointed out an easier path to the top and Hackett thanked him. The two chatted as they climbed, Louie boasting to the young woman that he knew the area well. They watched the setting sun for a few moments and then, as Hackett turned to leave, Louie followed.

"Oh, I take it you're ready to leave too?" Hackett asked, feeling a slight flicker of anxiety. "I think I'm going to jog for a bit," she announced and started in a slow canter down the gradual incline, hoping that her new companion would stay behind. But Louie was right on her heels.

Hackett now realized that something was not quite right. She stopped and turned toward the stranger. "If we're going in the same direction, we might as well walk together," she told him. Louie nodded.

"Now I was getting nervous," recalled Hackett. "But I didn't want to run because I thought that might provoke him. If you run from a guy, he is definitely going to run after you and catch you."

As they walked down the path, Hackett started peppering Louie with questions. He said his name was Louie. He told her he lived on Elmwood Avenue; went to Burlington High;

came to Rock Point often. All of his responses were brief and jittery. Hackett sensed he was tense and she did not like it. She kept talking, asking him questions, trying to relax him.

"He was giving me quick, popcorn answers," the young woman remembered. "Maybe he thought he was being cool by not talking much. It wasn't until I asked him if he liked to write that he showed any spark of interest. He said he liked to write poetry."

Hackett was relieved to hear the teenager contribute something to the conversation. By now they had come to the railroad tracks and Louie suggested that the path alongside it was the best way back to town. To Hackett it appeared well traveled, the snow packed with cross-country ski tracks and snowmobile treads. "Little did I know that the trail would pass alongside a bunch of abandoned boxcars, completely out of public view."

With the snow piled on either side of the path, the two marched single file, Hackett first. The sun had set and dusk was beginning to settle in. Hackett stopped at one of the boxcars, still talking. "Wow, look at these old cars. Must be a great hideout for drunks," she exclaimed.

But Louie had fallen silent. Hackett realized that he was not listening to anything she was saying. "Then I shut up. God! I was getting nervous. I wasn't about to run out on him because I was decked out in a couple of layers of wool and there was a lot of snow on the ground. We kept walking and I was whistling. Then the next thing I know there's a knife at my throat."

Louie commanded the young woman to sit down. But with a quick movement that she had learned as a lifeguard, Hackett grabbed Louie's arm, slipped from the chokehold, and whirled completely around to face her attacker. In an instant Louie had been taken off his guard. Hackett gripped the pressure points of his wrist and elbow and squeezed the arm holding the knife as tightly as she could.

"Now what did you do that for?" she asked. Hackett was reacting on instinct, too surprised even to panic. "You don't have any reason to pull a knife on me."

"Shut up!" Louie shot back.

Hackett kept her grip on Louie's wrist, making sure that the knife in his hand was not going to move. "Okay," she said calmly. "Okay."

Louie kept his eyes downcast. "Don't provoke me," he snarled. "Sit down!"

Hackett refused to sit. "You can't tell me what to do," she said firmly.

Louie repeated the order and Hackett again refused to obey. He glared at her, but made no effort to loosen Hackett's hold on his wrist.

"I can almost feel the tension you have built up in you," she said soothingly. "Why don't you hold my hand instead of the knife?" The young woman, petrified with fear, was bluffing for time. "He could have easily overpowered me," she later recounted. "You have so much strength when you have that much built-up tension inside. He was mad at the world. He was burning. I could tell. I could feel it, the way he answered me. The way he kept his head down. He had a very distant look in his eyes and he could have done just about anything to me at that point. He might have killed me."

Slowly Hackett convinced Louie to put the long, silver-bladed knife back into its sheath. She then took both of his hands in hers to make sure he would make no sudden move to retrieve it. Together, they walked back toward town, talking, always talking. Louie became docile, confessional. He told Hackett he had no friends and nobody liked him; that his brother was always provoking him; that he had just fought with his mother.

Hackett began breathing easier as they approached the streetlights of the Old North End. On Lake Street she said, "I guess this is where we part ways." Louie apologized and thanked her for listening to him, then walked off.

An hour later Hackett was at the Burlington Police Station, telling officers that the man who attacked her was named Louie and lived on Elmwood Avenue. They nodded; they knew who it was. At the end of her session, the officer asked, "Candy, do you have anything else you might want to add to your statement?"

"I just hope that no one else has to encounter this person who may not be as strong and communicative," she replied.

• • •

Louie agreed to plead guilty to a simple assault charge for attacking Candy Hackett. "We charged it as a simple assault because there was no bodily injury," explained Deputy State's Attorney Bob Simpson. "And that's all we could have done. Our major concern—since we knew that he would get little or no jail on a simple assault conviction—was that he would get some sort of psychiatric care."

Probation officer Niel Christiansen had come to the same conclusion. After Louie's plea, Christiansen was told to prepare the recommendation for sentencing. He met with Louie, with his parents, with Burlington High personnel, with caseworkers for the state's juvenile authorities, read the extensive police file on the Hackett assault, and checked for any history of criminal or delinquent behavior.

"Louie had no previous record," Christiansen recalled, but there were complaints against the young Hamlin in police files. He had been picked up for "causing a disturbance," for stealing a bike, on suspicion of car theft once, and once for sexually assaulting his younger sister. But in all those cases Louie was a juvenile, under sixteen, and no formal hearings were held. "None of those things would have turned up on an official record check," said Christiansen. "Even one that included juvenile information. Why? Because they did not result in an adjudication. And in juvenile terminology that means conviction."

Christiansen knew that there was more to Hamlin than the juvenile record showed, but he had no choice but to treat Louie as he might have any other first offender and recommend a suspended sentence. "First offense, sixteen years old, living with his family, doing satisfactorily in school. So what would you do, lock the kid up? Put him in jail? A good defense attorney would have been all over you."

But that did not satisfy Louie's attorney, John Ambrose, who sought to have his client's case transferred to juvenile court where the proceedings would be secret and the records sealed. In Vermont, though a person was an adult in the eyes of the court at age sixteen, the court judge still had the discretionary power, for sixteen- and seventeen-year-old defendants, to transfer the case back to the juvenile system.

At first Louie claimed he thought Hackett was a girl who
had yelled at him a few days before, and he wanted to scare
her. Later he would admit the lie: "The story that I told the
police was just to get out of trouble. That's all it was. My
intention at the time was that I was going to rape her. I didn't
tell the police that because I was afraid they were going to
charge me with something more serious."

To get Louie's case transferred to juvenile court, Ambrose
tried to show that Louie's actions were those of a confused
youth. "Louie needs to learn to better deal with his anger," the
defense attorney told the court. "Nevertheless, the report does
show he's a bright individual." The attorney then asserted that
Louie's grades "have been really rather good grades over all,"
and "this young man has not been or is not a general troublemaker."

Ambrose told the judge that Louie looked forward to being
a military policeman; a criminal record might ruin such hopes.
The attorney's most telling argument was a very simple one:
Louie was a victim of the calendar. "This young man was just
a few months over age sixteen," said Ambrose. "If he had
committed this stupid act a few months earlier, then he would
definitely be in juvenile court."

But Deputy State's Attorney Bob Simpson thought that the
luck was on the public's side. "We believe not only was it a
stupid act," Simpson told Judge John Connarn, "but a dangerous act." Simpson was aware that once the case went to the
juvenile system, it would be as if no crime had been committed.
Louie, he felt, should not be protected from the "taint" of
criminality.

When Simpson had finished, Judge Connarn complimented
defense attorney Ambrose for making "a persuasive argument."
"But I can't buy it, I'm afraid," he said. Then Connarn looked
toward Louie Hamlin, who had been sitting impassively at the
defense table.

"Louie, what makes you so angry?" asked the judge.

Louie shrugged.

"Why are you so angry?" Connarn repeated.

This time Louie responded. "I don't know," he mumbled,

looking down at the tabletop. "Just once in a while I get really mad."

"Why do you think that is?" Connarn probed.

"It's just events that lead up to things," said Louie. "Just things in my everyday life. I just get mad."

If Louie had no explanation for his anger, could he be expected to quell it on his own? Louie told Judge Connarn that he was working on it.

"You've got a lot of years," said Connarn. "This young lady, if she hadn't been so brave—I guess she got the knife away from you somehow—I can imagine what may have happened. There could have been an aggravated assault or murder here."

Connarn told Louie he did not want to jeopardize his chances to join the military or find a job. "But I don't really feel this warrants juvenile treatment. I think you need help." The judge then imposed a suspended sentence of zero to twelve months and ordered him to "get some alcohol counseling." Except for the fact that he now had a "record," Louie walked out of court a free young man.

On a drizzly, cool Saturday morning in April, just two weeks after his sentencing for the knife assault, Louie's violent psyche was given some macabre nourishment. Louie and his father were riding with Louie's uncle, Ernest Hoffman, along the small back roads toward Joseph Safford's farm, some twenty miles south of Burlington. Safford was Mary Hamlin's brother and Hoffman was married to Mary's sister Joyce. The two men each owned a half interest in seventeen pigs they kept on Safford's farm, and they had asked Louie and his father to come out to help with the butchering of the hogs.

When the three arrived, Safford escorted them to the holding pen where the pigs were wallowing in the mud. Safford had not seen much of Butch or Louie since moving to the farm a few years before. When the group arrived at the pen, Safford and Hoffman wrestled one of the pigs out of the fence and around to the back of the barn. "If you shoot the pig in the pen with the other ones," he explained later, "the other pigs could abort the little ones." Butch and Louie followed.

Hoffman, carrying a .22 rifle, carefully positioned himself between the pig and the rest of the men so a ricocheting bullet would not hit anyone. He put the muzzle of the gun almost directly on the soft spot behind the animal's right ear and fired. Louie, standing next to his father, watched as the pig lurched and squealed but failed to fall.

Hoffman was annoyed that his shot had not even brought the animal to its knees, but Safford, who had slaughtered a thousand pigs in his life, told him not to worry. "Some of these things have double skulls," he said, "and it makes it impossible to kill. Had one two years ago that took seven shots to bring down."

Safford handed Hoffman another rifle, this one powerful enough to kill almost any four-footed animal. Hoffman aimed against the spot behind the ear, and this time the bullet blast knocked the pig to the mud, where it lay flailing and kicking in pain.

Quickly Safford ran to it with his razor-sharp double-bladed "sticking knife" in one hand. "Once the pig is down," he instructed them, "you got to stick him before he gets back up. They have to bleed good or the meat's no good." The slaughtering process had little to do with being humane, said Safford. "A pig more or less quivers, and that's how it makes them bleed. You have to make sure it quivers good so it bleeds good."

He plunged the knife through the tough skin of the animal's throat, working the blade back and forth as he drove it in. As Safford had hoped, the pig refused to die. The knife wound sent it bounding to its feet, screeching and bleeding, lurching across the barnyard twenty-five feet before collapsing.

When he was sure the animal was dead, Safford turned to Louie with the knife and asked him to take it to the house to have his wife clean it. By this time both the knife and Safford's hand were covered with blood. Looking squeamishly at his uncle, Louie stepped back.

"I don't want to get my hands all bloody," he protested.

"Take it!" ordered Butch Hamlin. "A little blood ain't goin' to hurt you."

Hesitantly, Louie reached for the knife and slowly marched it over to the house.

By the time he returned, the teenager seemed to have over-come his distaste for the blood. He bent down and helped his two uncles drag the lifeless carcass to the barn, tie its hind feet together, and hoist it up off the ground. When the butchering was complete, Louie helped Safford throw all the bloody en-trails and innards into a wheelbarrow and take them behind the barn for disposal.

Throughout the day, except for his initial refusal to touch the knife, Louie rarely spoke. But he had watched intently. Frequently in the days that followed he would describe the gory details to his friend Jamie.

A few weeks later, as Louie and Jamie waited in the leafy shadows of Maple Street Park for their prey that Friday after-noon, the vivid picture of the pig slaughter moved back and forth in Louie's consciousness, blurring any distinction his clouded mind might have made between things animal and human.

CHAPTER 8

Frantic Hours

JANET LEFEBVRE WHEELED the old blue station wagon up to the side of the house and began unloading bags of groceries from the back. She was later than usual getting home; the heavy traffic coming through Five Corners that Friday afternoon had slowed her considerably. Police cruisers had been peeling out of the station on Pearl Street and rushing through the intersection. "It was loaded down there," she told her son John as she marched toward the house.

"Ma," announced Jamie's brother excitedly, "a kid got murdered over there."

"Oh, that's awful," said Janet, realizing that was probably the cause of the heavy traffic. From the south, over the housetops, sirens were wailing, but Janet didn't stop to think about her son's statement. She was in a hurry to prepare dinner for Jamie's stepfather, Bernie. After two weeks of duty with the National Guard, his homecoming was a special occasion.

Boarder Cathy Bailey had finished watching her late-afternoon television soap operas. She was on the front porch, trying to finish her letters, when she glanced to her left and saw Jamie walking up the road from Railroad Street. He reached the house, quickly bounded up the front steps, and pretended to hide behind the half-open front door.

"Is my mom home yet?" he asked.

"Yeah," she told him, "she's in the house putting away the groceries." Bailey thought Jamie seemed excited about something. That he bothered to talk to her, which he seldom did, seemed to indicate he was in a good mood. "Where's Louie?" she asked.

Jamie put his head out from the behind the door. "Oh, he's in the park." He chuckled. "And he's goin' to kill me when he comes home 'cuz I left him there." Jamie quickly disappeared into the house.

"I didn't think nothing of it," Bailey later explained, "because Jamie and Louie always horsed around together. He didn't act scared or nothing. He was his normal self."

Ten minutes later Louie arrived at the Lefebvre house. He came from the rear along the short path that ran across the vacant lot from East Street. His combat boots were muddy and Bailey noticed that there was sand and dirt on the bottom of his pants. "He was sloppy," Bailey remembered, "but he's not a great dresser anyway. He was just a little dirtier than usual, that's all."

"Is Jamie home yet?" he asked as soon as he had stepped onto the porch.

When Bailey told Louie that Jamie had gone in the house, Louie went in, but a few moments later he came back out and started down the steps.

"Where are you going?" Bailey queried.

"To the store," said Louie as he started off down the road. "His mom said he was at the store."

"But he's not at the store," the young woman told him.

The front door squeaked open and Bailey saw Janet and Jamie putting their heads out, smiling. "He thinks I went to the store," Jamie chortled.

"Janet and Jamie were standing in the doorway laughing at

him," recalled Bailey. "Louie thought it was funny, too, when he found out. Apparently they had played a little joke on Louie. Horsing around. It was a normal thing around the house."

Janet returned to her kitchen to continue preparing the dinner. From time to time she would think about "how terrible it was that the kid got killed," but she had a dozen chores to occupy her mind. Her other children—John, Jesse, and Julie—ran in and out of the house or sat in front of the television set in the living room. Jamie and Louie then went into Jamie's room and closed the door, telling Janet they wanted to change clothes.

Janet was too busy in the kitchen to do more than nod. "They acted funny, like they were in a hurry," she said afterward, "but I only thought it was because they wanted to go to Louie's house."

When the teenagers emerged from the room fifteen minutes later, Louie was wearing a pair of Jamie's dress pants and carried a shopping bag under his arm. He asked Janet for a ride to his house in Burlington. Jamie's mother often generously ferried the young Hamlin back and forth to Burlington, usually when he was working with Jamie at the Lincoln Inn. But tonight, she told him, she could not; Bernie would be home any time.

Louie was in an exceptionally agreeable mood. He borrowed bus money and left with Jamie. On the porch Cathy Bailey kidded him about his new pants and Louie laughed in response. On his muscular frame the light-blue polyester slacks stretched over him like dancer's tights. "Yeah," he said, "they're Jamie's. Kinda tight, but they fit."

The two strolled down the wet gravel road toward the village center, three blocks from where a bleeding Meghan O'Rourke was being lifted into an ambulance. As police and ambulance lights flashed through the gray air a few hundred yards away, Jamie Savage and Louie Hamlin calmly waited under the little plastic shelter behind the railroad station for their #5 CCTA bus to Burlington and the Hamlin home.

At the same moment, at the small police headquarters in the center of Essex Junction, the usually casual rhythm now took on a frenzied hum as the attack dominated police communications. Orders, requests, and questions from policemen in Maple Street Park, at the hospital, in their cruisers, and on foot searching the village, poured in and were recorded with urgent brevity.

5:07 Walkie-talkie #7 radioed, "Has coroner been advd?"
5:10 Cruiser M196 said, "Send SA."
5:12 Mobile Unit 2 reported, "Have child; poss witness, at United Maple Products."
5:12 M192 radioed that he was "10-23 at United Maple."
5:21 M191 radioed to "have 183 come up to last diamond at Rec Center; will meet him there."
5:23 M191 asked to "have someone bring 3-4 raincoats to scene."

The State Police Crime Lab and the medical examiner were summoned. At 5:25 Sergeant Robert Horton, the chief of Troop A State Police Bureau of Criminal Investigation, was called away from his dinner table to Maple Street Park. The four other officers attached to Troop A's BCI were also summoned. A State Police sketch artist, to work with Meghan at the hospital, was located in Lamoille County. At 5:30 all off-duty Essex police officers were ordered back to work.

Armed with Meghan's brief description of her attackers, police fanned out through the neighborhood, racing up and down the railroad tracks, going house to house, along Camp Street just behind the woods, down Grant and Jackson and Wrisley streets, searching for clues and witnesses.

One man who lived on Wrisley Court told police that he had been startled at about 4:30 by screams and shouts, and had gone out to his backyard, which bordered the woods. He had seen a little girl covered with blood and two men on the railroad tracks, but no one who matched the descriptions of the suspects. One woman had seen two men in the park who did match their descriptions, but that had been on Tuesday. The most promising lead came from two park employees who, seated in their pickup truck by the ball field just before four o'clock that afternoon, had seen two men ("dirty looking, creepy, and grubby") who "appeared to be in a big hurry."

Some residents of the area said they saw two suspicious men driving a light brown or tan, older model, large station wagon, possibly a GMC. Police stopped several cars whose occupants matched the descriptions, but the drivers and their whereabouts checked out and no arrests were made.

Mark Keller soon realized that there would be no quick solution to this case. Though a half dozen homes were less than fifty yards from where the two girls were raped, police found no one who had seen or heard the attack. Keller could only hope that Meghan O'Rourke would be able to offer more information, some additional clue to the identity of her attackers.

When State Trooper Stanley Strusinski, the police sketch artist, arrived at the hospital to see Meghan O'Rourke, he was shocked. As he stood by the little girl's bed, watching her suffer the tubes, the oxygen mask, and the probing hands of nurses and doctors, the tall, blond officer was not sure he should be there. Meghan looked close to death. He was torn between his instinctual reaction to leave her in peace and his professional sense that he had to command every minute possible with her. Meghan was the only one who, from her mind's eye, could help him "draw" her attackers.

For a few endless moments Strusinski stood with his book of facial parts, feeling strangely misplaced, consoled only by the thought that doctors would not have consented if his presence would harm Meghan. "She looked like she'd been through hell," Strusinski recalled. "So what do you say to this child?" Eventually, Strusinski found a feeble voice. "Hi, honey, how are you?"

When Meghan gave no response, the policeman looked up at Susan Via and James O'Rourke standing by the bed as if hoping they would order him to stop. But Meghan's father and the prosecutor resisted the temptation to intervene.

Strusinski again bent down to Meghan. "I realize you can't speak," he whispered in her ear, "but you and me are going to make a sketch together. I'm going to show you some pictures, and I want you to nod yes or no if it's the same or not."

Strusinski expected the young girl to whimper "No, no." Instead, Meghan looked at him as if to say "Okay."

"She was on the fringes of conking out. Yet somehow I started questioning her," recounted Strusinski.

But in a few minutes Meghan had indeed passed out. Strusinski left, worked at his sketch in the hall until Meghan regained consciousness, then returned for a few more precious minutes of questioning. "Okay, Meghan," he said, holding a page of paper and transparent overlays in front of the little girl's face. "Here's where we are now. Is the hair okay?"

Meghan looked but gave no response.

"Is it too short?" prompted Strusinski, placing his ear directly to her mouth. He heard a slight, hoarse whisper from behind the mask. "Yes."

Meghan soon lost consciousness again. Strusinski retired to the hall, where he pulled a nurse aside. "What's going on?" he asked, seeking reassurance. "Is she going to be okay?" The nurse didn't know. He waited, feverishly drawing, waiting for the next word that Meghan was awake.

During those first few hours Strusinski strained to create a picture of the attackers. Other than saving Meghan's life, his drawings had become the center of hospital attention. "Everybody was anxious," he recalled. "Even doctors were coming by and saying 'I'd like to cut the fucking guys' throats.' I mean, these were doctors and they were getting down to gut police talk."

In the hallway, waiting for Meghan to regain consciousness, Strusinski noticed someone who resembled the brief description she had given Susan Via and sketched him. When a doctor with a beard walked by, Strusinski coaxed him into Meghan's room and asked the child, "Does he look like this guy?" Occasionally Meghan nodded a "Yes"; sometimes she moved her head to signify "No." Invariably she drifted back to unconsciousness. For four hours Strusinski single-mindedly tried to create a picture of Meghan's attackers. "Anything. Anything at all to help get a description. Everybody wanted one that evening and I knew goddamn well I couldn't do it. It was impossible."

Meghan was trying her best, but she was too weak to hold on. During those crucial four hours Strusinski saw Meghan for a total of less than fifteen minutes: a few minutes of questions, then unconsciousness, followed by long minutes of waiting, then a few more queries. "I would be talking with her one minute," explained the trooper, "and bam! She'd be gone."

It was almost midnight before he gave up for the night. "I knew it was going to be slow and there was just nothing I could do about it. Rather than be satisfied with something that wasn't accurate, I'd rather take two or three days." That night, Strusinski improvised, using his composite kit to piece together a broad outline of two faces. He showed it to his superiors, but he cautioned them that it probably was not even close. He needed more time.

In Essex, residents were soon engulfed in fear and outrage, fulfilling Mark Keller's prophecy of the town going crazy. In this small rural state little remained private for long, and the news spread at a panic rate before it even reached the media. From the hospital, minutes after arriving with Meghan, Judith Stafford had called the mother of a girl who was giving a party at which Mrs. Stafford's daughter and several classmates of Meghan and Melissa were guests. She told the woman to make sure the children stayed in the house.

Policemen who had children called their homes as soon as they could get to a phone. "The first rule that got passed on to my wife was keep the doors locked, don't let the kids out of your sight," said Patrolman Taylor, who lived in the neighboring town of Colchester and had two children at home. "Up until that point, our door being locked was a haphazard thing. If we remembered it, we did; if we didn't, we didn't. But at that point, it was the door stays locked and you don't unlock it. Period."

By early evening the streets of Essex Junction were deserted. A grim and fearful watch began as parents gathered their children indoors, paralyzed by the fear that the killers were still at large in Essex. "This is a very active community in the evening," Taylor went on. "Early evening, up to about nine or ten, there is a lot going on during May. People walk in the streets, walk their dogs, kids out playing, riding their bicycles. That ceased immediately. The minute it was learned that the girls were attacked and there were no suspects, there was no one on the streets."

In the absence of solid information, fear prompted rumors. Already, false word raced through Essex that Melissa Walbridge's body had been found hanging from a tree.

The phone of Althea Kroger, a local state representative, was busy with callers wanting information and demanding action. Kroger, who came to Vermont in the 1960s, now realized that the state's mountain peace could no longer be taken for granted. "We love Vermont so much because it is so laid back. But when I received news of the killing, I realized for the first time I had to sit down with my eleven-year-old son Andrew and explain to him that there are bad people out there, and that you don't talk to strangers. Essex changed overnight. Nobody walked on the streets; nobody left their houses. It was absolutely astounding."

In a state with only a half-million population, smaller than scores of American cities, and with one of the lowest crime rates in the country, the assault was a blow to everyone's sense of security. The attack on the two girls was an attack on everyone's daughter. If there was panic and fear, there was also a wish for vengeance.

Michael and Patty Garvey, who lived down the street from the Walbridges, and for whom Melissa often baby-sat, were bitter. "I want to do something," said Mr. Garvey. "It's a violation of society is what it is. My wife wants to get a gun now."

Essex psychotherapist Toba Gladstone, who had worked with serious cases of abuse against women and children, could not recall a local crime so violent. She and her husband resided in the large colonial house at the corner of Church and Main, the house where Marie Walbridge had lived as a teenager. "The people in this community wanted to kill the guys," Mrs. Gladstone remembered. "It's not like New York City, where if you picked up the paper and read about this people would say, 'Oh isn't that terrible but it happens all the time.'

"People were angry; they wanted to see these guys dead. My husband is not at all a violent person, but he felt that whoever did it should be shot. People who usually aren't like that were saying that nothing short of death would be good enough—a hanging in the town square."

At 5 Gaines Court in Essex, Jamie Savage's parents thought he was acting strangely that evening. The teenager had already finished his second pack of cigarettes, had skipped dinner, and now sat vacantly in front of the television "just staring in a daze," according to his stepfather. "He just didn't talk very much. Usually Jamie's always got something to say about the events or something that's happened during the day."

For Jamie Savage the events of that day buzzed in his memory like a swarm of unorganized hornets, and not until the evening news did he find a measure of clarity. "A small army of law enforcement officers are searching for two men tonight in connection with an attack on two young girls in Essex this afternoon," the newscaster intoned. Jamie tightened. "One girl is dead. One is hospitalized."

The facts were suddenly there, arranged neatly and simply, even for his immature mind. Jamie could understand the meaning of "a small army" of cops, and he was now truly worried. One of the girls was still alive. "I was thinking if maybe I was going to get caught or not," he later said. "Like should I turn myself in."

Jamie rushed to the kitchen phone and dialed Louie's number.

Louie had come home to Elmwood Avenue late that afternoon, Mary Hamlin remembered, deposited a sack of dirty clothes in his room, and asked his mother to cut his hair and beard. She often acted as the family barber for her husband and two older sons.

"Louie's hair grows just so long. I usually trim it and I do his beard and mustache when it gets where he wants to shave it off and can't take it anymore," Mary later explained. Louie had discussed trimming his hair a few weeks before, but had not pressed his mother about it until today.

Mary complied and scissored her son's hair and beard. Afterward, Louie took a bath, shampooed his hair, and shaved off the rest of his beard. He left the little bathroom with smooth chin and cheeks, babyfaced again except for the dark bush of eyebrow that hovered above his eyes.

Louie stayed home that night. He went into his room unusually early, at 8:30, and did not leave it until his father called him to the phone a few minutes after 11:00 P.M.

"Are ya listenin' to the TV?" On the other end of the line was Jamie Savage's voice, speaking in a muffled and excited whisper.

"No," Louie said. "I been in my room."

"Well, go watch it. And call me back."

Hamlin hurried into the living room and turned the television set to Channel 3. As the tube flickered on, a young reporter was standing under bright lights in front of the Essex police station speaking into the camera in a somber voice. ". . . a white male, said to be in his twenties, approximately six feet tall with short brown hair and a close-cropped brown beard. The second suspect, also a white male, is said to be younger, taller, with blond curly hair. Anyone with information has been asked to call the Essex Police Department."

Louie walked to the kitchen and called Jamie. He felt safer now that he was clean-shaven. He had not expected one of the girls to live, but her description of him was not that good, he thought. On the phone, Louie told Jamie there was nothing to worry about.

"He just told me that if my mother was looking at it when I was, don't act scared," Jamie later recalled. "But my mother could tell I was scared because I was smokin' so much."

If they didn't act scared, Louie warned Jamie, they weren't going to be caught. Jamie hoped Louie was right.

CHAPTER 9

The Manhunt

EARLY SATURDAY MORNING the silhouettes of two dozen men could be seen between the trees, moving like steady-eyed scavengers through the woods. The policemen walked in rows back and forth, sometimes crawling on their hands and knees, examining every inch of the underbrush for a clue to the identity of the attackers of Meghan O'Rourke and Melissa Walbridge. They fanned out along the railroad tracks, walked the path beside the woods, the path inside the woods, and pushed their way through the branches and bushes where there was no path. When they finished searching an area, they went back and searched again.

"For the first time in my short career in law enforcement," said Patrolman Gary Taylor, "I didn't hear anybody complaining about getting a lousy assignment. The guys just hopped to it. They were in the bushes, crawling around looking for evidence with forty- and fifty-dollar dress slacks on. We were all doing it. And then we'd go back and check the scene again. I've done some pretty thorough crime searches before, but there was nothin' like this."

The police picked up anything that could be remotely connected to the crime, from candy bar wrappers to shards of broken glass. They found a used CO_2 cartridge and a pellet canister they thought might give them a lead on the BB-like wounds found on both Meghan and Melissa. They found articles of clothing that the O'Rourkes and Walbridges identified as belonging to their daughters, but they were unable to locate what the parents told them they should find: a green knapsack, a bright blue travel bag, a burgundy jacket with a plaid lining, and a pair of new blue jeans. More than two hundred different items were tagged by State Police Crime Lab analysts that morning.

During his lunch break, Zane Snelling of the Essex Police Department returned to the woods and obstinately began to plow through the same thicket once more. To his surprise, Snelling found a paring knife a few dozen yards from the small clearing where Melissa was killed.

In the center of the village, the squad room of the old colonial police station resembled a battlefield command headquarters. "The entire building was taken over by the investigation," recalled Robbie Yandow. Police officers from all over the county were arriving to volunteer their services. They came from Burlington, Shelburne, Colchester, South Burlington, the State Police barracks in Colchester. Federal authorities offered their assistance; police departments from other parts of the state, even outside the state called with leads. The St. Albans police chief volunteered to send his entire fifteen-man squad to Essex. The chief of police from the town of Richmond called, apologizing that he could not spare anyone from his two-man department.

The morning newspaper hit the stands displaying a startling headline: GIRL, 12, KILLED, COMPANION HURT IN ATTACK AT ESSEX JCT. PLAY AREA. In its 155 years "serving Vermont," the discreet Burlington *Free Press* had never run such a front-page story. It was a dismal piece of news beside the announcement that PRINCESS ANNE GIVES BIRTH TO DAUGHTER; sad in proximity to another article stating that Pope John Paul II was recovering from the terrorist bullet wounds that felled him three days before.

That morning Essex was in a state of siege, locked in, angry and apprehensive, its public places deserted. On the streets, Judy Safford remembered, "you could hear a pin drop. I always go down to get doughnuts for the kids Saturday mornings and there's always people out. But not that day. No one was there. I took my daughter and we bolted town that morning and went to our camp."

The flag at Lawton Middle School was flying at half-mast. Inside, at an emergency meeting, officials were contemplating closing the school on Monday. They formulated a plan for safety precautions for the children: to call home if they needed a ride; to encourage parents to call the school if their child was going to be absent.

Across the street, at the Little League field in the Maple Street recreation area, a game was being played as scheduled. But it was not a typical Saturday morning. There was more than the usual turnout of parents, on hand to stand watch over their children. They had considered canceling the game but decided against it, concluding without enthusiasm that the youngsters should play rather than stay home and think about the grisly attack.

The newspaper story and the description of the attackers repeated regularly on the radio brought the police a flood of leads. One man telephoned to report that he had seen a car matching the description parked in front of Mazza's General Store on Malletts Bay the previous evening; a woman relayed the news that her paper boy had seen a suspicious-looking man at the bus stop at Steven's Park; another woman reported seeing a suspicious vehicle being driven at a high rate of speed by two men up Brigham Hill Road; another man called to say his two teenage daughters had been "verbally accosted" by two men in April.

People reported on neighbors they thought were acting suspiciously. Girls informed on their former boyfriends; hitchhikers gave the identity of drivers who had offered them rides. In more than one case fathers came into the stationhouse with their daughters to tell police about men who had made sexual advances toward them.

Two special telephone lines were installed to handle the calls coming in from all over Vermont, from Massachusetts, Rhode Island, Connecticut, even New York. "The calls just kept coming in," Lieutenant Yandow recollected. "At the minimum there must have been ten times the normal amount."

The inventory of fear and gossip did not include the dozens of people who walked into police headquarters in person to relate their stories or, oddly, the cases of frightened men offering their own names to police because, unluckily, they had a beard or matched the description of the suspects. "Everybody became very suspicious of anyone who in any way, shape, or form fit the description of these two guys," said Lieutenant Yandow.

The pressure for a rapid solution to the mystery was channeled into an impromptu, hectic, but efficient manhunt organization. Swarming through the pine-paneled squad room and overflowing to the other half dozen temporary offices, the police worked on folding chairs and folding tables, answered phones, screened tips and leads among them, asked questions, scratched heads and elbows.

A giant yellow plastic vat on a corner table, mystically filled with seventy-five cups of hot coffee every morning, emptied steadily during the day and into the night, long after its contents were cold and mudlike. The men's diet consisted of fast-food burgers and fast-fried chicken, or hurried meals at the Inn across the street where the town had made arrangements with owner Kourkoulis to let the cops sign for the check. Occasionally, village women would relieve the food boredom by bringing in a home-cooked morsel. The air was funky and the ashtrays full.

"All of a sudden the building was more than just a structure," explained Gary Taylor. "It wasn't empty. It wasn't 'Oh, God, another day another dollar.' All of a sudden it was a command post! Everyone had the same goal. These two guys can't get away. They aren't bank robbers who are going to East Horseshoe now to enjoy what they got. These guys are kid rapists and kid killers. We had to get them."

The Essex officials cooperated by offering a substantial reward. Saturday afternoon, the board of town selectmen met and voted unanimously to offer $10,000 for information leading to the arrest of the attackers; another $10,000 was appropriated to cover expenses incurred by the police and investigators during the manhunt. According to Town Manager Kevin Ryan the attitude of the town administrators was "no-holds barred on the costs."

The focus of operations was a large table in the center of the squad room where Mark Keller, Robbie Yandow, and State Police Detective Nick Ruggiero huddled around stacks of papers, police files, soda cans, and boxes of index cards filling steadily with tips. With no real suspects in mind, it soon became apparent that they needed a system for coordinating information and assignments. Bob Simpson had suggested three-by-five index cards. Every piece of information went on a card, was alphabetized and dated. "We don't want to miss one call," Simpson had said. "That could be the one we're waiting for."

Twice on Saturday the investigators believed they had received that crucial call. Summoned to the Lincoln Inn early Saturday morning to quell a fight, police questioned a man named Charles Carosa. Carosa, who was staying at the Inn, had once been charged with aggravated assault against a child, and fit the description of the dark-haired suspect. Police told him not to leave town and released him while they checked his alibi.

That night, when New York State Police called that they had picked up a Charles Carosa and a blond-haired companion driving a stolen vehicle, Keller felt sure he had his killers. But when he was informed that Carosa's companion was a woman, Keller quickly instructed Susan Via to question Meghan again: Make sure that the youngster was absolutely positive that both her attackers were men. Via called back a few moments later with the deflating news. Meghan was sure.

Carosa had disappeared as the primary suspect but, almost immediately, police received another tip. "We thought that with this one we had the whole case solved," Keller remembered. "Somebody called up to say that they saw two men working on the grounds that adjoined the railroad tracks Friday afternoon. They fit the description. He said, 'This is them. It's *got* to be them, scruffy-looking, everything fits.'" Keller and a half dozen other investigators spent the rest of the evening trying to locate the head of the company contracted to work on the IBM grounds.

"After we got his name we called his home," said Keller later. "No one was there so we called all over town, to the bars, to the business clubs, all over. Finally, we found him and got the names of the two guys on the crew. Then we had to find the two guys." When Keller and Ruggiero located them, well after midnight, the men said they were nowhere near the woods at that time and gave the investigators the names of people who would vouch for their whereabouts. It was after 2:00 A.M. before Keller and Ruggiero, after checking the alibis, knew they were on the wrong investigative path.

For the second time in less than twelve hours, they plunged from the confident sense that they were closing in on the killers back to their depressingly long list of slim leads. There were hundreds of them. The fact that they were arriving from all over the state confirmed the investigators' hunch that the killers were flatlanders who had left town immediately after the crime. Keller groaned as he looked through the mounting pile of teletype messages on the squad room table:

ADV MURDER SUSPECTS WERE IN MIDDLE GRANVILLE AT ABOUT 1330 HOURS, WENT INTO CHAPMANS STORE AND BOUGHT BEER AND THE SUBJECT WITH BEARD BOUGHT SHAVING KIT....

WAITRESS AT CHARLMONT REST. RT 15 IN MORRISVILLE. SHE ADV TWO SUBJECTS WERE IN THERE THIS MORN FOR COFFEE, ACTED STRANGE...ADV DARK-HAIRED SUBJECT COULD BE A MATCH....

A KATHY GRACE FROM WATERBURY SAW A SUBJ YEST MORN AROUND 0915 MATCHING DESC OF DARK BEARD SUSPECT. SUB HAD NO JACKET ON AND WAS WALKING UP AND DOWN STREET. HAD SHORT SHIRT ON AND COULD SEE HIS STOM-ACH....

There was some tangible evidence at the scene of the crime. It was the battered corpse of Melissa Walbridge. Sunday morning, in the morgue of the Medical Center Hospital, Melissa's body lay on a stainless steel grating in exactly the same condition as when it was discovered.

"The body is that of a naked young female," the medical examiner, Dr. Eleanor McQuillen, dictated into the microphone, "extensively covered by blood anteriorly and coated with brown plant material." For McQuillen, a mother of five children, a doctor for more than twenty years, and the state's chief medical examiner since 1978, this was a particularly unpleasant autopsy. "A turquoise-aqua terry shirt is used as ligatures to bind the wrists behind," she continued. "There is a pair of blue cotton slacks around the neck knotted with scalp hair behind. There is a gray sock tightly tied through the mouth, compressing the cheeks, left more than right, and knotted behind the neck."

Dr. McQuillen had cut short a trip to Massachusetts to return for the autopsy. As she began, an unusually large crowd of police officers, doctors, and medical assistants stood silently to her side. Officers Hollwedel, Bouffard, Bolduc, Larose, and Yandow came from the Essex Police Department. Two Vermont State Crime Lab officers were present, ready to tag items that could later be used as trial evidence. Susan Via was there. Dr. Lloyd Novick, the state health commissioner, and Dr. Nicholas Hardin, who had come to the murder scene when Novick sought help, also observed.

Noticeably absent was State's Attorney Keller. Despite his reputation for cool detachment at autopsies, Keller had passed. "I had finally gotten myself together," he explained later, "and I didn't want to get all messed up again. At that point, it wasn't important for me to know if she was shot five times or six times."

As Dr. McQuillen was to find, Melissa had been shot six, perhaps seven, times with a BB gun: once in the back, once on the thigh, twice in the stomach, once in the neck, and once in the left eye. The wound to the eye must have been excruciatingly painful. Because of the surrounding bruises, the medical examiner knew that the shot was fired while Melissa was still alive. The BB had lacerated Melissa's cornea and was found by Dr. McQuillen lodged in a bone.

The autopsy was both clinically tedious and, even for the professional observers, wearing. Inch by inch Melissa's little body was inspected, her wounds described in scientific detail, her organs extracted, weighed, and measured. The policemen who had seen her lying in the mud in the woods just after the attack once again strained to control their anger.

Throughout the long procedure, physicians from the hospital looked in and, with unusually unmedical candor, unburdened themselves. "I think that every doctor at the Medical Center at some point stopped into the autopsy," recalled Susan Via. "Overnight the killing had become quite notorious and they just kind of wandered by, came in and said, 'This is the most disgusting crime that I have ever seen,' and walked out."

The autopsy, however unpleasant, was not just an exercise in morbidity. For the medical experts and law enforcement personnel it carried the significance of a judicial hearing, Melissa Walbridge's last chance to testify to the world. "It is my opinion that there is another witness in all of these homicide trials," Dr. McQuillen would later explain, "and that is the deceased; in this case, Melissa Walbridge. She had left a message regarding her attack and her attackers." That message was unmistakably clear: Melissa had been tortured.

McQuillen counted twenty-nine separate wounds on the body. There were cutting knife wounds, stabbing knife wounds, BB gun wounds, "blunt impact" wounds. Most of the extremely painful ones such as the blunt impact blows to the face, the BB shot to the eye, and some of the knife wounds were delivered while Melissa was still alive. Others were inflicted after the knife fatally pierced Melissa's heart.

Multiple slashes crisscrossed Melissa's chest. There was a laceration just inside the hairline on her forehead, a stab wound in her neck, fractured bones and cartilages in her neck, a swollen bruise on her cheek. Hemorrhaging of the larynx, trachea, and eyes had resulted from strangulation and asphyxia.

The shallow incisions carved back and forth across Melissa's chest and neck could be interpreted only as inflicted to cause increased suffering. "They look like teasing," said McQuillen, "as the weapon is teased across the skin. They are not lethal ... but they are clearly before death."

The three deep and long stab wounds in Melissa's chest that caused her death showed that her attackers had carved and slashed at her. The wound that the medical examiner determined was the fatal one penetrated Melissa's chest and passed through both the left and right ventricles of her heart. "The upper two stab wounds," Dr. McQuillen later explained, "were part of a three-inch long, half-inch gaping incised wound." On close examination the medical examiner could determine that the wounds had a "fishtail appearance that is due to the fact that the blade is drawn out at a slightly different angle than it was put in due either to motion of the body or motion of the hand holding the instrument."

Dr. McQuillen photographed every wound, documenting the extent of Melissa's injuries for possible use at a criminal trial—if her attackers were ever apprehended. "It was not pleasant to do," the medical examiner acknowledged. "But it is Melissa Walbridge's message to all."

The child's mutilated body was testimony to the fact that something was amiss in Vermont, that somewhere there were two assailants who had violated not only two innocent girls, but had ruptured the sense of security of a whole people.

Somberly, Susan Via carried part of that message upstairs to the Intensive Care Unit where Meghan O'Rourke, still in fragile condition, was recovering. On the advice of physicians, Stephanie O'Rourke had told Meghan Friday night that Melissa was dead. Susan Via, patiently repeating to Meghan that she should feel no guilt about her friend's death, now explained what an autopsy was and how it showed that Meghan could have done nothing to prevent the tragedy.

"Meghan told me that she felt that the Walbridges were going to be really mad at her and that they must hate her," Via recalled. "And we assured her that that was absolutely not the truth. That they wanted her to get well real quickly."

Everyone was rooting for Meghan, which, Via explained, is not always true about rape victims, some of whom find themselves having to absorb the blame for their own victimization. "The only thing I needed to do, and you do it with all rape victims, is reassure them that they are not to blame for their situation in any way."

"As difficult as it was for Meghan to resolve this," commented Essex therapist Toba Gladstone, "she had all the community supporting her, believing her. She turned out to be a heroine, while many rape victims aren't even believed."

Meghan's hospital room filled with flowers from well-wishers. Cards from her classmates lined every inch of shelf and windowsill space. "Her room looked like a florist shop," Via recalled. "There were flowers, balloons, and kites, and pictures and eight million cards." Her twenty-four-hour police guards, Paul Duprat, Malcolm Kingsland, and Zane Snelling, brought Meghan a huge stuffed bear, decorated with the patches from each of the different police departments taking part in the manhunt. Via and the officers, with their constant vigil and good humor, became like family.

Susan Via had assumed the role of protector to the injured girl. The deputy state's attorney knew that the trauma of rape can be profound, and she and Keller decided that there would not be dozens of cops pressing Meghan for information. Only Via was to ask Meghan what happened—not the guards at her door, not even State Trooper Stan Strusinski. The fewer people that Meghan had to tell her story to the better. And it would be better still, they believed, if that person was a woman.

"It was important that Meghan not hold anything back because it could mean the difference between catching these SOBs or not," Via later explained. "Mark agreed with me that there was no way that we were going to have a male police officer talk to this child about what happened. Because of her age and sex and her lack of experience, I just felt that she ought to have a woman. Her doctor even assigned Dr. Wendy Marshall personally to Meghan and didn't want male residents, if at all possible, around her."

From the time Meghan was taken to the hospital late Friday afternoon, Meghan's parents, brother, and sister had kept a constant bedside vigil, taking little rest until Sunday, when doctors assured them that Meghan was out of danger. "I made it my business, based on everything the gynecologist and the medical examiner told us, to explain to her parents what I could," recalled Via. "But we made it clear to Meghan that she didn't have to talk to her parents or the psychiatrist or anybody. If she wanted to, fine. She should feel comfortable to know that the psychiatrist, especially, would keep it confidential. If she had nightmares, things like that, she should talk about them. And people would help her to get through it. But her personality is such that she didn't feel the need to talk about it."

On Sunday afternoon, in the Intensive Care Unit, Meghan's doctors reluctantly told Susan Via that Meghan was strong enough to answer questions. They did not have to remind the prosecutor that the attack had left the little girl in a delicate emotional and physical state.

Despite her pain, Meghan soon surprised everyone with her resilience as she refused to flinch under the prosecutor's patient requests for her to remember. "She is a smart little girl," Via stated, "and she understood that unless she gave us a description of these guys and what happened, we would never find them."

"I know this is hard to do," Via began. "When you answer, can you try to say yes or no?"

"Okay," Meghan responded.

"Okay is fine, too," Via said soothingly. "Now you told me that the man that assaulted you, that hurt you, was the blond-haired man?"

"Yes," said Meghan.

"Okay," Via continued. "Can you try to tell me in your own words what he did to you first. Did he grab you, did he drag you, did he say anything?"

Meghan answered very slowly, in a voice made hoarse from the strangling, and almost impossible to make out. "Well, he came up behind us, and they had guns. They grabbed our mouths and all of a sudden they dragged us along. I just had to go because I was too scared. And he held the gun to our heads and he said, 'Come this way and don't try to yell; it's a .45 and I'll shoot you if you do.'"

Meghan winced. After surviving a rape, a punctured lung, and strangulation, Via was amazed that Meghan could talk at all. "Try to tell me as best you can," Via calmly prompted the child, "and go as nice and slow as you want, everything that the man with the curly hair did. Just tell me what you can remember, sweetie."

"Well, first, he told us to take off all our clothes. The guy with the curly hair. The black-haired man did the same with Melissa."

"Did you do that when he threatened you with the gun?"

"Well, I hesitated," Meghan said in her tiny voice. "But then I—I was scared."

"Sure, sure you were," Via soothed the girl. "You did what he said because you were afraid he was going to hurt you with the gun?"

"Yes." Meghan still sounded embarrassed.

"Okay, that's okay," said Via. "So you took off your clothes?"

"Yeah."

"Did you see whether Melissa did the same thing? Did she take off her clothes?"

"She started struggling," Meghan whispered.

"She started struggling with the black-haired man?" Via repeated as if in disbelief.

"She goes, 'No, no, I'm twelve years old. I don't want to,'" Meghan told the deputy prosecutor. "And then finally he took them off."

Meghan's voice dropped away, as she averted her eyes from the adults at her bedside.

Via knew that victims of sexual assault are more reticent about an attack that produces not only pain, but guilt. The difficulty was compounded by Meghan's age, and the fact that Melissa had died and she had survived, but Via also recognized that Meghan had the type of emotional strength that many adults lack. "Meghan is a very remarkable young lady," Via later commented. "Very strong. That is one of the reasons she is still alive. She is a real tough lady. I think children are stronger than adults anyway. We lose a lot of resiliency as we get older."

From experience Via knew that there was no better way to deal with sexual assault victims, even small children, than being direct. "Okay, sweetie," Via pressed gently. "You took off your clothes because he ordered you to. Okay? Right?"

"Yes," said Meghan softly.

"And what did he do first? Did he make you lie down or what did he do?"

There was a long silence. Meghan hesitated. "He made me suck on him," she finally mumbled.

Meghan told of being raped, being forced into anal sex. She explained that she was gagged with Melissa's sock and her hands tied behind her back with her own shirt. She remembered the murder knife, a brown-handled kitchen knife with a six-inch blade.

Melissa struggled against her attackers, Meghan recounted, and tried to talk with them. "Melissa kept saying, 'Oh, I really like you. I wish you wouldn't hurt me,'" Meghan explained. But Missy's attempt to reason with the men was futile. They pushed her to the ground, choked her with something, and "stomped on her back."

At one point, Meghan said, the dark-haired man held the gun to her own neck. "And he goes, 'What do you think we should do with you, lady?' she told Via. "And then I go—I go, 'I think you should leave and run away.' And he goes, 'I don't do that,' and he shot me in the side of the neck."

Meghan's account was all the more tragic for its childlike narration. Although not complete, the account was studded with the type of detail, even innocence, that lent her story the unassailable ring of truth. "The black-haired man hit me in the back with something," said Meghan. "I think it must have been a sleeping dart because it was so sharp. It put me to sleep for a while."

Meghan was tiring rapidly. As her responses became increasingly monosyllabic, the state's attorney decided to end the session. "Okay, I'll let you rest now, all right?" she said. Meghan nodded, forced a tiny smile, and closed her eyes.

Over the next few days, Meghan worked hard for Via. Rather than shunting aside the images of the assault, she struggled to resurrect them. Her voice, never more than a whisper, had a hummingbird coarseness. Via, after hours without sleep, had almost lost her own voice. "The two of us together," the attorney later said, "sounded like Tallulah Bankhead interviewing Lauren Bacall."

Meghan's recall was uncanny. She remembered that the dark-haired man wore jeans and black boots, and had "mean-looking eyes." The curly-haired man had on tennis shoes with yellow stripes. The pistols the two held looked "fakish" and "plastic." She had been gagged with Melissa's sock, not her own. She recalled a silver cartridge that the dark-haired man was holding. It looked just like the one she had found in the park on Wednesday with the word "Daisy" printed on it. She remembered him showing it to her saying, "If you move, this one will definitely kill you."

Meghan was able to reconstruct flashes of conversations, remembering how Missy had stood up to the two men. "Melissa swore at them," Meghan told Via. "What did Melissa say?" Via asked. Meghan hesitated. "It's okay to say what she said," Via assured her.

Meghan finally answered, her voice trailing off in an embarrassed whisper. "She said 'Fuck you!'"

"What happened when she said that to these guys?" Via asked.

Meghan's memory was clear. "Well, he said, 'You think we're just fooling around, don't you? We're not.'" Meghan repeated the remark, offering even the sarcastic inflection. That subtle detail alerted investigators to the possibility that the suspects were younger than they had thought.

"Who said that?" asked Via.

"The black-haired man," said Meghan.

"And what other conversation do you remember?" Via pushed. "Tell me anything else you remember, about killing you or anything."

"They said, 'Now you're going to get yours,' and 'You're going to know what it's like to get shot five times and you're going to know what it feels like when a pig gets slaughtered.'"

Susan Via never revealed her shock at both the facts of the attack and Meghan's ability to recall them. "The way doctors who work with children explain it to me," Via later said, "after a person has suffered a traumatic injury, like a car accident or a stabbing, they often have a kind of amnesia about the event. It is their way of coping, pushing it very far back in their memory, so far back that they can't recall it in their consciousness. In that way they can remain an integrated person and aren't immobilized by this horrible fear. It is a survival mechanism." But, Via added, Meghan refused to forget, a sign of her strong ability to cope.

Meghan's visual memory of her attackers also amazed State Trooper Strusinski. "Maybe because of all this trauma there was such a powerful mental picture in her mind about what happened," he later theorized. "She was able to reach far inside and bring it up. She knew that the only way we were going to get these animals was to do this picture."

Strusinski had left the hospital late Friday night with little hope that the traumatized girl would be up to the task of re-creating the faces of her attackers. But he returned to the hospital early Saturday morning and stayed until late in the evening. Meghan was better, but she was still weak. Each of their sessions together on Saturday lasted only about five or six minutes, and by nightfall, Strusinski had better sketches of both suspects than during the first night. But still, he warned the investigators, more refinement was necessary.

Strusinski, who had been the preeminent police sketch artist in the state for some ten years, appreciated the difficulties witnesses and victims have in recalling exactly what their attackers look like. "Mental pictures are funny," he explained. "It's even hard for people to leave a room and remember in much detail what that person looked like even after talking with someone for a while. Most victims or witnesses see these people for only a split second and they have to rely on that minimum contact to build a composite. But some witnesses are better than others.

"I think children make better witnesses as a whole because they are simpler by nature. They have more vivid recall, and their memory is more conditioned at that age. In school they have to constantly memorize. But they're not so good at judging. For example, height. These kids are usually four-foot-two,

and anybody five-five or five-seven is gigantic to them. Anyone
who has whiskers is automatically an older man, not a sixteen-
or seventeen-year-old kid."

Strusinski knew that in working with Meghan he faced a
very complex situation. Her physical condition alone was a
major hindrance; in addition she had suffered mental and emotional trauma. But finally, Meghan and Strusinski had completed a composite of the two attackers. While it did not fully
satisfy Strusinski, the sketch was the first visual lead to the
rapists.

On Sunday morning the composite sketches of the two suspects were published in the Burlington *Free Press*, the state's
largest daily newspaper, stimulating the tempo of the intensive
manhunt. "Here are the police descriptions of the two men
being sought in the death of Melissa Walbridge and the wound-
ing of Meghan O'Rourke," the paper announced below the
large front-page portraits. As residents all over the state studied
the photos that Sunday, the phone lines in the Essex Police
Department jammed with callers.

By Sunday afternoon, the search for the criminals had become the largest manhunt in Vermont history. Keller sent his
deputy, Bob Simpson, into a corner room by himself "just to
think." With the door closed, Simpson shuffled through the
dozens of lead cards, lists of suspects and possible suspects,
notes of interviews with witnesses and potential witnesses. His
job was to weigh theories about the type of persons who would
commit such a vicious crime and point investigators in direc-
tions they might not have considered.

Based on the information gathered at the scene, from Meghan,
and from the autopsy, original theories about the suspects were
changing. Meghan at first had described her attackers as "men,"
and investigators assumed they were adult, even middle-aged.
An early State Police bulletin had described the dark-haired
suspect as being in his "mid-forties to early fifties" and the
second suspect as being "younger, approximately mid-twenties."

But the emphasis began to shift when the state's best-known
forensic psychiatrist, Dr. William Woodruff, offered a suggestion. Woodruff reminded investigators of the sadistic Chicago

murderers of the 1920s, Leopold and Loeb, and hypothesized that sadists of this type were often very intelligent. At once police began to realize that their initial theory about the killers might be false. It now seemed possible that the suspects could be younger than they had thought. Police quickly began a search through the yearbooks of local colleges. "We thought maybe it was a sick college kid off on his last fling before graduation," recalled Susan Via. "Someone really twisted."

A copy of A. Nicholas Groth's classic study of sexual assaultists, *Men Who Rape*, was pulled off the shelf of the state's attorney's office. Chapters on "Myths about the Offender" and "Sadistic Rape" and "Male Rape" were photocopied and passed out to the investigators.

Police began compiling what became known as a "Who's Who of sexual perverts" in the county. "We got together quite a working list of sexual offenders," said Yandow. "People would call in and say, 'This guy did this to my daughter and I wasn't going to report it before, but now that this has happened, how do I know, maybe he did this to those little girls.'"

The college-age-criminal theory seemed plausible, but one aspect of the case did not fit. It was the BB guns. "That didn't make sense," said Via later. "If they were trying to hurt these girls, why BB guns? Why not real guns? Why would a grown man or even a college-age youth use a BB gun? So we said, 'Maybe it's high school,' and we started to pull out the high school yearbooks."

Reluctantly, police were also changing their theory about the origin of the killers. No one wanted to believe they could be from Vermont, but the more investigators thought about the information gleaned so far, the less likely it was that the culprits were flatlanders. The woods in Maple Street Park were not a place that transients would easily find, and Meghan had seen the same men two days before.

"It looked like they were staking the place out," Susan Via explained. "They knew exactly where to bring them. They either put the mattresses there or knew of them. They knew that this place was where a lot of kids passed through. It didn't seem to me that they were transients. Perhaps they moved here six months before, but they definitely knew the area."

The investigators reluctantly began to adopt a new theory: The rapists and murderers, if not homegrown, at least lived on Vermont soil.

The police officers prayed for a concrete lead, but ironically, when it came their way, they dismissed it. On Sunday morning, a nervous woman walked into the small station holding her copy of the *Free Press* tightly under her arm, and hesitantly asked to talk to someone about the murder. Before that Friday such a request would have brought the entire Essex Police force racing to interview her. But now, after two days of sifting through a constant stream of false leads, the dispatcher simply asked the woman to take a seat.

Behind the locked door to her right, she could hear the muffled voices of the policemen in the squad room. In a few minutes a buzzer sounded and Gary Taylor emerged, notebook in hand. The woman explained that she worked at Henry's Market and had just seen the composite sketches of the suspects in the newspaper.

"They look just like these guys that are always coming into the market," she told Taylor. "I don't know if it means anything, but I thought I should mention it."

"Do you know who they are?" asked Taylor. "Their names, or anything about them?"

"Yeah." The woman responded hesitantly, as if unsure whether she was doing the right thing. "One's Jamie Savage and the other one, the guy with the beard, his name is Louie Hamlin."

"Okay." Taylor was writing. He knew both kids. Hamlin he remembered only as a silent shadow of Rene Savage. After Taylor had busted Rene for car theft, the teenager often came by the police station to brag about his exploits. Hamlin was often with him, but never said much. Taylor was more familiar with Jamie Savage. The policeman had been to the Lefebvre house a number of times to quell a "domestic disturbance," and remembered Jamie. "One time," Taylor recounted, "Jamie was running his mouth about how he was going to kill his father or something. His father and him had been fighting and he had a little paring knife. He was sputtering about his father and how he would like to kill him. He finally threw the knife in the sink."

Another time Taylor found Jamie roller-skating down the middle of Pearl Street, the main thoroughfare from Essex into Burlington. "He wouldn't stop for me," Taylor related. "I put my flashing lights and siren on, and he wouldn't stop. Talking about feeling stupid. I have a slow speed pursuit with some guy on roller-skates. But he always did things like that. That was Jamie's style. He was stupid. The thing with the roller-skates was a big joke for him. He had a big smirk on his face when he finally stopped. I said, 'You hear the siren?' He says, 'I heard the siren.' 'How come you didn't stop? Get out of the road?' He says, 'Man, I didn't know it was against the law to roller-skate down the road.' That was Jamie."

"You know, I don't know anything about the murder or anything," the woman told Taylor. "It just seems that they look like these guys in the paper and they always hang out together."

"Anything else?" Taylor asked. "You see 'em on Friday?"

"No, I wasn't working Friday."

"Okay. Thanks, ma'am, for coming in."

Taylor went back to the squad room, wrote the information on one of the cards, and dropped it on the stack already sitting on the table. He didn't think much of it. He barely knew Hamlin, and Jamie was just a mouthy kid. A couple of local teenagers. Troublemakers, maybe. Killers, no.

CHAPTER 10

Staying Cool

THAT SATURDAY MORNING Mary Hamlin washed her son's clothes. Curious about what he had been up to all week, she exercised her motherly instinct to give the laundry a quick "read." She noticed that all of Louie's clothes were still wet and soggy—as if he had been caught in a torrential rain. His long-sleeve white shirt with the snap buttons was grimy and his new jeans were streaked with dirt and sand. "Just looked like maybe he had been fishing or something like that," Mary later commented. "Or maybe he had knelt down in the mud."

In Essex Junction, at the very same time, Jamie Savage was washing his own clothes. Cathy Bailey, who watched him spread his brown turtleneck sweater and undershirt on the floor, then hang his jeans over the door to dry, thought that for Jamie to wash his own clothes was a "miracle." Later that morning Jamie went to work at the Lincoln Inn, but he did not seem the same gangly goof-off co-workers had become accustomed to. "I just remember him being very quiet," recalled waitress Melody Petrides.

After lunch Jamie took a bus into Burlington, where he met Louie. As they walked to their haunt near the dump and along the tracks, over the Blue Bridge to Winooski, talking about the television news the night before, the two teenagers decided that if they were not caught immediately, they would be all right. There was nothing to worry about, they reassured themselves, if they played it cool.

Jamie and Louie had considerable experience with the game of cops and robbers, but their paths of lying and stealing had thus far been sheltered by the community and the forgiving juvenile law. To them, there was no right and wrong behavior. Good and bad acts were judged solely by their own instincts of pain and gratification. Theirs was a moral measuring rod inscribed "I felt like it," and "Don't get caught." Even with the blood of two little girls on their hands, they had no other yardstick by which to judge.

At one point that evening the manhunt was only yards away. When Jamie returned to the Inn to work, he glanced across the street to the police station, where cruisers were pulling in and out of the parking lot next to the Brownell library. A television camera crew was climbing into its van.

Inside the Inn, Jamie hustled dishes back and forth between the kitchen and the coffee shop and restaurant. Business was slow for a Saturday night, usually a good family time, but policemen in crumpled uniforms with big leatherbound notebooks in hand came in, gobbled sandwiches, and drank cups of hot black coffee before quickly dropping coins on the table and leaving. Everyone talked about the killing.

The once secure town now envisioned danger in every shadow. It was after nine and dark when Melody Petrides, who was ready to go home, expressed concern about walking alone to her car in the back parking lot. "Because they hadn't caught these guys yet, it was just a sort of eeriness everywhere."

The twenty-five-year-old woman, who was working part-time at the Inn while earning her social work degree from Champlain College in Burlington, liked Jamie and sympathized with him for the difficulty of his home life. "Here was this big lanky kid who rode around on a little bicycle that was four times too small for him," she recalled. "But all the poor kid did was work. He probably should have been out doing other things."

That night Jamie, who was tall for his age, seemed like security to the frightened waitress. "Some nut's running around out here," she told him, "and I'm not about to go out there by myself." She asked Jamie to walk her to her car.

Jamie wiped his sudsy hands across his apron and smiled a mischievous grin. "Oh, you're just chicken," he laughed, then accompanied Petrides out the kitchen door and to her car, where he politely said good night.

Jamie was up early Sunday morning. He walked over to the Lincoln Inn at 7:30, before most of the employees were there and quietly made his way to the empty bar on the far side of the sprawling building. Reaching into the cash register behind the counter, Jamie grabbed a roll of dimes and one of nickels, stuffed them in his pocket, and quickly went back to the kitchen.

It was not the first time that he had stolen from the Inn, but he generally took only food from the freezer, which he would bring home for his family, telling his mother that the manager, Arthur Kourkoulis, had given it to him. But this was the first time he had taken money. "I wanted to go roller-skating and I didn't have no money," he said later.

At noon Louie Hamlin came into the Inn. Arthur knew Louie, and sometimes called him in to do dishes, peel potatoes, clear tables. But the Inn manager considered Louie a troublemaker, and lately had called him to work less frequently.

Even though Louie had not been called to work this morning, Jamie's mother had dutifully driven to Burlington to pick him up. Janet thought Louie was "a nice kid," and did not enforce her husband's edict to keep him away from their house. "Louie was usually pretty good and usually quiet," Janet remembered. "Once in a while he and Jamie would get mad at each other, but I figured that was just normal, you know."

As they drove into Essex, the car radio crackled with news of the rape and killing as it had every hour for the past thirty-six. "Isn't it awful what happened to those two girls," Janet said to Louie, who did not respond. Janet noticed that Louie had shaved off his beard and mustache, but did not discuss it with him.

The waitresses at the Inn who knew Louie thought the clean shave made him look younger, and considerably neater. But this morning the women were more involved in reading the front page of the *Free Press* than in noticing Hamlin's appearance. Between trips from the kitchen to the dining tables, the waitresses hovered over the newspaper spread out on the counter behind the coffee shop area. Each deplored the crime, wondering who could have done it. To one another, they whispered their theories about the suspects, ruefully recalling the times the Walbridges came in to eat with little Melissa.

It was another banner front-page news story, headlined MEN HAD CONFRONTATION WITH GIRL in bold two-inch type across the top of the page. By now everyone knew about the "men" and the "girl." The large color photograph showed four investigators huddled around "evidence uncovered in woods." In the right-hand column, staring out at the waitresses and more than 40,000 other Vermonters that morning, were the two composite drawings, the first look anyone had of the suspects.

Jamie and Louie were standing by the entrance to the kitchen, a few feet from the women. Pretending to talk, they kept glancing at the newspaper. When there was space, the teenagers walked over and sat on the stools to peer down at the black-and-white likenesses.

Surprised, even exhilarated by the attention unknowingly being lavished on them, Jamie and Louie were relieved that the composite sketches were far from exact. Missing was the unmistakable bush of brow between Louie's eyes. The picture showed him with a thick beard instead of the rag-tag growth he had carried on his face until Friday. The description stated he was in his mid-twenties and weighed 185 to 200 pounds— ten years and twenty-five pounds too high. Jamie's likeness was equally miscast, even though the description of him as being "younger and taller" was accurate. It missed his baby-faced puffy nose and lips, and his acne scars. In the rain on Friday, Jamie's hair may have resembled the short, tightly packed curls drawn on the second suspect. But normally his hair rolled in waves over his ears and forehead.

A waitress looked at the newspaper over their shoulders. "It's just awful what happened," she exclaimed, shaking her head, and moving on to the high counter where the plates of food sat warming.

"Yeah, it is," Jamie mumbled without looking up.

The manhunt was circling around them, but Jamie and Louie felt safe, untouched at the center. The faces of the suspects were a foot in front of their own faces, and even though waitresses were talking about nothing else but the murder, it appeared that no one suspected them. The regular diners at the tables a few feet away were contemplating ways of "hangin' the sons-a-bitches" when they were caught.

As Jamie and Louie sat at the counter that morning, they felt that fate was on their side despite the proximity of the crime and the search. At police headquarters across the street, police were charging about, making their lists of suspects, and responding to hundreds of phone tips. The Maple Products lot to which Meghan was first taken was only a 200-yard dash out the back door. A few hundred yards farther away were the woods where Melissa was found.

The newspaper article had said that "police are not close to an arrest," and neither teenager even considered running away from Essex and Burlington. They sat quietly as the others spoke of nothing except their crime.

The phone call from Arthur Kourkoulis Monday morning did not surprise Jamie, for the Lincoln Inn manager often called when he was short of help. But when Kourkoulis said that he wanted to "talk," Jamie became nervous. His concern proved to be accurate. At the Inn, his boss accused him of stealing the rolls of coins; Jamie denied it.

In these encounters Jamie was a stubborn but bumbling showman. With shop owners and store managers, parents and teachers, his defenses of innocence were paper-thin, but his galling thickheadedness and a capacity to weave a half dozen contradictory lies into his protests usually succeeded in frustrating his accusers. Although they knew the youth was not telling the truth, they generally threw up their hands and uttered the hapless comment: "Just don't do it again."

But things were different that morning. Hemming, his eyes searching aimlessly about the room, shuffling his feet, Jamie insisted, "I didn't do it."

"Look, Jamie," the manager said, "if you don't tell me the truth, I'm going to call the police."

On other occasions, Jamie gladly would have accepted that challenge; he was no more frightened of police than of any authority figure. He knew that the police could do little to him except take up his time, and of that he had an abundance to waste. But not this morning. Now there was something threatening about meeting with the police, who, without knowing it, were turning the village upside down looking for him.

Quickly Jamie confessed to the petty thievery and offered to pay the money back. Kourkoulis, described by one employee as "having a rough exterior but a heart of gold," told Jamie he would deduct the money from the pay he was owed. Then he told the youth that he was fired.

On Monday afternoon, Louie Hamlin was sitting quietly in a hard-backed chair in the kitchen of a little house on Malletts Bay Avenue in Winooski. The old mill town, settled on the lazy slopes above the Winooski River between Burlington and Essex, was only a twenty-minute walk, by way of the railroad bridge over the river, from the Old North End in Burlington. Louie had made the trip a few times since Friday looking for his girlfriend, Jeanie Parker, but now that he had finally found her home Louie discovered he had little to say. Jeanie thought he must have something on his mind because "he was acting strange, not talking, just staring ahead."

Jeanie was a full-fleshed girl of sixteen, an eighth-grade dropout with long hair. Though she had boyfriends other than Louie, she was Louie's only girl. With him, Jeanie shared sex and offered a sympathetic ear. To her, he confided his secrets of self-hate.

The first thing Jeanie noticed about Louie that day was that he had shaved. She was upset about it. Jeanie didn't mind the absence of the beard, but she had liked his mustache.

"So why'd ya shave it all off, Louie?" Jeanie asked.

But Louie wouldn't say anything more than, " 'Cuz I felt like it." His voice was distant and his statement had no finality to it, which was unusual for the normally gruff teenager.

"Did you hear about that girl?" Jeanie asked.

Louie said, "Yeah," then fell back to his staring and ruminating.

"He just kept starin' at things," recalled Jeanie, "like pencils and pens, and walls and things that don't even—like not even nothin'."

Eventually, the two teenagers left the house and walked downtown, past the large Grand Union shopping center and to the Blue Bridge spanning the Winooski. As they talked about the murder, Louie began to feel more relaxed, realizing that Jeanie had been out of town all the previous week and had not read any of the newspaper accounts. She pressed Louie to tell her what had happened.

"She got stabbed bad," Louie said, "like in the heart and the back and the throat."

Had Jeanie been reading the newspaper, she would have realized that she had just learned something known only to the police and the medical examiner. As the *Free Press* had reported, police were "tight-lipped" about the details of the murder. It was known only that Meghan had a stab wound and a collapsed lung, and that the crime had "sexual connotations." That morning the *Free Press* had reported the medical examiner's conclusion that Melissa "died after a knife pierced her heart," but said that Dr. McQuillen "refused to elaborate on additional findings." The public, though outraged, still had no idea how brutal the killing was.

Louie realized that he had said too much. "He looked away all of a sudden and was staring at the water for no reason at all, watching it go by," remembered Jeanie. "And about a half hour later, he turned back to me and said, 'Do you know anything else about it, or only that?' " Jeanie assured him that was all she knew, unaware that she already knew more than anyone else.

Later that afternoon, Louie called Jamie from Jeanie's house and asked if he wanted to meet him and Jeanie at the bridge. Jeanie's younger sister, Barbara, would be there, he told his friend. Jamie said he would be right down. For Louie and Jamie, Jeanie and Barbara were safe females, and they had been a friendly, if sometimes argumentative, foursome for the last year. They would sit and talk under the old railroad bridge, or go to Jamie's house in Essex Junction, or walk around Maple Street Park while Jamie and Louie hunted squirrels and chip-munks along the way.

Barbara, a fourteen-year-old eighth-grader, would later comment that she was not fond of Hamlin. "He was funny-acting. He was too quiet. I don't like quiet people." Barbara had noticed that Louie's silences were often accompanied by vacant staring. "It drives me up the wall," she would say. "When he did something he wasn't supposed to, like one time he went to Jamie's house and he wasn't supposed to—and he was staring at things."

When Barbara got home from school that afternoon she found Louie in front of the television, but "he was just staring at the floor." He kept up that strange behavior for five minutes or more, Barbara remembered. "He was like that before, but never this much. He would look at something and he would sit there and look at it for a long, long time. He stared at a fly for about half an hour."

"My mother asked me if he was all right because he didn't say anything," added Jeanie. "He was jumpy. My mother dropped the salt shaker and he jumped almost to the roof."

That afternoon, Louie brought the same distant look to the river. Jamie arrived with his BB rifle and was shooting at anything that moved on the rocky riverbank while Louie, Jeanie, and Barbara watched from higher up the hill, under the shadows of the bridge. Louie continued his silence, gazing vacantly at the water while Barbara and Jeanie chatted about school.

From the bank Jamie shouted that he had just shot a wood-chuck. But after scurrying frantically about the boulders, he bounded empty-handed up the hill. As he sat down next to Barbara, the girl moved a few inches away. She did not fully trust Jamie, who, in seeming jest, would sometimes throw a knuckle punch at her arm. Once Jamie had broken Barbara's belt buckle while trying to pull her to the ground. Barbara had also noticed Jamie's rough treatment of his younger brother and sister. "He would hit Julie all the time. She aggravated him a lot and he'd pick up his fist and whack her one.... One time when Jesse took his bike he lost his temper because he warned Jesse three times not to take his bike. He just shot [threw] Jesse on the ground—picked him up and shot him down."

It was quiet under the railroad bridge as the deep brown river curled swiftly along below the four youngsters. The isolated spot in the brambles a hundred yards from the main road between Burlington and Winooski was a popular meeting ground for teenagers. The currents were too rapid for swimming, but the empty beer cans and wine bottles littering the shady shore were evidence of youthful lingering. With a fishing pole and a six-pack a boy could pass idle hours, the silence broken only by the four-o'clock freight clattering over the bridge.

Lulled into lethargy, Jamie, Louie, Barbara, and Jeanie sat, throwing stones and twigs into the water. Eventually the girls brought up the murder again.

"Why did they stab them in so many places?" Jeanie asked without expecting an answer.

Barbara agreed that it was brutal. Jamie and Louie, looking off toward the river, just nodded.

"I wonder who did it?" Jeanie asked.

For a few long minutes no one said a word.

"Actually," Louie began, rousing himself from his self-imposed silence, "we did the killing." He laughed as he spoke.

Jeanie and Barbara jerked their heads up in unison. To the two teenage girls, the rape-killing was not a subject for jest. Neither did Jamie think that his friend's unexpected statement was funny. He squinted at Louie with what Barbara later called an "evil eye."

"Shut the fuck up!" Jamie snarled.

Louie quickly changed the subject and asked Jeanie about her trip to West Rutland with her father. The murder was soon forgotten, at least in conversation. By five o'clock the foursome had tired of their sitting and wandered back home.

• • •

Mary Hamlin was surprised by her son's behavior that week. Louie was pleasant, was back in school, and was home early every night. Mary did not know the reason, but it was enough that, as she thought at the time, Louie acted "as good as gold." He invited no badgering from his sister or brother, and even helped his mother with the dishes. Shorn of his bushy frieze of facial hair, Louie had become lamblike.

He provided another surprise for Mary that week when he brought Jeanie home and introduced her to his mother, something he had never done before. "I don't know when she came into his life," Mary Hamlin remarked. "I don't know anything about her except she lives in Winooski. She's taller than I am, a little bit longer hair than I got, on the blond side." Louie did not tell his mother everything about Jeanie, especially about the time he had shepherded her into the house late at night and had sex with her in the little downstairs bedroom by the kitchen.

That Wednesday, after baby-sitting for her brother's children on North Street, a few blocks from Louie's house, Jeanie walked to Louie's and they snacked on potato chips in front of the television. Louie was still acting funny, Jeanie thought, staring at things. He called Jamie and asked him to meet them at the bridge, but Jamie begged off, said he was digging a hole by his house. "It's big enough to fit you in," he told Jeanie when she got on the line, "and Louie, and Barbara, and your mom too." Jamie didn't like Jeanie's mother. "Maybe I'll bury you all in it and keep you there." He laughed. "So what's it for?" Jeanie asked. "Nothin' special," said Jamie.

Since the incident on Monday at the Blue Bridge, Jamie had been avoiding Louie. As dull-witted as he was, the youngster understood that he was safer away from his partner-in-crime. Louie would call and ask Jamie to meet him and Jeanie. "Jamie would say 'Yeah,' but he never showed," remembered Jeanie.

In Essex, Cathy Bailey thought the number of telephone calls from Louie to Jamie was unusual. Instead of coming to Essex as he normally did, Louie would call on the phone; but Jamie acted as if he preferred not to talk to Louie. "Tell him I'll call him back," he told Bailey, "tell him I'm out in the yard."

Jamie was staying protectively close to his house that week, only occasionally dropping in at the Lincoln Inn to talk with the cook and waitresses. Otherwise he spent his time by the television set or in his room with his stereo and Rene's strobe lights. "He's usually asking if he can go to the store and do an errand for me," related Cathy Bailey. "He always wanted to be out doin' something instead of sitting around the house. But now he didn't even want to go out."

Jamie took a sudden interest in the daily newspaper and asked Cathy to let him see it each morning, which surprised her. "Jamie's mother would get on his back about a job when he wasn't working at the Lincoln Inn, and he'd pick up the paper just to show her he was looking," Bailey later explained. "But now, he was reading it every day even before I did. He always asked for the news pages and never even bothered with the job section."

Bailey assumed that he was taking a special interest in the attack in Maple Street Park. One day, she asked: "Do you know those girls or something?" Jamie just shook his head, but it was the second time someone had posed an upsetting query about the crime. Louie's mother, on the phone the day before, had wanted to know if Louie had been at Jamie's house all day Friday. Jamie said yes, but wondered why Mrs. Hamlin was asking.

Mary had asked her son the same question. "Where were you last Friday afternoon?" "At Jamie's." "Were you at his house *all* day?" "Yeah." "Okay."

Other than being "like his old self again," Mary Hamlin did not notice anything unusual about Louie's behavior. But ever since she'd heard the news of the killing in Essex, something had been troubling her, "just a feeling," as she said. There was the haircut and the shave that very day. She tried to tell herself it was not unusual, but she knew that Louie preferred to wear a beard until the weather got hot. There was also the dirty, sandy clothing on Saturday morning, plus the upsetting information that her sister, Joyce Hoffman, had just passed along.

Joyce's friend on the police force had told her that little Meghan O'Rourke was able to remember quite a bit about the attack. The details, she understood, were more gruesome than anyone would believe. When the policeman informed her that one of the attackers told the girls that they would be slaughtered like pigs, Mrs. Hoffman remembered that her husband had driven Louie and his father to a pig slaughter a few weeks before. After Joyce confided this news to her sister, Mary Hamlin told Joyce that Louie had shaved off his beard the day of the murder. It was not good, they agreed; there were too many coincidences.

By Wednesday Mary Hamlin was becoming increasingly concerned. She held the suspicions about her violent, hulking son within herself as long as she could, but when she walked out the door with little Mark in her arms that afternoon on the way to the pediatrician, she felt her burden was becoming too heavy to contain. "I had to tell somebody," she later said. "It was just a feeling, those awful feelings. I didn't even think such a thing—but if he did it, he needed something more than he was getting at home. God!"

CHAPTER 11

The Roundup

JAMIE AND LOUIE had no idea of the storm raging around them. The blood on their hands, unsettling in the way of a nettle in the shoe, only numbed their sense of reality further.

For a time, they were lucky. The massive statewide manhunt yielded little but frustration despite the efforts of dozens of obsessed law enforcement officers who were working overtime without pay, missing dinners at home, and going without sleep. Then on Monday afternoon, the fourth day of the investigation, Ted White, the principal of H. O. Wheeler Grade School in Burlington, called the Essex Police Department. He said he didn't want to talk on the phone, but explained that the sketches of the two suspects published in the paper looked like two of his former students, Louie Hamlin and Jamie Savage.

That evening Bob Simpson dropped a couple of cards on the desk in front of Mark Keller. "This is something you might want to pay attention to," he told his boss. Keller looked at the names on the cards, but didn't recognize them: Jamie Savage and Louie Hamlin. Simpson explained that he had once prosecuted Hamlin on an assault charge; the state's attorney said he would assign someone to do more checking.

On Tuesday morning, Ted White called the Essex police again. He had been speaking with his home-school coordinator, Joyce Hoffman, who was Louie Hamlin's aunt. She, too, felt that the sketch in the paper looked like Louie. A few hours later, a waitress from the Lincoln Inn came to the station to report that one of the sketches looked like a fellow employee, Jamie Savage.

The telephone at the Essex Police Department had not stopped ringing for days. People were calling in possible suspects from all over the state, but the names of Hamlin and Savage were beginning to attract serious attention. "As more people called about them," remembered Lieutenant Yandow, "we realized we had to start looking at these guys a little harder."

Shortly after noon on Wednesday, Ruggiero, Yandow, Simpson, Horton, and Keller retired to the town selectmen's room and closed the door. They needed privacy. Their leads were drying up and they were running out of theories. All the suspects were "checking out"—at the time of the crime they were in jail or working or at home or out of town. The police feared that if there was not a break soon, they might lose the thread of continuity. "After three days if you don't start getting something, you might as well bag it all," explained Sergeant Horton. "I was thinking for sure we had lost it."

The investigators began a review of everything they had. Keller went to the blackboard, wrote names in chalk, then crossed them out as his colleagues called out the results of their inquiries. On all the suspect lists there were always two names that still did not check out: Louie Hamlin and Jamie Savage.

They were both local boys and terribly young, facts that could not be reconciled with the savagery of the crime, nor fit in with Meghan's estimate of their age. But other details fit well. There were the BB guns, a weapon for youngsters not adults; and tennis shoes; and adolescent remarks. "It sounded more and more like younger guys," Keller speculated. "When one of them told Meghan to perform fellatio and she refused, he says, 'Forget it then.' That sounded like a kid."

The investigation of Hamlin showed that he had been kicked out of school that week, had previously pulled a knife on a girl, had been accused of raping his sister, and was a constant companion of Jamie Savage. The two looked increasingly like good suspects. With all other leads dying, the five lawmen decided to take officers away from other assignments and focus on Hamlin and Savage.

By that afternoon there were eight policemen tracking the youths. Sergeant Horton assigned a state trooper to visit Joseph Safford's farm in Ferrisburg to ask Hamlin's uncle about the pig slaughter. Jay Fish, a sergeant with the South Burlington police, was told to put together a photographic "lineup" that included pictures of Hamlin and Savage. Stakeouts of both homes were organized.

At the Wheeler school, Principal White told Lieutenant Lee Graham and Patrolman Bill Laurenson that neither Jamie nor Louie was a good student, and that he always had trouble with Louie. White then called Joyce Hoffman, Louie's aunt, into his office. Though reluctant to talk at first, Mrs. Hoffman gradually told the police what she knew. "She was afraid that Louie would seek revenge on her for giving information," reported Graham. "She said she couldn't predict what he was going to do, that he had rages of temper and just went crazy."

"I hate to admit it," she told the policemen, "but I know that it is him."

Graham and Laurenson next located Louie's brother John at a foster home on North Champlain Street. The eldest Hamlin son, taller than Louie but not as stocky, was cooperative from the beginning. He gave the police a tour of Louie's hangouts, including the cabin in the city dump made of discarded lumber. The police were hoping to find items taken from the victims, but the shack contained nothing except soggy girlie magazines, empty beer and wine bottles, and reefer butts. At the riverbank by the Blue Bridge, where John said Louie often hid things, the police searched for evidence but found none.

As they walked along the river John talked about Louie

honestly, but without animosity. He said, almost casually, that he thought his brother Louie was capable of murder. John also speculated that Louie and Jamie engaged in some homosexual activities, but, he added, "Louie didn't want people to think he was queer." He believed Louie experimented with this out of frustration, and did not think his brother was truly homosexual.

"John Hamlin painted a picture of Louie that made him sound like a pretty cold person. And the more he talked, the more convinced I became that we were on the right track," recalled Graham. "From what little psychology I knew, he seemed a classic sociopath. Just a classic no-conscience guy."

As they were talking, John suddenly saw a young man and woman crossing the bridge on the way toward Winooski. "There goes Louie with his girlfriend now," John said, pointing at the pair.

"Oh shit," Laurenson and Graham exclaimed in unison. Not wanting Louie to see them with John, they hid under the bridge on the riverbank until Hamlin was out of sight.

The two policemen kept John Hamlin with them all afternoon and evening, holding him incognito, what Mark Keller called "sitting on him." Since no charge had been filed against John, it was legally risky, but Keller decided that it was worth it. The police were on firmer ground with Jamie's brother Rene, who had been caught driving without a license two days before. Patrolman Taylor picked him up on that charge and brought him to the station.

At police headquarters, Rene was met by Nick Ruggiero, who waved a copy of the composite sketch at him, followed by a barrage of questions about his pellet gun. Sensing trouble, Rene said he was leaving. "We didn't trust the guy, so we arrested him and just kept him there," Keller said. "He got pissed off so we'd give him a doughnut. Then he got real pissed so we said, 'Keep your mouth shut, or you'll go to jail.' He finally said 'All right,' and began to cooperate."

Rene looked at the composites. "Yes," he believed that they looked like Jamie and Louie, and felt it entirely possible that they were involved. Rene was sent home to find a picture of Jamie, a threat from the police in his ears: "Your ass will be grass if you don't come back." He returned with the photograph and stayed at the stationhouse.

Other officers, meanwhile, were out canvassing friends and relatives of the youths and staking out the homes of both Hamlin and Savage. The police received another lead late that afternoon when Niel Christiansen called Susan Via to tell her he had just gotten off the phone with Mary Hamlin and her pediatrician. Mrs. Hamlin, the probation officer explained, suspected that her son Louie was involved in the murder.

As night fell that Wednesday, the pace of the investigation quickened. In the police squad room, a heated debate was under way about the number of photographs Meghan should be shown to accomplish an identification that would stand up in court. The consensus finally settled on the number twelve: eleven photos along with Louie Hamlin's; eleven more photos with Jamie Savage's.

The investigators' greatest concern was how to proceed against Hamlin and Savage without solid evidence. Should they arrest the two? Or merely call them in for questioning? Bob Simpson was one of the few who argued against premature arrest. "I was afraid the way we were building up such momentum and that if it turned out not to be them, it would be a tremendous letdown," Simpson explained.

A compromise was reached in which Essex Lieutenant Yandow would ask a judge for a non-testimonial identification order. It would allow the police to pick the suspects up, photograph them, fingerprint them, and take blood, urine, and hair samples without officially charging them with a crime. At the same time, Meghan O'Rourke would be shown the lineup books. If she could identify the two, they would be formally arrested and charged.

The timing was worked out in detail. Jamie and Louie would be driven to the State Police barracks in Colchester. To maintain secrecy, particularly with the press, the police planned to move the manhunt headquarters out of Essex. Each officer was told to "sign off" at Essex that night to confuse news people monitoring police radios.

At eight that evening Chief Terry, chatting with a reporter

outside headquarters, confided: "I think we're going to crack this case." But, he cautioned, they were not ready to make an arrest. At eleven o'clock, police representatives appeared at the home of Vermont District Court Judge Edward J. Costello in Burlington to ask for the non-testimonial identification order. Costello readily obliged, providing police with a legal scrim for a bold bluff. Without solid evidence, their best chance was to have the teenagers cooperate voluntarily, hoping they would eventually incriminate themselves.

At the Essex Police Station Mike Donoghue of the *Free Press* was becoming suspicious. "Something's going on," he told Keller. "Robbie Yandow doesn't sign off at Judge Costello's house at eleven at night for no reason at all." But Keller played innocent, coolly misinforming the reporter. "Nothing is happening."

The frustrated reporters had been camped out in front of— and even inside—the stationhouse all week, awaiting news of a break in the case. Keller had been dissimulating all evening, telling them there was nothing new to report. Meanwhile investigators were secretly switching their headquarters from Essex to the State Police barracks in Colchester, a few miles away. "We didn't want all the cameras taking pictures of the guys coming into the office," Sergeant Horton explained later. "Supposing it isn't them? You've kind of screwed up their whole life."

One by one the investigators were trailing out of the Essex stationhouse on their way to Colchester. A little before midnight Keller announced, "I'm going home," and put on his jacket. "Let's go home, 'Mildew,'" he said to Steve Miller, the state policeman assigned to Keller's office. The two left by the back door, got into Ruggiero's car, backed out of the lot going the wrong way, turned up a one-way street, and sped away. They drove on back roads all the way to the Colchester barracks, three miles west of Essex, to ensure that no reporters had followed them.

As midnight approached, the police were getting worried. All the evidence against the teenagers was circumstantial: Hamlin's shave and haircut, the pig slaughter, the teenagers' friendship, their being in Essex on Friday, their love of BB guns, Hamlin's previous assault conviction. Still, the four policemen thought they had their killers. "I know everybody is supposed to be innocent until proven guilty," Horton recalled, "but according to us they're not. That's for the court to decide. Our feeling, even before we grabbed them, was that we got the right guys. Then when they came in here and looked so much like the composites, we were even surer that they did it."

At the new command post, Yandow, Graham, Horton, Simpson, and Ruggiero began to prepare for the interviews with Hamlin and Savage. But it was not something they could count on. The plan was to pick up the teenagers at their homes at midnight and hold them in custody, but without a charge. The two suspects would have to consent to the interrogation. If they did, the police could employ the classic bluff—make the suspect believe he has been caught with evidence in hand, then let him admit to the crime himself.

The other test rested with Meghan, who, in the early hours of the morning, would have to identify the photos of Hamlin and Savage as her attackers. If she failed, it would be a major setback. "A lot of things depended on that photo i.d.," Ruggiero said. "Confessions are useless nowadays," Horton added. "They're rarely admitted into court for one reason or another. There's always some technical reason somewhere."

"At that point," Keller explained, "it was a matter of waiting until we got a phone call from the hospital." Only little Meghan O'Rourke could seal the case.

It was a few minutes after midnight when police officers arrived almost simultaneously at the homes of Jamie Savage and Louie Hamlin. They were met at the front doors by people in bathrobes and pajamas, their faces staring blankly, unaware why they were being disturbed at such a late hour. The officers gave only brief explanations of the court order they were serving. Jamie and Louie were to come to the State Police offices immediately, they said, for certain police tests related to an investigation of a crime committed in Essex Junction on May 15th. No mention was made of Hamlin or Savage being suspects in the murder case; the policemen were told not to offer any more information. Although they did not inform the suspects, police had orders to stay at their homes and await further instructions should either Hamlin or Savage refuse to go with them. The police knew that if this happened, there was little they could do. There was not enough evidence to arrest them.

The night air gusting in off the darkened front porch was cold as Cathy Bailey eased the door open at 5 Gaines Court, suspicious of the late-hour ring. Officers James Penniman and Brad Larose quickly identified themselves. "We'd like to talk to James Savage," said Penniman. The police knew that Jamie was home. The officers on the stakeout, following every movement around the house since that afternoon, had left only when Penniman and Larose arrived.

Leaving the two policemen on the porch, Bailey jogged up the stairs, and a few minutes later Janet Lefebvre stumbled back down, followed by her husband. "What do you want?" Janet asked, still trying to shake herself awake. She and her husband, who had to be up before six, had already been in bed for a couple of hours. Larose explained what the court order meant, that Jamie and a guardian would have to come to the police station for some tests.

Janet motioned for the two men to come in, asking no questions, then walked to a door a few feet away. "Jamie, get up," she shouted, banging on the door.

The group stood in silence, waiting for Jamie. They could hear him inside his room, shuffling around, drawers opening and closing. "Come on, Jamie," she said, "the police want to talk to you." Ten minutes passed before he finally emerged from the bedroom, barefoot, carrying a pair of tennis shoes in one hand.

"This is a non-testimonial identification order," Penniman told the sleepy-eyed youth. "It's for now, twelve midnight, this date, at the Colchester State Police barracks. We'll give you a ride down." Jamie glanced at the document but made no attempt to read it. Without a word, he sat down and put on his shoes while Bernie and Janet assured the police they would come to the barracks as soon as they dressed.

In the dark, outside the tumbling wicker fence of the Gaines Court home, Jamie was asked to put his arms on the police cruiser. The officers quickly searched him for weapons and placed him in the backseat. Ordered not to interrogate Savage, they made the ten-minute ride to the barracks in complete silence.

At the same moment, in Burlington, Louie Hamlin was riding in a police cruiser to the same rendezvous. In the little house on Elmwood Avenue, a pale and frightened Mary Hamlin waited with police officers Fraga and Searles for her mother-in-law to arrive. Her husband was at work and with her little son still sick, she could not leave until Butch Hamlin's mother, Delphine, who lived across the street, came to baby-sit.

Mary was nervous, not sure how much trouble her son was in. Louie had thrown a cardigan sweater over a white T-shirt and left with the police without speaking to his mother. Mary was troubled whether she had done the right thing confessing her suspicions to both Louie's probation officer and the family pediatrician that afternoon. It had all happened so quickly and unexpectedly; this middle-of-the-night visit by police surprised her. She was very cooperative, but unprepared for the suddenness with which the consequences seemed to be descending on her.

Asking Delphine to call Butch at Koffee Kup, Mary Hamlin accompanied the police officers to their car and drove with them through the deserted streets to the Essex Police Station. There, she consented to be interviewed. Mary told about Louie's school suspension, the fact that he had stayed at Jamie's house all week, the haircut and shave she gave him Friday evening, and the sandy clothes she washed out on Saturday.

She was unburdening herself to police when a call from Butch abruptly interrupted the interview. Mary had already told her husband of her conversations with the pediatrician and Niel Christiansen that day. He had scolded her about talking to the authorities, worried that she was inviting trouble. Mary had answered, "Yes, but I had to tell somebody."

When the phone conversation with her husband was completed, Mary returned to the small office to resume the interview with Searles and Fraga. She seemed shaken.

"I'm going to start with the time you saw him come home," Patrolman Fraga began.

Mary raised her hand diffidently. "Could we stop just a minute?" she asked.

"Sure," said Fraga.

"My husband doesn't want Louie questioned without his attorney present," she said meekly, trapped between conflicting duties. "Okay? I don't know if maybe he told you."

"He told Lieutenant Searles that," Fraga answered, "and that's why we are going to finish this off so you can be up there to make sure that all those things are going to be done. Okay?"

Mary Hamlin nodded. For the next ten minutes, in a soft and wavering voice, she continued her account of what she knew of her son's activities on Friday and the days that followed. Neither Searles nor Fraga mentioned the rape and murder. The police merely wanted to know whether Jamie was with Louie when he came home that day, whether he still had the pellet gun that he had shown her that morning, whether he had friends who drove a car. Mrs. Hamlin answered all the questions without hesitation. As if relieved to be talking about such seemingly inconsequential matters, she often volunteered small details, putting off, it seemed, the inevitable.

"No, come to think of it," she offered at one point, "he didn't have the green shirt that day. He had the white shirt. He may have had the green jacket over it 'cause he had a white shirt, the one that has slot buttons something like this. Snaps down the front."

But the heart of the matter could not be postponed indefinitely. When it finally came, Mary Hamlin was unprepared. Patrolman Fraga picked up a piece of paper and stepped toward Mrs. Hamlin. "I want to show you this composite, all right," he said, holding an eight-by-eleven sheet in front of the dark-haired woman. "It's a pink copy composite. It has two people pictured on it. Can you tell me anybody that may look like that?"

Mary Hamlin glanced at the paper but quickly turned away. She had seen these faces on television and in the paper for the last four days, but with a police officer now holding them in front of her, she saw her suspicions materialize. Below the sketches it read, WANTED FOR: HOMICIDE OF 12 YEAR OLD FEMALE; ATTEMPTED HOMICIDE OF SECOND FEMALE. She covered her eyes with her hands.

"Just be as honest as you can," Fraga urged gently, seeing the woman start to tremble. "We know it's hard."

"I could not," she began, and burst out in sobs. "God help me," she moaned, "I can't help it."

Meghan O'Rourke, through State Trooper Strusinski's skilled hand, had finally created a telling image of her attackers: the dark, pondering eyes; the mussed, disheveled hair, parted on the left and slanting across the forehead just above the eyes; the scraggly beard. It was not an exact portrait of Louie Hamlin, but it was enough of a resemblance to bring Mary Hamlin to tears.

"I know this must be very difficult for you," the patrolman sympathized. As Mary Hamlin cried, he tried to console her. "It's okay. It's okay." She continued to moan. "Who do you think—"

"Jamie, too," Mrs. Hamlin blurted.

"It looks like Jamie, too?"

"Yes," Mrs. Hamlin agreed.

"Subject number one looks like your son?" said Fraga, wanting Mrs. Hamlin to confirm out loud what her sobs were so eloquently stating.

"Could you just speak out once, yes or no? Subject number one?"

"I'm—it looks like it might be Louie." She put her head in her hands and cried.

CHAPTER 12

Jamie's Confession

IT WAS 1:30 A.M. Thursday, May 21st, almost a week after the
attack. Susan Via, Sergeant Jay Fish, and Detective Stephen
Burke were in the police cruiser riding to the Medical Center
Hospital, clutching two "books" of photographs. As Via recalled, "We had our fingers crossed. You could hear all three
hearts pounding."

When the three arrived at Meghan's room on the pediatrics
ward, Meghan was asleep. Via had called the hospital earlier
and asked doctors and nurses not to give the young girl any
medication that might make it difficult for her to be awakened
in the middle of the night. Patrolman Zane Snelling, then guarding Meghan, told the investigators that she had been up earlier
that evening and had been given no sedatives.

Meghan's sister, Jennifer, came out of the room. In addition
to the police guard, either her mother or sister stayed with her
all night, every night. In the hallway, Via explained to Jennifer

that they were there to show Meghan photographs of suspects for identification. Jennifer was concerned, she told Via, because her sister had not been sleeping well that night; she was in pain.

Via and Jennifer went in first to wake up Meghan. "She was whiny and said she was in a lot of pain," Via remembered. "I sat down on her bed and said, 'Meghan, how would you like to do a little work?' She shrugged her shoulders. And I said, 'I have two friends from South Burlington Police Department whom I want you to meet. And I want you to look at some pictures. Do you think you're up to looking at some pictures?' She kind of groaned and said 'Yeah.' But she was very uncomfortable. She said, 'I don't like this pillow.' I got her another one. Then she wanted to get on the cot because the hospital bed wasn't comfortable. We were fluffing pillows. It seemed like it took forever to get her comfortable."

"Okay, I'll go get the officers," Via finally said. "Their names are Steve and Jay." Jennifer left the room, whispering to Via that she was too nervous to watch the proceedings.

Via brought Fish and Burke in, and introduced them to Meghan. Patiently, Fish explained to Meghan that there were twelve photos in each of the two books, and that the people who attacked her might or might not be among them. The photos might have been taken a while ago and might not look exactly like her attackers, Fish warned the girl. Their hair length could have changed; their facial hair could be different. Fish was going to great lengths not to prejudice Meghan in any way. The two dozen law enforcement officers then pacing the floor of the State Police barracks were awaiting the outcome of her identification, and no one wanted a legal challenge to this crucial session.

Fish told Meghan to look at *all* the pictures before deciding if there was anyone who looked like the man who attacked her. By examining all the pictures first, there would be less chance that Meghan would choose the first photo that resembled her attacker. The officers wanted no mistakes, no confusion, no approximations. From experience, Fish knew that people sometimes felt obligated to defend their first choice, even if they saw a closer likeness later on.

Because Hamlin was now clean-shaven, the police had had the problem of finding an appropriate photo. Fortunately, they had located a picture of him with a beard, a high school yearbook photo of Hamlin on the wrestling team. To have it match the other mug shots, they had tracked down the original group photo and rephotographed it so that only Hamlin was visible, then enlarged it to the same size as the others. The photo of Jamie was the one taken by police at the Colchester barracks.

Fish carefully placed the first book in Meghan's lap. Via, supportively holding the child's hand, could not see the photos, but she watched Meghan's face as the girl slowly turned the pages of the album. At one point Meghan hesitated, her eyes opened wide. Via could see a sudden intensity as Meghan focused on the page. She then turned the page, saying nothing, as Fish had instructed.

None of the investigators dared tell Meghan the true importance of her task. If she did not recognize Hamlin and Savage, the investigation would be irrevocably damaged. It would mean that either Meghan was a bad witness or that police were after the wrong suspects. Either alternative was fatal to the case, for at this point investigators had no other suspects.

"Do any of these pictures look like the man who assaulted you and Melissa?" Fish asked when Meghan had completed turning all the pages.

"Yes," said Meghan.

Fish began turning the pages again, one by one, photo by photo. "Now, Meghan," he said, "you tell me when you see the man who you think assaulted you."

At photo number 6 Meghan stopped him and put her finger on the picture. "That's him," she said without hesitation as she pressed her finger to the picture of Louie Hamlin. She did not look at the adults for a sign of confirmation, nor did she ask if she had chosen the right one. Meghan was sure.

"Okay, thank you, Meghan." Fish, fighting desperately to restrain his excitement, made a note on his pad. Via glanced up at Burke who was behind Meghan. A smile broke across the policeman's face, and he raised his hand and gave the prosecutor the okay sign. "I just kind of felt, 'Oh God, don't let me just die right here,'" Via related. "My heart was going kaboom, kaboom. And I was saying to myself, 'Come on, Meghan! You can pick these guys out!'"

Fish then slowly picked up the second book and gave Meghan the same instructions. Meghan went through the procedure, and when she had finished Fish asked again if she recognized any of the people as her attacker. Meghan said, "Yes," just as firmly as before.

She pointed to photo number 3. It was the photograph of Jamie Savage.

"We could barely contain ourselves," Via remembered. "Burke was smiling from ear to ear; you know, this big shit-eating grin."

Via got up, gave Meghan a buss on the cheek. "Thanks, sweetie," she said. "Sorry to bother you."

"You get better quick," said Fish.

"Bye, Meghan," said Burke. "Thanks, you're a doll."

In the hall outside, the three met Jennifer and Zane Snelling, their faces lit with anticipation.

"She did it!" Via almost shouted, hoarsely but jubilantly. Everyone hugged one another. Jennifer O'Rourke sobbed. Snelling was exploding, "All right! All right!," wrapping his arms around everyone in sight.

Fish broke at a trot down the hall toward a telephone, then dialed it as quickly as his exhausted fingers would allow. "We got 'em!" he screamed into the phone. "Perfect i.d.! Both guys!"

By then Via and Burke had caught up with Fish and the three left the hospital, unable to speak. "We walked out in tears," Via remembered.

When Nick Ruggiero walked through the troopers' room of the State Police barracks to pick up the phone, everyone knew it was news from the hospital. It was now almost two in the morning, but the police were still in the building, milling about the large room in the rear. No one, even those police with little to do, wanted to leave. If Meghan O'Rourke identified Hamlin and Savage, the massive manhunt would be over. If she did not, the search might never end.

So far the operation was proceeding as planned. The press

had been successfully eluded as the command headquarters was transferred to the State Police offices at the old army barracks near St. Michael's College. Louie Hamlin, his fingerprints taken, sat quietly in a small office in the front of the building next to the bathroom, a police guard at the door. Mrs. Hamlin, down the hall in the motor vehicles office, was alone, waiting.

In another room, Mrs. Lefebvre looked on as a state police evidence technician was completing tests on her son, Jamie Savage. His parents were cooperating, as was Mrs. Hamlin. Only Butch Hamlin was balking. Lieutenant Searles informed Mark Keller that the elder Hamlin did not want his son interrogated. If he were, even with the permission of his mother, Louie Hamlin, Sr., insisted he would deny everything both of them had said. For the state's attorney, it was only a minor inconvenience. At the moment all he cared about was how twelve-year-old Meghan O'Rourke would perform.

Silence fell over the police officers as Sergeant Ruggiero disappeared into the small office to answer the phone. Ruggiero was back out in less than a minute, his ruddy face glowing. "She's got 'em both!" he shouted.

The room exploded in exultation. After five days of steely, controlled behavior, everyone was leaping, shouting, hugging. Some of the burliest men displayed tears; broad smiles spread over their faces. "This is the beginning of the end," Robbie Yandow thought as he looked around at the ecstatic men, some of whom had been without sleep for more than thirty hours.

Mark Keller, hearing the noise, ran into the room. "Everybody was jumping up and down," he recalled, "yelling 'Great! Great!' and hitting each other on the back."

Keller smiled, then lifted his yellow legal pad and said, "This is what we gotta do next."

"Jesus Christ!" someone shouted. "Can't you at least give us five minutes to celebrate and shut up about your goddamn things to do?"

"Yeah, sure," Keller reposted. "You've had fifteen seconds. Now let's get going."

Yandow and Ruggiero entered the room where Jamie Savage and his parents were sitting and closed the door. The two policemen were now convinced that Savage and Hamlin had committed the murder, and Meghan's identification gave them ammunition to persuade the teenagers to confess. The room was small, cluttered with metal filing cabinets, bookshelves, and a gray rubber-topped desk. There was only a single dark window high on the wall. Janet and Bernie sat upright, uncomfortable in their metal-backed chairs. They turned slightly so they could see Jamie, who sat stone-faced next to his mother.

Ruggiero began slowly, explaining for the first time that Jamie had been brought in because they believed he knew something about the murder. Janet, hearing the word "homicide," slumped in her chair.

"You have the right to remain silent and you may refuse to answer any questions asked of you," Ruggiero continued, reading from the Miranda Warning that the Supreme Court had made a prerequisite for any police interrogation. "Anything you say can be used against you in any court of law. You have the right to talk with a lawyer and have him present with you while you are being questioned. If you cannot afford to hire a lawyer, one will be appointed for you before any questioning, if you so desire."

Yandow and Ruggiero were now at their Rubicon. Miranda warnings were sufficiently clear to give any suspect hope that he could delay the reckoning. He did not have to talk; he could call an attorney. If the Lefebvres or their son had any misgivings, this was their opportunity to back out. If they did, Ruggiero and Yandow knew, no attorney would permit his client to confess.

But as Ruggiero read on, he noticed that the blood seemed to rush from the faces of Bernie and Janet Lefebvre, ashamed at the thought that Jamie might be involved in such a brutal crime. They both stared at Jamie, sitting with his head down, his hands kneading the white denim over the flab between his thighs. "The parents were sitting there in total shock," Ruggiero recollected. "We weren't sure how they were going to react to all of this, especially when they realized how serious it was, whether they'd let him talk to us. But you could see in their faces that they wanted to find out as much as us what the hell he was going to say."

With a brief attempt at cool confidence, Jamie said, "I'll talk about that, sure. I ain't got nothin' to hide." Janet, Bernie, and Jamie all signed the waiver form. Yandow and Ruggiero, knowing they had overcome a major hurdle, began their questioning.

The expected denials began immediately. Ruggiero's first question was "Tell us to the best of your recollection what you did on Friday, the fifteenth."

"In the mornin' I went to work. Got done at one-thirty. I was home at three-thirty."

It was obvious that Jamie had already given the question some thought. His reply had come quickly, the times he gave were precise. He made no mention of the fact that he had gone to Burlington with Louie and visited Louie's probation officer, information police already had. Being home at three-thirty, about the same time that Meghan and Melissa were attacked, sounded convenient.

But it quickly became apparent that the fidgety teenager was more confused than conniving. After answering a few questions about his work, Jamie clarified his statement. "I was home from one-thirty to three-thirty. Then I went to the park with Louie."

Neither Ruggiero nor Yandow expected the break Jamie was now offering them to come so quickly. "And we were shootin' at squirrels," Jamie continued in his monotone. "So Louie decided to go get the girls."

"What were you shooting squirrels with?" Ruggiero asked.

"With a BB gun," Savage replied.

"What kind of BB gun?"

"Hand pistol." Jamie's replies were slow, quiet, and brief.

"Whose gun was it, Jamie?" Yandow interjected.

"Louie's."

"Do you know where Louie got it?" Yandow continued.

"No."

"Do you know how long Louie had this gun?"

"No."

Janet Lefebvre was watching her son intently, seeking to help, desperately wanting to know what happened. "Is that the one that Junie had?" she asked Jamie, referring to her son Rene by his nickname.

"Junie's was a pellet." Jamie responded to his mother's question.

"This was definitely a BB gun, then?" asked Yandow.

"Yeah."

"Okay."

"Nothin' but BBs."

"Could you shoot pellets in it?" asked Janet, not unversed in the guns her sons and their friends used.

"No," said Jamie.

"So go ahead, go ahead," prompted Ruggiero impatiently. "You were shooting squirrels."

"Yeah," said Jamie. "And Louie wanted to go out to do girls. Which I didn't do anything—I just went with him. He told me to stop the girl, so I stopped her. And then he started hittin' the girls and takin' their clothes off—which I just held the other girl without doin' a thing."

That Jamie would cast the blame onto Louie came as no surprise to Yandow and Ruggiero, who now realized that extracting the real story from Jamie was, as Ruggiero suspected from the beginning, "going to be like pulling teeth."

"Because the parents were there this kid was not going to sit and tell us he raped two girls and had them perform oral sex on him and then killed one of them," he explained. "No way. But he was watching the papers every day just like everybody else in that community, so he was abreast of that. He knew he was had. He didn't know what we had, obviously, so the easiest way out was to say that Louie did it all."

In his stumbling manner, Jamie did exactly that. He was apathetic, his voice without inflection, unemotional. "When Louie saw 'em," he told Yandow and Ruggiero, "he yelled to me. I was ready to go home cuz it was rainin'. He yelled to me, so I was dumb enough to go back and he went after the girls. He told me to hold this one, so I holded her."

The lanky figure squirmed in the chair, his baby face still marked by pimples, with cheeks puffy and lips pouty. The mantle of murder did not seem to fit. He seemed a pathetic anachronism, nothing like a hardened criminal. "When I first saw him in the barracks," Ruggiero would say, "I thought, 'My God, he's young. Looks just like a young kid. No way that he's the one.'"

"Okay, so what happened?" asked the State Police sergeant.

"So then Louie went after the other one," Jamie said, "started slappin' her, beatin' her up, takin' her clothes off. I just stand there and just hold that girl."

"Did you have a gun?" Ruggiero asked.

"No."

If not for Meghan's contradictory account, Jamie's story might have sounded plausible. Within his jangled presentation, there was evidence that he had already considered this eventual showdown with police.

"You didn't have a gun?" Ruggiero pressed, knowing that Meghan O'Rourke had said that Jamie held a gun to her head.

"I threw mine down," Jamie responded.

"Did you have anything at all in your hand?"

"No."

"You threw your gun down?" Ruggiero continued. "Where did you throw it?"

"Over the bank."

It was obvious that Jamie was lying, but Ruggiero wanted the teenager to tell his full story before confronting him with discrepancies. Instead, he subtly dropped hints that perhaps Louie was talking to police as well.

"So why don't you give me a brief thing about what happened," Ruggiero suggested politely, "and then we'll go over the details. How's that? Then I can compare it to what Louie said. What happened then?"

"Well, then he started—he took his knife out and started hittin' her with it. Then when he was done with her, he went after the other one."

"What do you mean, hitting her with it?" Ruggiero interrupted.

"Slicin' her," said Jamie, with no emotion in his voice.

"You mean he stabbed her?"

"Yeah."

"Could you see them?"

"Yeah, I saw 'em."

"What happened when he stabbed her?"

"She started to bleed and she went—she laid down. When she went down on the ground, Louie went after the other one." Jamie talked as if the events he was describing were a television episode, saving his emphasis for denying responsibility. "'Course, when he took the other one, I left."

Ruggiero and Yandow let the obvious invention pass, urging Jamie to tell them more about the direction he took to go home, the clothes he was wearing, the time he got home, what Louie did that day. To anticipate possible insanity or defective state-of-mind defenses, they asked Jamie whether he and Louie had been drinking any alcohol, smoking pot, dropping acid, or taking any drugs at all. He said "No" to each question.

Jamie denied ever going to Maple Street Park before that Friday, but his mother interjected skeptically: "You didn't go there before?" Jamie also denied having seen the girls before that Friday. In his recounting, he omitted any mention of rape, claimed he left the park as soon as Louie started stabbing the girls. He had no idea what happened to the girls' clothes and other belongings.

"Okay, I have to say something." For Ruggiero the time had come for confrontation. He halted the questions about the details and looked directly at Savage. "Are you being totally honest with us, James?" Ruggiero used the formal Christian name, unaware that "Jamie" was in fact the youth's given name.

Jamie stared back briefly, then looked away. "Totally honest," he said with an almost wounded belligerence.

"Are you sure?"

"Positive." But it was not a positive statement. Jamie's voice cracked slightly as he spoke. It was a transparent answer, made more to satisfy the authority represented by the interrogators than to address the substance of their words.

Ruggiero and Yandow instinctively assumed almost a paternalistic attitude. "We have a little conflict here," Yandow offered without rancor.

"Well, there's a lot of conflicts," Ruggiero interrupted bluntly. He then lectured Jamie with part-truth and part-bluff. "But the thing you got to realize, James, is not only the conflict between what Louie says and what Meghan—the girl who's alive, that's her name—Meghan says. There's also certain things that our Vermont State Police Crime Laboratory picked up at the scene that can verify a person doing a certain thing. Okay? Physical evidence. That is why Corporal McMaster in there took hair from you, right? Took hair samples, had you spit onto that disk. Certain things we can say you did or did not do based on those things. And I think it's very important for you to understand that you be totally honest about everything you did, because if we could prove differently, well, then we're going to say, well, who's being honest with us? Is it Louie? Or is it Jamie? Okay?"

At that moment, Louie Hamlin was sitting by himself in a small room down the hall, still awaiting his time for interrogation. Ruggiero was counting on Jamie's fear that his partner-in-crime might already have talked.

When Savage again denied ever seeing Meghan nude, Yandow drilled in.

"Do you remember what I said about us all being very honest about this whole thing?" he asked.

Jamie delivered a muffled "Yeah."

"Yet Meghan's saying some things that you did that you're not admitting to," he told Savage.

"Wha'd'ya mean? What's that?" Savage asked in a barely audible voice.

Yandow, a young, mustachioed native Vermonter who dressed in tailored three-piece suits, was normally unflappable, but his frustration began to show. "We're talking about a sexual assault, Jamie," he said. "We know it happened. And it's not going to do anybody any good if you deny it. Because we know it happened. But we would like to get your side of the story." Yandow stopped. "The girl did not have her clothes on, did she, Jamie?"

"Noshedidn't," Savage said, rushing through his admission.

Without gloating about his victory, Yandow simply continued. "Okay. Now, did you take her clothes off, or did you just tell her to take them off?"

"Just tol' her."

Jamie was giving up his story piece by piece, but as Ruggiero had expected, the single admission did not open the confessional floodgates. Savage clung to his Louie-did-it safety jacket, denying that he had made Meghan do anything to him after he ordered her to disrobe.

"Remember, truth time," said Yandow. "Now, what did you make her do to you?"

"Nothin'."

Nick Ruggiero, who had excused himself from the room a few minutes earlier, now returned. When he sought to, the thirty-year-old detective, born in Naples, Italy, and raised in the Bronx, could turn his altar-boy expression to big-city stone. Standing by the desk, he was somber.

"We're going to start getting into some details here which we have to get resolved one way or another," Ruggiero said, looking at Janet Lefebvre, small and nervous in her heavy topcoat, her eyes filling with tears. He was letting Jamie know that he was prepared to stay all night if necessary. "I don't know if maybe Mrs. Lefebvre might want to stay here. If you'd like to leave, that's okay too. But I want one of you people here for James, okay? But that's your decision."

The police knew that because of Jamie's age a guardian had to be present during the interview. Bernie and Janet looked at each other, unsure of themselves. "I will reiterate that these details are not going to be pleasant," Yandow added, "so we just want to make sure that you know fully what we're—"

"I don't have to stay?" asked Janet, tears streaming down her cheek. She mumbled and started to rise. Janet now understood exactly what her son was accused of and, despairing of the interview outcome, she wanted no more. Ruggiero escorted the sobbing mother out of the room.

With only the men and Jamie now present, Yandow and Ruggiero sought to unravel the details of the rape.

"Did you make the girl perform any sex act on you?" Yandow asked the teenager.

"No."

"Did you perform any sex act on her?"

"No."

As Savage continued to deny the sexual assault, Ruggiero pulled out a sheaf of papers from a manila folder. "I have Meghan's statement here," he told Jamie, "word for word.

Okay? I'll read it to you." The detective read quickly, without emphasis, from the transcribed interview between Via and Meghan in which the little girl said that the curly-haired man "made me suck on him."

"It's not true," Jamie responded vigorously.

"Why would she fabricate something like that?" Ruggiero countered.

"I don't know, but it's not true." For the first time there was force to Savage's rebuttal.

"Okay," Ruggiero said calmly. "Why do you think we had you spit onto that disk?" The detective was bluffing.

Suddenly Savage was silent, as if thinking. Then, quietly, he said, "I don't know."

"That's to help us determine these things," said Ruggiero. "See what I mean? Because sometimes stories are fabricated and we have to determine the truth. And I think it would be very helpful in this case if you'd be totally honest."

"I am," Jamie said, discovering again his refuge of denial, "on that."

"Okay. Well, if you say it's not true, I'll go along with you for the time being on that." The detective changed the subject momentarily, but Yandow quickly picked it up again.

"Did you try to have intercourse with her?"

"Nope," the youth mumbled. "No, I didn't."

On a hunch Ruggiero interjected, "Do you know what intercourse is?"

"No," Savage replied.

Slowly the detectives were beginning to understand what Mark Keller meant when he characterized Jamie as a "little Neanderthal."

"Do you know what being laid is?" asked Ruggiero.

"Yeah," said Jamie.

"What?"

"Sex."

"And when I say sex, what does that mean to you?"

"Laid down with her."

"And what?" coaxed Yandow and Ruggiero simultaneously.

"Start fucking her."

For the next ten minutes, Jamie continued to deny engaging

in any sexual acts with the victims.

Yandow then took up the combined preachy-patronizing cudgel. "Jamie, you're not going to be able to go through this thing and say 'I didn't do anything,' because we know you did," he said emphatically, his voice rising. "We know that you had or attempted to have sexual intercourse with that girl. We know that. And we know that Louie did not inflict all the harm on both of those girls. Louie was not the only one that stabbed them. Louie was not the only one that shot them with the BB gun. We know this!"

"And Louie didn't choke Melissa, okay?" said Ruggiero. The detectives spoke with the assurance of eye witnesses. "So let's at least start being honest about things." Ruggiero paused. "Okay?" He paused again. "You ready? What did you use to choke Melissa with?"

"A sock." Jamie was now staring at his knees.

The detectives quickly fired a succession of questions at the agitated teenager. Just as rapidly, Jamie admitted that he tied Melissa up and choked the little girl.

"You know what I think might be easier now that we've had this little moment of honesty here," Ruggiero finally said, almost sympathetically. "Why don't you start over again, telling the story again, but exactly what you did. And please don't leave anything out or don't add anything that you didn't do. How's that, Jamie?"

Jamie began again, repeating his story, adding the changes. He included Louie's statement about knowing what it would be like to be slaughtered like a pig, but continued to deny taking part in the sexual assault or knife attack. He described the "fucking," the six-inch knife blade, the "slicin'," and blamed it all on Hamlin. He told the detectives how he used the sock "all red" to choke Melissa. Louie, Jamie recounted, "stabbed her heart," pushing the blade in "five or six times." As he described the gory incident his voice was without emotion.

"There were no outward signs of remorse about any of it," Yandow recalled. "You know, he never choked up while he was talking about it. He wouldn't look at anybody, but his manner was pretty consistent during the whole interview."

Jamie's stepfather, however, was bristling in his chair. "He was just going crazy," Ruggiero remembered. "He wasn't yelling or anything like that, but you could see it in his eyes. It was just killing him. He just kept looking at Jamie and shaking his head. And he wouldn't even look at me."

At one point Ruggiero asked Jamie if he thought Louie was a crazy person. "Yeah," said the youth, adding, "even he said he's crazy."

"Would you say you're crazy?" asked the sergeant.

"Yes, I would."

"Why?"

"To go along with it," Jamie said, "I'd have to be crazy."

Ruggiero was concerned that no court could later interpret that remark as a claim of temporary insanity. Ruggiero quickly asked Jamie: "You could still tell the difference between right and wrong?"

"Yes."

"Okay, and you know what you did is wrong?"

"Yeah."

"Did you know at the time what you were doing was wrong?" Yandow asked, hoping further to obviate a mental-disease defense.

"Yes."

"Okay," Ruggiero continued. "When you saw those girls— now, you're a young man. Were those girls attractive to you?"

"Yeah," said Jamie, following the detective cautiously along the new course.

"And you got excited by looking at them?"

"Yeah."

"What did it do to you? Inside? How did you feel?"

"I felt like going after them."

"Just like that?"

"Yeah."

"You just got the urge to have sex with them?"

"Well, I didn't have sex."

"Well, I'm asking—"

"I just had the nerve to go after them—just for the hell of it."

"For what?"

"Just for the fun."

"When you first saw the girls, did you get sexually aroused?" Ruggiero continued.

"Yes."

"Did you get an erection?"

"Yes."

"Okay. So if you got an erection—what does that mean?"

Jamie was silent. "I don't know," he admitted.

Ruggiero knew he had to find a common language with which to communicate with Jamie. "You said it sexually stimulated you. You know what stimulate means?"

"No."

"It aroused you. Do you know what arouse means?"

"No."

"You got an erection. Do you know what an erection is?"

"No."

"You know what a hard-on is?"

"Yeah."

Gradually, the light shone. Just as the rape and murder occurred in a demented world all its own, so Jamie Savage— crossing and uncrossing his legs, his baby lips barely moving as he spoke—recognized it only in primitive terms.

"I didn't have enough nerve to get 'em," Jamie protested as Yandow and Ruggiero pushed him closer to an admission. "To actually fuck 'em."

Back and forth the adults went with the fifteen-year-old, listening as Jamie Savage tracked and backtracked, from one moment to the next.

"What do you mean?" asked Ruggiero. "You took off her clothes, you had her naked right there in front of you. You had a hard-on."

"Yeah, but then I lost my nerve."

"You lost your nerve?"

"Yeah."

"But did you try?"

"I tried."

"And what was that trying, what did that consist of?"

"Just helped Louie get their clothes off, and that's it."

"Did you try to put your penis in her?"

"No, I didn't."

"Not at all?"

"Not at all."

"Why would Meghan say you did?"

"I didn't. Louie did."

"Yeah, she said Louie did too. But she also said you did. You tried, but you couldn't do it."

"I did try, but—"

"You couldn't get it in her, she said."

"No, I couldn't."

"But you did try to do it."

"I tried, but I didn't."

"Did you stick your penis up against her?"

"No, I didn't."

Ruggiero had moved slowly to the edge of the desk. Looking down on the teenager like a disappointed father, he asked again, with a disapproving edge to his voice, "Did you?"

Jamie leaned back under the gaze, shrugged, then drawled in submission, "Yesss."

Bernie Lefebvre quickly looked away from his stepson, as if sick. "Oh my God," he mumbled.

It was now almost three-thirty in the morning, more than an hour since the intense questioning had begun. Jamie had not admitted everything, but he had traveled far since his first inept denials. Ruggiero and Yandow maintained their pressure, confident that, though the confession lacked all the detail of Meghan's account, it was a solid corroboration. Once Jamie admitted that he helped Louie hide the girls' belongings after the murder, they began to wind down. Savage even said, "I could take you there."

"After questioning him again and again and again and again," Yandow would recall, "and catching him in lies and confronting him with the lies, at the end I figured we had a lot of the truth. I don't think we had all of it. He didn't always make a lot of sense. But I was convinced we had the basic story of what had happened to the two girls."

"We knew he was lying about his own involvement and throwing everything on Louie," Ruggiero added. "But Robbie and I knew that we weren't going to get a full admission. So once there was a possibility of us recovering the clothes, we said, 'Let's go for that.'"

In the small Arson Investigation Office a few doors down the hall from where Jamie Savage was accusing his friend of murder and rape, Louie Hamlin sat like a rock. The back of his hard chair touched a set of drab green metal lockers, his arms were folded over his chest, his square, clean-shaven chin steady. He gave no indication that he was suffering any anxiety during his two hours of detention. His mother, seated at Louie's right on an identical chair, was turning her knuckles white twisting on the strap of her enormous purse, her fingers clutching a wrinkled white handkerchief. The huge woman, in her tight polyester slacks and frayed overcoat, was as agitated as her son was stony.

Sergeant Horton settled into a chair behind the desk. Lieutenant Graham sat in front of the desk, Louie and his mother on his left. Though the two officers now felt confident they had their killer, Horton's first impression of Louie was that he was "just another kid off the street." In some respects, that impression would not change.

After Searles's account of what Butch Hamlin had said, neither officer expected Louie and his mother to accede to the interview. Nervously, Mary Hamlin said she didn't know what to do. "My husband said not to talk, but I feel like my son should clear up any problems that have come up." She looked nervously at the officers, then at Louie.

"Yeah, I don't care what he says about it," Louie retorted. "I'll talk about whatever they want to talk about."

Surprised, Horton and Graham read Louie his Miranda rights and Hamlin and his mother signed the waiver form. Horton looked at Mary Hamlin and bluntly told her that Jamie Savage had already confessed; he was now accusing her son of murder. The woman turned away, as if at the dawn of another nightmare, and began crying quietly.

"Do you understand why you were brought here?" Horton then asked Louie.

"Yeh," said Louie, "a little bit."

"Why do you think you were brought here?"

"I was accused of killing and attempted killing of two girls." Louie spoke without looking at either Graham or Horton. His voice was calm, matter-of-fact.

Both Horton and Graham quickly surmised that, though a kid, Louie Hamlin would be a tough adversary. Unlike Jamie, he seemed to know all the right answers. He had shaved his beard because "he felt like it," he said. Between three-thirty and four-thirty that Friday afternoon he was at the bus stop in Essex. Yes, he was familiar with Maple Street Park, had been there a couple of times with his girlfriend. Yes, he used to have a pellet gun, but he had sold it a couple of days before that Friday "to a guy." He didn't remember the guy's name. No, he wasn't at the park on Friday around four o'clock, and he didn't know whether or not Jamie was.

"See," Louie explained voluntarily, "what I did was I went out for a walk 'cuz he said he was going to go over and try to borrow some money at the Lincoln Inn." It was the same story Jamie had told, with a crucial difference in sequence. Louie had failed to explain away two hours, but he spoke confidently, unhesitatingly.

"Talking to him I had the feeling he was your typical antisocial, smug, screw-you kid," recalled Horton. "He knew why he was there—I'm sure of that—but he didn't seem at all concerned. It wasn't the kind of behavior of an innocent person who, if you tried to tell them that they did this, would pass out and fall on the floor. Louie was the kind of kid who had probably been accused of crimes any number of times. Maybe not so serious, but he'd been through it before."

As Graham listened, he found it difficult to maintain his professional demeanor. "Emotionally, it was hard to interview Louie knowing the torture he and Jamie had committed on this young girl," he explained. "Sitting across from an animal like that. We have to have some justice, but it was very hard to sit there and listen, just look at him be as cold as he was, not showing anything. His voice didn't quiver, waver or anything. He sat there displaying no emotion, none whatsoever. The kid was like ice. He just sat there with his hands on his knees, staring down and saying, 'No I didn't do it.'"

But as Horton and Graham confronted Louie with contradictions in his story, the teenager became angry. "He began to rant and rave," Horton recollected, "saying 'What the hell you talking about,' that kind of thing."

"We have a problem," Horton tersely told Louie. "I'll tell you what the problem is. We've got people who say you were there, that you were in the park. They saw you there, they saw you play with the pellet gun, they saw you and Jamie together. In fact, Jamie says you were there with the pellet gun."

"I wasn't!" Louie growled.

"Jamie has even confessed," Horton continued. "He says you did it. He told us how you did it, when you did it. He told us how you sexually assaulted them, how he held the girl, how it was all you who did it."

As Horton spoke, Mary Hamlin began to squirm in her seat. Confused and shaken, she suddenly blurted, "Maybe we should talk to a lawyer or public defender."

Once she said that, it was all over. "Louie was squirming around in his seat," Horton recalled. "I think it was just another five minutes of conversation, we would have gotten him to admit to it." But now the two officers knew they could do nothing more until an attorney came, and they knew that no competent attorney would let his client talk.

"He needs to talk to someone—" Mrs. Hamlin reiterated, then collapsed in tears. Her sobs grew louder, and through her hands, cupped over her face, she half looked at her son and cried, "May God have mercy on your soul!"

Louie, leaning back in his chair, stone cold, spat out in a flat, even voice, "What the fuck did He ever do for me!"

With that Mary Hamlin shrieked and crumpled onto the floor. As Lieutenant Graham reached and helped her up, her wails echoed down the hall, bringing other investigators out of the offices where they had been working. Graham leaned the distraught mother against the wall, asking if she was all right. She sobbed that she had to talk to a priest, and as Graham released his grip, Mrs. Hamlin collapsed again.

CHAPTER 13

Getting Away with Murder

JAMIE SAVAGE'S CONFESSION was welcome news for Mark Keller. As soon as he received word of it, Keller arranged for a priest and a lawyer for Mary Hamlin, then picked up the telephone and dialed Kell & Mahoneys in Winooski. "I need all the beer you got," he told a startled bar manager.

It was three in the morning. After twenty-four hours without sleep, the chief law enforcement officer in the county was now conspiring to break at least three different laws: no take-out liquor sales from a bar; no liquor sales at all after two in the morning; no credit sales of liquor.

The nervous barman at first suspected a crude attempt at entrapment, but Keller laughed. When the state's attorney explained the reasons for the request, he had to pull the phone receiver away from his ear to avoid a deafening Yankee exclamation. "You got it!" the man on the other end shouted.

The investigators, elated that the manhunt was over, also

decided to have some fun with the media. Ruggiero dialed Mike Donoghue, the *Free Press* reporter who had queried him that night about rumors of an imminent arrest. Donoghue answered the phone. "Mike?" said Ruggiero. He didn't wait for a response. "Nick here. You were right." Ruggiero hung up. "He was there about thirty seconds later," Ruggiero recalled.

Susan Via, who had returned from the hospital to help with the legal work of processing the suspects, was just as exultant. She left the State Police barracks at five in the morning, exhausted, but pleased. "I went home and showered because I couldn't stand myself. Not having slept or bathed and being around a lot of cops who smoked like chimneys, I had to take a slow shower. Then I went back to the Essex Police Station where they were processing Savage and Hamlin, met Chief Terry, who had put on a clean uniform, and we went to the hospital to tell Meghan the good news—that we had arrested them."

The strain of the late-night session with the investigators and an increasing surge of pain had left Meghan sleepless. She looked drawn. But at her bedside, Terry gave the pale little girl the news and watched her face suddenly flush with emotion. Meghan burst into tears, the first time since the attack that she had permitted herself to cry.

The police at the Colchester barracks were ecstatic, filled with pride in their work. But at the same time, they were suffering the age-old frustration of cops. After being driven for a week by an obsession to "get the bastards" who had killed Melissa Walbridge, they were now denied the opportunity to see their primal instincts satisfied. The icy demeanor of Louie Hamlin only sharpened their anger. Lieutenant Lee Graham, who that night sat across from Louie and listened to his cold denials, had a strong desire to hack at the stone-faced suspect. "And for me," he would later explain, "it was less emotional than it was the guys who had been there to see the girl that day."

After the fruitless interrogation, police handcuffed Hamlin to bolts imbedded in the wall. The teenager sat calmly, a guard at the door, seemingly unconcerned with his situation. He dozed on and off, nestling his chin against his chest as if listening to a dull Sunday sermon. Throughout the early morning hours his expression did not change, and as the night wore on, his cool reserve became an affront to police officers who were wandering up and down the halls. At one point during this frustrating vigil, an officer walked into the troopers' room, pulled his pistol out of its holster, and loudly emptied the gun of bullets. "You better take this," he said, handing the weapon to a colleague. "I might be tempted to blow the son of a bitch's head off."

Meanwhile, as soon as the first light appeared, Jamie Savage had been whisked away to the woods. Police had brought him to the scene of the crime so that he could show them where the girls' clothes were buried. The leaves on the trees and underbrush were still wet with dew as four officers followed the youth down the path, retracing the line of attack he and Hamlin had followed five days before.

The task was one torn by conflicting emotions for the policemen involved. Leading them to the girls' belongings was another signature of confession by Savage, a step closer to sealing the case, for which they were grateful. But having to return to the woods, now haunted with gruesome memories, was oppressive. They burned with rage at the skinny youth, marching casually beside them, who had caused so much pain.

"It's over there," Savage announced, pointing across the small ravine to their right.

With Savage in the lead, Taylor, Burke, Larose, and Sgt. Leo slipped down the embankment. Their clothes now wet, the officers complained as they made their way haltingly to the swampy creek bed. "It ain't my fault, man," said Savage haughtily, responding to the policemen's frustration.

"Shut up!" one of the officers snapped.

Savage looked unconcerned, his pose of innocence an affront. They expected nervousness, shame, guilt, but Savage offered none.

Steve Burke, dressed in a suit, stepped into the mud as he crossed the tiny creek. The slime slid up his calf. "Goddamn it!" he muttered.

Jamie Savage smiled. "That's too bad," he chirped, as if enjoying their discomfort.

Burke's eyes revealed his feelings. He wanted to break the youth in half.

Taylor shoved Savage ahead, ordering him to hurry up. "The stuff is buried right there," Jamie said.

Sticking out from under a pile of leaves a few feet ahead, the officers could see the edge of a blue bag. Carefully, they pushed the leaves aside, revealing several mud-caked articles—the girls' clothes, a book bag, school books, a pair of shoes.

As the memories struck with a vengeance, the policemen growled their disgust at Savage. The youth shrugged, further angering them.

Taylor, afraid there might be trouble, quickly moved his charge away. "I had to get him outta there because he was getting on Detective Burke's nerves."

At 6:30 A.M. officers at the State Police barracks were getting ready to transfer Louie Hamlin to Essex, where he would be formally booked on a murder charge. The handcuffs were removed from the wall and locked on his wrists in front of him. Sergeant Ruggiero clamped his hand around the youth's elbow and led him down the narrow hall; the other men in the building stopped what they were doing and watched in silence. Hamlin too, his face taut, staring at the floor as he walked, said nothing.

Outside the barracks, a group of newsmen were waiting for Hamlin in the morning mist. For a moment, just as the husky youth appeared at the entrance, an uncharacteristic quiet fell over them. Rather than crowding around, pressing microphones and cameras to the subject as he walked expressionless through them, they only stood and looked. Finally, someone from the group spoke up, echoing the sentiments of the reporters. "You fucking bastard!"

As Vermonters drove to work that Thursday morning radios crackled with the news. On television, a special morning report announced the arrests. "A major breakthrough has been made in the Essex Junction stabbing today. Two youths have been arrested following a week-long probe into the stabbing of two twelve-year-old girls, one of whom died."

Relief spread rapidly throughout the state. Drivers hung out the windows of their cars and yelled to the cops as they drove through Five Corners in Essex. "Way to go!" Across the street, a large homemade banner was quickly attached to a telephone pole: I'M PROUD OF OUR POLICE. AREN'T YOU?

The tired cops walked through the rest of Thursday, writing their reports, conducting searches of Hamlin's and Savage's homes, interviewing more witnesses, swept along by success. As the afternoon wore on, rather than returning home to sleep, they began drifting over to Brian Searles's house in Essex Junction for the delayed celebration. The six cases of beer that Keller had purchased on credit in the middle of the night were opened.

"We were all kind of in a trance," Gary Taylor explained. "Nobody had been eating right. We had been drinking coffee until, God! I felt like a cup of coffee! We had lost track of time. From the minute that the murder occurred I couldn't have told you what day of the week it was. It wasn't until that morning and somebody said 'Five days,' and we all started counting on our fingers to figure out where we were. So when we finally went down to Brian Searles's house for the little get-together and the celebration of solving it, everybody was drunk on the first beer. I mean, I had been on for thirty-eight hours and it had been about twenty-one hours since I had eaten! And I think that was the rule rather than the exception. Everybody, everybody was drunk after beer number one. It was just a matter of degree after that."

Robbie Yandow left the Searles house late in the afternoon. As he glanced about, he saw grown men in uniforms sprawled about like big stuffed animals. "People were lying all around, on the furniture, in the corners, on the floor, sleeping. They'd just had too much. Not necessarily too much to drink. But just lack of sleep. And it was just time to lie down."

The entire state was first jubilant, then unnerved by the arrests. And along with the relief came more outrage as details of how brutally Melissa Walbridge was killed were revealed to the public. Keller told reporters that the killing was "sadistic" and involved "calculated actions to cause as much pain as possible."

Almost as shocking was the news that the suspects were native Vermonters, homegrown youngsters. In a state so compact that it is often referred to as a community, the killing had become almost a family affair. Just as the killing had brought together police from various communities without bickering, so the residents were unified in both their anger and their soul-searching.

In Vermont, a common reaction to murder was to make reference to "big-city" criminals, but the news that Louie Hamlin and Jamie Savage were born and raised in Burlington was an affront to the state's self-image. "It would have been a lot better for everybody if it had been some transient escaped rapist from Georgia," said local newspaper publisher Rosalyn Graham. "This puts more of a load of responsibility and guilt on the community, asking, 'Could we have done something to prevent this? How come we didn't keep this kid in a situation where this wouldn't have happened?'"

A Saturday morning *Free Press* editorial asked: "What kind of a person would so cruelly inflict so much pain on twelve-year-old girls? And why?" Psychiatrist Dr. Brij Seran of the Vermont State Mental Hospital in Waterbury said people who commit such crimes "take pleasure out of producing pain," adding that "when the opportunity arises, he takes what he wants." Dr. Seran, said the *Free Press,* "linked the increasing number of violent sex crimes by teenagers to broken homes, the media's preoccupation with sex and violence, and the proliferation of hard-core pornography, which, he said, is accessible to nine- and ten-year-olds right here in Vermont.'"

Neighbors, friends, and acquaintances of Hamlin and Savage were immediately sought out by the press. SUSPECTS CALLED BOTH QUIET, TEMPESTUOUS was the headline the day after the arrests. "To me he was a nice kid with just a bad temper," a North End neighbor told the *Free Press* about Louie Hamlin. "The other child, the only thing I know him as is trouble. My next-door neighbor, she was telling me that Savage was over in her yard one day just crumbling up the vinyl siding." Yet at the Lincoln Inn a pot washer said that Jamie Savage "was a good worker."

Students at Burlington High who were asked about Louie said he was a powerful arm wrestler, "as strong as an ox," "a drifter," "polite," "kind of all alone." Newspaper reports revealed that "Hamlin has a history of assaultive behavior toward family members and women" including, said one early report, "an alleged sexual assault on a younger girl a few weeks after his fifteenth birthday."

Editorial writers searched for answers, lessons to be learned from the trauma. "We are troubled . . . by the fact that the crimes may have been committed . . . by boys of ages fifteen and sixteen, for they are the victims of a society that failed to meet their needs," opined the *Free Press*. "No child is born to kill. And we must wonder whether each of us is not partly to blame for the crime. Certainly there were warnings. . . . Someone should have heeded their desperate cries for help, for their need for love was not met by those of us who could have provided help."

But the paper's theorizing did not sit well with all of its readers. John Pratt of Castleton fired off an angry response. "Baloney, baloney, baloney!" he wrote. "You sanctimoniously ask . . . 'Where have we as a society failed these young men?' We haven't failed them, we have failed the young ladies."

That Hamlin and Savage were natives, that they were so young and their victims even younger, was to embroil the state in one of the nastiest debates in its long democratic history. "If we weep for the victims and their families, we must weep for ourselves as well," editorialized a local weekly, the *Suburban List*. "There is no place in all of this to seek comfort. If the police are right about the suspects, they are our own. They are not a pair of randomly brutal transients, against whom we might protect our towns and our homes by increased vigilance. . . . Are there other youngsters out there like these two? . . . We have all got to ask ourselves whether there is anything in our own lives that can contribute to a sickness like this."

• • •

"Louie Hamlin is being held for lack of $100,000 bail and will face a sentence of life in prison," announced television newsman David Frankel. Hamlin's bail had been set unusually high to ensure that angry locals would not produce the release bond and lynch the young suspect.

Vermonters' sentiments were no secret. "As for where to put these scum," an Essex man had written the *Free Press,* "they belong in the most vile, uninhabitable place possible." The judicial system might vent the residents' outrage, but this crime had changed their definition of justice. Said another Vermonter after the arrests, "I think they oughta give 'em a fair trial—then hang 'em."

But there was even more disquieting news to come.

"James Savage is facing the same charges," commentator Frankel continued, "but his case will be handled by a juvenile court. If Savage is convicted, regardless of the severity of the sentence imposed, under Vermont juvenile law, he will be set free on his eighteenth birthday." As quickly as the relief at the arrests had swept the state, it disappeared; even the hope of legal retribution was dashed.

The legal import of Savage's age and his special status as a juvenile sent the state reeling with disbelief: One of Melissa Walbridge's killers would go free in less than three years no matter what the court decided. Could it be possible that one of the most vicious crimes in the state's history would go unpunished?

"I can remember feeling a sense of elation when we learned, 'Oh, we've got them,'" Susan Via recounted. "And then this sinking, sick feeling when I learned that one was fifteen." The deputy prosecutor, having worked in the office that handled the cases of juvenile delinquents, knew immediately the legal significance of Jamie Savage's age—that while Hamlin could face life in prison, Savage, just a few months younger, would automatically be set free at age eighteen, without a criminal record. But the public, sheltered from news about its juvenile justice system because of the state's strictly enforced gag rules on all juvenile proceedings, was not so prepared. However, in

the days following the arrest of the two teenagers the press
sadly educated its audience.

Each news account pointedly reminded the Vermont public
of Savage's privileged legal status as a juvenile. "Two teenaged
boys—one of whom cannot be convicted because of his age—
were accused Thursday of the 'sadistic' rape, torture, and stabbing death," began one early report. "Authorities said a fifteen-
year-old Essex youth also was arrested," said another. "His
name was not officially released under state law requiring persons under sixteen to be handled in juvenile court where proceedings are kept secret."

But no one in the press, and few of the police investigators,
had much sympathy for the nuances of a law meant to protect
the identity of the most hunted man in Vermont history. As
soon as reporters revealed that officials had refused to divulge
the name of the juvenile suspect, they invariably continued
"but he was identified by sources as James Savage, fifteen, of
5 Gaines Court, Essex."

The Rutland *Herald*, the state's second largest newspaper,
attempted to teach its readers the arcane juvenile law. "If Savage
remains in detention after a detention hearing, a hearing on the
merits of the case (the equivalent of a trial in adult court proceedings) must take place within fifteen days, a short period
of time to develop or defend a murder case," the *Herald* explained.

The paper then pointed out what would *not* happen after
that: "Under state law, youths under sixteen cannot be charged
with a crime. They can be ruled delinquent and put in the
custody of the Social and Rehabilitation Services Department
until their eighteenth birthday, when they must be released."

Death threats were soon phoned to the homes of Hamlin
and Savage, and even the court-appointed attorneys felt the
sting of a frustrated and outraged community. "Tell that goddamn fucking lawyer of yours that if he gets Savage out, that
dozens of us are ready to blow his head off!" one anonymous
caller told the secretary of Savage's attorney. "Make sure he's
aware that his fucking head will be blown off and that a lot of
us are ready to do it. Just give him that message."

Others were more polite, but equally outraged by the juvenile escape hatch. "An abomination to society," wrote a woman from New Hampshire to the Burlington *Free Press*. "Actions involving murder should not be dealt with as though the category was stealing candy from the candy store." Sean Moran, a native of Burlington, wrote from Los Angeles, "An eighteen-year-old in Winooski gets fifteen to twenty-five years in prison for robbery, but a fifteen-year-old has a chance to go scot-free for assault and murder involving a twelve-year-old girl? If we let this go, due to our own laziness or stupidity, then we are just as sick as those young men involved."

Vermonters found proof enough of Savage's adulthood in his crime. The law itself now became a "sickness," a declaration of "open season on Vermont females." "Crime has no age limits," an Essex Junction woman wrote. "Punishment for crime should know no age limit either. Our correctional departments have given up capital punishment to protect human life, but for the moment this choice gives anyone under the age of sixteen the legal right to take life. They don't even have to give a thought to hard punishment. A slap on the hand, three years' close supervision, and it's all right."

Another Essex resident offered "one last bone-chilling thought: with laws such as ours, what's to stop 'Big Crime' from outside states from hiring a fifteen-year-old youth to commit murder? The young man would surely know full well he'd be paid handsomely for his contract and be scot-free at the age of eighteen."

The criticisms were not limited to the circle of ordinary citizens. The state's attorney general, John Easton, called the law a "license to kill," and pledged to work for change. "The law in Vermont is such that a juvenile under sixteen is incapable of murder under the law, and that is terribly distressing to me," he told reporters. "Right now the juvenile who is treated in juvenile court and found delinquent is, literally, out of the system at age eighteen. At age eighteen the records are expunged, there is no record of the offense and the juvenile is walking around and nobody even knows he committed a crime."

As Louie Hamlin walked out onto the adult courtroom stage, Jamie Savage disappeared behind a legal curtain designed to protect "children." The courtroom doors were closed, his name deleted from all but the most top-secret official papers, and his identity disguised as that of "said juvenile." The names of his attorneys were not officially revealed, the name of his judge was secret, the charges against him unpublished. In this most celebrated of Vermont murder cases, for all the public officially knew, one of the two men who had murdered Melissa Walbridge was a phantom.

Even the sober editorial writers of the *Free Press* complained about the law. "The legislature must change the law that enables youths who have not reached age sixteen to be kept in custody only until their eighteenth birthday," they wrote. "To suggest that a person of fifteen should be less responsible for his actions than someone a year older is the thinking of an overly permissive society."

Suddenly, the focus of the state's attention had turned. What had been outrage over a senseless murder became livid frustration over the possibility that a killer would "go scot-free," that the law had made it not only possible, but definite, that Jamie Savage would get away with murder.

Lorraine Graham was in an "I-told-you-so" mood. For three years the fifty-six-year-old state representative from Burlington had been lobbying her colleagues in the legislature to pass a new juvenile law, but all her proposals had failed. "I could see that kids were committing more violent crimes at an earlier age," she recalled. "Not so much in Vermont, but I knew it would come."

When it came, Graham bitterly knew what might have been. At the end of 1979, the Democratic representative presented a bill to lower from sixteen to fourteen the age at which juveniles could be prosecuted in adult court for major crimes. The bill, H-301, passed in the House in a slightly amended form, then in the spring of 1980 died in a House-Senate conference committee for lack of one vote just as the legislature adjourned.

Graham returned for the 1981 session and began her crusade again. "I felt it was a very important bill and I reintroduced it," she recounted. Two juvenile murderers had already slipped under the age barrier. A fifteen-year-old killed his aunt in Pownal

in 1979 just as Mrs. Graham was proposing the new law. While
the 1981 legislature was in session, one of three youths charged
with the murder of an elderly North Danville couple turned
sixteen just a few months after the crime.

Graham worked feverishly for her new bill in the 1981
session. "I did everything I could," she recounted. "I wrote
every state's attorney, every police chief, every sheriff, judges,
the old attorney general and the new one, John Easton. Easton
endorsed it and I got endorsements from the majority of people
I wrote to. I went on television and radio and on panel discussions. Still, it wasn't even considered by the committee in
the '81 session." That session ended just two weeks before
Melissa Walbridge and Meghan O'Rourke were attacked.

When reporters came to Graham's door after the arrest of
Hamlin and Savage, the mother of Lieutenant Lee Graham and
six other children told them: "I am very disgusted and angry
with the chairman of the [Judiciary] committee. I asked every
member. They kept saying the chairman wants to study it. . . .
Well, I think it's been studied to death."

Representative Norris Hoyt, a Harvard Law graduate and
chairman of the Judiciary Committee, resented Mrs. Graham's
attack on him. "We are not going to be swept away on a tide
of emotion," he told reporters. But, like most of the other
lawmakers, he admitted that the Essex rape-murder would probably result in a change in the law. "The legislature must have
had reasons to treat young people this way," he continued,
referring to the current law. "Basically it's out of sympathy for
the young offender. . . . You get a case like this, and it makes
you wonder if maybe your sympathy wasn't misplaced."

The juvenile law had been passed in 1968 at the height of
a national outpouring of sympathy for young offenders. Until
that time anyone in Vermont who committed a crime that carried
a possible life sentence, no matter at what age, could be tried
as an adult. Hoyt was correct about the intentions of the 1968
law: It stated clearly that it sought to "remove from children
committing delinquent acts the taint of criminality."

James Jeffords, a co-sponsor of the 1968 bill, and now a
member of the U.S. House of Representatives, regretted the
age loophole that enabled Savage to kill without real account-

ability, but he explained the intent of the legislation: "The idea at the time was that you should treat the young differently, that young people make mistakes. What we wanted to do was avoid giving them criminal records so they could do better later on. It seemed as if the five years between sixteen and twenty-one were long enough for rehabilitation. But back then, you were talking mostly about crimes that would merit about that long a sentence, not things like rape-murders."

Unknowingly, the state legislature compounded the problem in 1971 by lowering the age of majority from twenty-one to eighteen. That meant the state would have only three years to rehabilitate fifteen-year-old juvenile criminals. At the time, no one paid attention to the effect the change had on the juvenile justice code. "Everyone was saying, 'If eighteen-year-olds can go and die, they should be allowed to vote and drink and get married and do all the rest,'" explained Emory Hebard, then a state representative. "Back then, nobody really thought about these things, young kids being involved in murders and all. We thought of them as children."

Few people now thought of Jamie Savage as a child. Lorraine Graham was receiving accolades from the public and getting as many as fifty calls a day from citizens expressing their disgust with Savage, Hamlin, and the law. "I got calls you wouldn't believe," the legislator said. "A lady from Waterbury, scared to death, says, 'My goodness, I have two grandchildren in Essex. What can I do?' And I can't describe how angry the men were. Tell me that the men at IBM weren't outraged. They were just sorry that they couldn't have gotten to Hamlin and Savage before the police. In all my seventeen years in the legislature I had never seen such a public outcry. All I could say was, call the governor and tell *him*."

CHAPTER 14

People vs. the Juvenile Law

GRAHAM WAS NOT the only one advising Vermonters to call the governor. The morning after the arrests, Vermont radio show host Jack Barry was on WJOY advocating an immediate change in the law. He suggested the unusual step of an emergency session of the legislature, urging his listeners to tell the governor.

Governor Richard Snelling's Montpelier "Hotline" was immediately jammed with calls, but Barry's idea was shunted aside by an aide who argued that a special session of the legislature was "not the answer at this point." Knowing that Jamie Savage and the Essex murder were the catalysts, the spokesman said simply, "If the legislature were to meet tomorrow, they couldn't make the law retroactive."

The idea of a special session was also quickly rejected by legislators. Norris Hoyt said a change in the juvenile law could surely wait until the next regular session. The Senate Appropriations Committee chairman, Robert Gannett, complained, "What's needed is a long-range solution and not a knee-jerk reaction." The lawmakers had only just finished their last marathon session on May 5th and few were anxious to rush back to Montpelier, especially at the $30,000-a-day cost to taxpayers for operating the 180-member legislative body. "Nobody in the legislature wanted it," recalled Lorraine Graham.

In Essex Junction two angry housewives—Hope Spencer and Carol Hathaway, both of whom had children in Melissa's and Meghan's class—saw the situation differently. Friday morning, sitting in Hathaway's kitchen drinking coffee and listening to Jack Barry, the two women turned the problem over in their minds. "We were very angry to think a boy capable of doing such a crime could be out on the streets in three years," recounted Hathaway. "We said to ourselves, 'What can the public do? Do we have any power at all?'"

Hathaway was thirty-three and had three young children. An attractive, athletic woman, she often wore jogging clothes as she bustled her brood around. She was born in Essex, went to school in Essex, married in Essex; her husband, too, was born in Essex. Hathaway's house was only a block away from where she grew up, a home in which her parents still lived. From her front yard she had watched the ambulances and police cruisers screeching to a halt at the Maple Products lot where Meghan was first placed after the attack. Ever since the crime her eleven-year-old daughter had been experiencing nightmares.

Hope Spencer, a soft, plain-spoken, small woman with short black hair, had a distinct mind of her own. Born in Quechee, Vermont, a tiny east-central village, Hope, her two children, and her husband, a native of the same town, had moved to Essex ten years before. The Spencers lived in a small house on a wooded lot less than a hundred yards from the spot where the girls were attacked. "My husband usually walks to work at IBM and he goes right by the path in the woods," Hope related. "And it was funny because that day he changed his mind at the last minute and took the car. If he hadn't taken the car, he would have been coming by there, walking home from work between four and quarter past that day."

In the week following the murder, Hathaway and Spencer experienced a fear they had never felt before. Now, after the arrests, it had become transformed to anger. "You wouldn't have believed what everybody was saying about those two," Spencer said. "What they wanted to do to them. I think if some of the fathers had gotten a hold of them, they would not have made it to court. The women just wanted to torture them. The men wanted to find them and shoot them."

That Friday in Hathaway's kitchen, their frustration over Savage's juvenile status precipitated a concrete plan. "I've never gotten myself involved in anything before," Hathaway said, "but when you're angry enough, you're forced to get involved. As parents, we were going to do everything possible to protect our kids."

The two mothers decided that writing a letter to a representative or registering their opinion on the Governor's Hotline would not be sufficient. "To think Savage could go right back out on the streets in two years was—it was just unbelievable," said Hope. And after a few moments, Carol brought out a dusty typewriter and the two began composing a letter of petition to the governor.

Dear Governor Snelling:

 We, the undersigned, as citizens of the State of Vermont, do hereby request an immediate Special Session of the Vermont Legislature to revise our current juvenile laws!

 We are appalled to think that in less than three years a young girl will again have to fear for her life because her assailant will be set free with no record whatsoever. Not only one girl will be fearing for her life when he is set free, but any one of our daughters or wives could be the next victim.

 We feel Vermont laws for juveniles are much too lenient and we will be watching to see what our elected politicians do on our behalf.

 We strongly urge immediate action before another incident occurs.

At first, the women had modest goals, intending to canvass only the neighborhood and village. They knew nothing about political organizing and did not understand that the most powerful politicians of the state, including the governor, would oppose their proposal. Nor did they have any idea how infrequently in Vermont history special sessions of the legislature had been held.

Lieutenant Brian Searles, who researched the subject for the State Police magazine, would later say that Hathaway and Spencer "set out to do what had seldom been done before, successfully, except in the case of natural and financial disasters." In more than 120 years there had been only twenty-two emergency legislative sessions. The first, in 1857, was called by Governor Ryland Fletcher because the Statehouse had burned down during the previous winter. In 1927 a special session was called to devise a way to help pay for the damages of severe floods that had devastated much of the state. Special sessions were called in 1861, 1898, 1916, and 1944 to vote on emergency wartime measures. To find a precedent for action on juveniles or criminal justice, one had to go back to 1875, when the lawmakers were called back into session because the Vermont Reform School for juveniles had burned down.

For the two politically naive mothers, their ignorance of political precedent was perhaps their most potent asset. Straight from the typewriter, and without consulting anyone (not even their husbands), Spencer and Hathaway took their letter to Richmond Office Equipment and had a hundred copies made. They made the rounds of the local stores, and, with a few petitions still left, drove to drop them off in neighboring towns. By that evening the two friends had distributed their letter to stores all over South Burlington and Essex before going home to make dinner for their families.

News travels rapidly in Vermont. Hope Spencer was home only a short time when a television reporter and camera crew from Channel 3 were at her door. That same night on the eleven o'clock news, she and Carol were on the air, and by eleven-thirty they had received the first of many calls. A woman from Burlington, a former neighbor of the Savages, wanted to help with the petition. More calls came in from people wanting to sign the petition and offering to help distribute it.

"From then on it was constant," recalled Hope. "A lady in Arlington, down in the middle of the Massachusetts and Vermont border, called me long distance. She wanted to do something down there. Then we had one from up on the Canadian border. It went from border to border. We never had to go out and ask people to do anything. I couldn't sit down to supper without my phone ringing. My husband was worried about getting crank calls, but I didn't get one."

When Hope walked into a store on Park Street in Essex on Saturday, the manager scolded her. "I need a petition," she said. "Forty people from IBM came in here yesterday on their way home wanting to sign it."

The reaction surprised Hope. "They stopped in to sign the petition even *before* it was on the news. They could only have heard about it from people that had stopped at another store where we had left it and who spread the word. I mean, we started at one in the afternoon and the people at IBM get out at four. That amazed me!"

Spurred on by the response, the two women expanded their expectations and, without organization or plan, applied themselves with the single-mindedness of crusaders. They enlisted family and friends. Carol and her family went to Windsor for the weekend and took copies of the petition with them, handing them out as they traveled. Hope's parents, who lived in Windsor, collected the petitions. Carol's sister passed them out and picked them up in the northern part of the state.

The women soon exhausted their first one hundred copies, and the next time they went to Richmond Office Equipment for more, the printing was done without charge. In the week that followed, Hope and Carol loaded their five children in the Hathaway's station wagon and drove the back roads of the county distributing their urgent call for a special session.

"We'd just get in the car and go," recounted Spencer. "We'd say, 'Well, let's go from here to Barre,' and we'd go. Not on the Interstate, but on the back roads and stopping at every store, leaving them and telling them we would pick them up in a week. That was it. We set a deadline for ourselves of about two weeks so we could get them to the governor as soon as possible. We went to as many as we could get around to, but we didn't get to half the places that we could have. It just was not organized."

But as the women trudged on and public support grew, Governor Snelling repeated his opposition to a special session. "Our Constitution rules out retroactive actions," he asserted. "A more proper thing to do would be to look very, very intensely at the problem and be ready to take action next January."

The two housewives from Essex Junction could not have chosen a more formidable adversary. The governor, a fifty-five-year-old businessman, had been a politician since 1961 when then-Governor F. Ray Keyser fired him from the Vermont Development Board. A self-made millionaire, Snelling had sold vacuum cleaners door to door as a college student, had sold used cars, new cars, and cable television parts. In 1959 he had borrowed $5,000 to start a company and soon built it into Shelburne Industries, a multistate hardware and sporting equipment manufacturing company which, among other things, sold more ski poles than any other company in the world.

His political career, with a one-term stay in the legislature in 1959 and the 1961 dispute with Keyser, had been a turbulent one. It included losing the race for lieutenant governor in 1964 and the race for governor in 1966 and 1972. Not a quitter, Snelling quickly retrenched after failing even to get his party's nomination in 1972, lowered his political sights, and won his second seat in the legislature that same year. He soon fought his way to House Republican leader and state finance chairman for the party. In 1976 he was willing to risk being a three-time loser by running once more for governor. By then, his political acumen sharpened, he won the race in a landslide, capturing winning margins in ten of the state's fourteen counties. In 1978 and 1980 Snelling was returned to power by large margins. Now, it was rumored, he had his eyes on a seat in the United States Senate.

The governor was vehemently opposed to a special session. As his spokesman said, "Let's not overreact to the problem. We can't make judgments of this magnitude based on emotions alone." Privately, some Snelling aides thought the call for a special session was more like the cry of a lynch mob.

Brushing aside the criticisms that their action was based on emotions, the two Essex mothers not only accepted the charge, they embraced it. "I'm sure it was," said Hathaway, "but it got done. You're not going to get any reaction unless something has happened to make people mad. I'm only sorry that the people didn't get mad when that elderly couple was killed by those kids in Danville. Because if they had forced it at that time, Savage would be in adult prison now."

In two short weeks, the women not only developed a sense for the political arena, but as they moved about the state, they formed a visceral opinion of politicians. "We learned a lot about politicians," Hathaway would later say. "And I'd never want to be one. They're all so wishy-washy. None of them really wanted the special session. The governor never believed in this."

But neither indifference from the legislature nor rejection from the governor stymied their petition drive. By the first of June, after just a week of frantic activity, Hathaway and Spencer estimated that they had almost 10,000 signatures. They had also mobilized others to action.

In Franklin County, Sally Hull of Richford, a small village on the Canadian border, was helping plan a pro-petition demonstration at the twenty-fifth annual Vermont Dairy Festival in Enosburg Falls on June 6th. Despite the decline of the state's once booming dairy industry, the festival was still a prominent Vermont celebration, one that Governor Snelling had agreed to attend.

Hull's husband, Carroll, principal of Richford High School (which had once received Jamie Savage's school records but had never had the young truant in attendance), had gathered some 2,000 signatures on the petition. With "concerned people" from the towns of Enosburg Falls and Richford, he was decorating a float and preparing a graphic skit for the festival. The float, whose theme was the need for a special session, would depict a courtroom scene and be scattered with the newspaper accounts of Melissa Walbridge's killing. The skit was designed to be even more lurid. Hull and his friends planned to display a bloodied body of a young girl with a mother hovering over it and an assailant standing nearby.

In the days preceding the Dairy Festival, as the petition drive gained momentum, Governor Snelling began to worry. He called a Washington, D.C., political consultant who had at one time given Gerald Ford campaign advice, and held intense discussions with aides to decide how to treat what appeared to be a major voter offensive. The consensus, according to one Snelling adviser, was that "If you do nothing, the public will hammer you."

The governor's first reaction was to avoid Hathaway and Spencer, who were regularly calling his office to arrange delivery of their petitions. Whenever they called, the secretary insisted that the governor was busy. How about next week? the women asked. Governor Snelling would be busy the next week as well, came the quick response. "What she was saying was that he was going to be busy from now on," Hathaway recalled with a smile. "So we asked if we could deliver them to an aide to the governor. 'No, all the aides are busy,' she said. Well, I didn't care. I would give them to the receptionist then."

Neither women knew that Snelling was already reacting to the public pressure and considering reversing his position. The next day, at his weekly press conference, he shocked the state by announcing that he might call the legislature into session. "We must stop waiting for tragedies before we identify with a need for action," he said. "Right now a very large number of people seem to be convinced we need to beef up our criminal justice system."

The governor deftly sidestepped the petition demand for juvenile law reform by presenting his own six-point package of crime measures, speaking as if he were the originator of the idea of a special session. At the Dairy Festival that Saturday, his change of heart forced organizers reluctantly to cancel their skit.

The Burlington *Free Press* candidly called Snelling's change a "sudden turnabout." The paper's capital correspondent, David

Karvelas, noted that "the move was uncharacteristic for Snelling, whose mathematical-like approach to problems leaves little room for emotion-laced decisions." But Karvelas pointed out how adroitly the governor had appropriated the issue as his own.

The following Tuesday Hope Spencer and Carol Hathaway called the governor's office to say that they would be in Montpelier the next morning with their petitions. The newly sophisticated public figures did not mention that they had already contacted the television stations, the wire services, and a number of newspapers. Nor did they mention that Eric Walbridge, father of the slain girl, would be coming along to deliver the petitions himself.

Early on the morning of June 10, just two and a half weeks after they had started their drive, Hope, Eric Walbridge, his brother Carl, and three other Essex residents met at Carol's home, piled the boxes of petitions into the back of the Hathaways' station wagon and headed toward the small capital city.

Outside the governor's office, a crowd of reporters watched as an aide to the governor appeared and sheepishly accepted the large boxes from Eric Walbridge. "These signatures reflect what the little guy wants from his government," Melissa's father said as he passed the box to the aide. "This is just a first installment," Carol Hathaway added. With the boxes was an unprecedented message to the governor: 27,350 signatures.

They had managed an incredible feat. In only two weeks they had forced the governor's hand. "Judith Stephany, a state representative, came up to me once and said what a good job we had done and how well organized it was and I just looked at her and I said, 'It was not organized at all!'" related Hope Spencer bluntly. "I don't know, but if we even had a couple more weeks we could have probably had ninety-five percent of the people in Vermont sign it. There was no question that people really wanted some action."

The state's politicians had gotten the message, one etched in passion by two politically inexperienced housewives. The governor was soon forced to admit that no one wanted the special session on juvenile crime diluted with a laundry list of anticrime measures. The people wanted a change in the juvenile law. Snelling grudgingly retreated. "I suppose I would take it," he said, "but not lying down."

Judicial committees from both the House and Senate soon voted that it would be a one-issue session: the problem of juvenile offenders.

For the next three weeks Vermont engaged in a debate that touched on almost every issue surrounding juvenile crime, from legal and constitutional intricacies to the moral and philosophical conundrum of defining who and what is a "child."

There were three different proposals for change of the juvenile code—Lorraine Graham's, the governor's, and the attorney general's, but they differed only in details. Each would lower the age at which a juvenile could be tried in adult court for certain serious crimes. These included arson causing death, aggravated assault, murder, manslaughter, assault and robbery, maiming, aggravated sexual assault, and kidnapping.

One proposal would lower the age from sixteen to fourteen; another would reduce the age to ten; and the third would have no age limit at all. Two of the bills would extend the state's authority to retain custody of delinquents beyond eighteen. Several lawmakers wanted that change made retroactive so that Jamie Savage could be held.

The vehicles for debate were public hearings of the Vermont House and Senate Judiciary committees. Though pressed by the deadline, the lawmakers, in the tradition of Vermont democracy, gave almost everyone a chance to speak, and asked their witnesses many questions. "Suppose a seven-year-old kills someone?" "What's the youngest juvenile that you had that had been charged with some sort of a serious crime?" "What injustices could happen on the juvenile court level that would not happen if you get rid of confidentiality?"

But for every large question asked, a dozen smaller ones followed. When does a person reach an age where he or she should be held accountable? Should the parents ever be held responsible? Is the best way to solve juvenile crime through the incentives of kindly social programs or the deterrent of stringent punishment? Should a juvenile be given a public criminal record? Should juvenile hearings be open to the public? There were disagreements on specifics, disagreements on philosophy, disagreements on approaches, disagreements on priorities.

Some witnesses urged moderation; a few even suggested that a special session was not the answer. When State Defender General Andrew Crane suggested as much, House Committee member Everett Clifford upbraided him for "trying to whitewash this whole thing back to the status quo."

But few witnesses sought to maintain the status quo. Even John Burchard, in charge of the Vermont Social and Rehabilitation Services Department, fulfilling the parental role of the state, admitted that something had to be done about violent juveniles. "I believe in the community-based program," he said of the system of foster and group homes that had taken the place of the state's juvenile detention center. "But I also know that we need a facility to hold over the few sociopathic kids who can't be reached any other way." Burchard said that of the 750 juvenile delinquents in state custody, thirty-one had been charged with major offenses like aggravated assault. But most of these potentially dangerous juveniles were either in nonsecure facilities or out on probation.

Implicit was the disturbing realization that at least two fundamental assumptions about the social order could no longer be taken for granted. It was clear that kids were no longer "just kids" and that parents did not always know how to be parents. The statistics were frightening. Vermont Attorney General John Easton pointed out that arrests had risen "254 percent since 1960 for those under fifteen for rape, murder, and aggravated assault." Perhaps most startling was the fact that young people were the major criminal offenders. Those under eighteen caused fifty percent of the crime in Vermont, said Easton. The consensus was that kids were somehow out of control.

But if they were, not everyone believed that throwing them in jail was the answer. "You and I know that changing the degree of punishment is not the real answer to the problem of crimes committed by young people," Dr. Paul Young, a pediatrician and chairman of the Council on Children and Families of Chittenden County, told the Vermont House Judiciary Com-

mittee. "I cannot say why any individual child or teenager kills
or commits a violent crime, but I do know that children who
are unwanted and unloved, who are not given caring, consistent
discipline, who do not learn right from wrong, who are abused,
neglected, or sexually exploited, are the potential murderers
and criminals of a few years hence, as well as the parents of
a future generation of lawbreakers."

Dr. Young, a soft-spoken Burlington physician, represented
the approach to juvenile crime that further infuriated those in
Vermont already outraged that Jamie Savage would be getting
away with murder. The advocates of the psychological and
sociological approach to juvenile crime saw themselves as the
voice of reason and viewed those who wanted a new "get-
tough" law as the proponents of irrationality.

It was in the rubble of broken homes and family incest that
those who sided with Young saw the causes of juvenile crime.
"We must have laws which allow, and indeed require, intervention at an early phase when parents are abusing, neglecting,
or not caring properly for their children so that this cycle can
be prevented," said Dr. Young.

But those clamoring for a change were screaming that such
a system was already scandalously lenient, that the emphasis
had been on kid-glove treatment of juveniles for too long.
Though they agreed there was some merit in the gentle medicine
prescribed by Dr. Young, these petitioners argued that it was
plain the present system was allowing Jamie Savage to get
away with murder. That, obviously, would not happen.

The Judiciary Committee found an articulate critic of the
juvenile law in Judge Alan Cook of the state district court.
Since 1972 Cook had seen the issue from every vantage point.
He had been an assistant attorney general in the Department
of Corrections and Mental Health, had spent one year as the
acting commissioner of mental health, and for four years had
been traversing the state as a district court judge handling both
juvenile and adult cases.

After agreeing that "there is no quick fix" to the problems,
Cook told the committee that confidentiality was one fault of
the juvenile system. By shrouding the process in secrecy, the
law effectively protected it from public accountability. "I think

the detriments outweigh any value in protecting the juvenile," Cook asserted. He reasoned that had the veil of secrecy been removed years before, the public might have reacted much sooner and been able to prevent the spectacle of a juvenile killer going free at eighteen years of age.

There was no "bottom line" for juveniles in Vermont, he also reminded the legislators. "As a practical matter, if a juvenile fails to cooperate in the process, there's very little that can be done." If a judge found the youth "delinquent," he had only three options: return the child to the custody of his parents; place him in the hands of the Social and Rehabilitative Services; or put him on probation.

While the hearings were in progress, David Karvelas of the *Free Press* took to the streets to ask the kids themselves what they thought of the lenient juvenile law. Tommy, a fourteen-year-old put in state custody for arson, told the reporter, "I knew I wouldn't go to jail." Asked if a law that made it possible to send kids ten and older to jail would make any difference, Tommy replied, "Yes. I wouldn't have done it if that law were passed. If the law was changed there wouldn't be so many crimes."

A fifteen-year-old found delinquent for breaking and entering agreed. "A lot of kids say, 'Do everything before you are sixteen and you won't get into that much trouble,'" he said. "They go out and steal a car because they know they're not goin' to jail."

On the evening of June 24th, the nine members of the House Judiciary Committee held a public meeting in Essex Junction. Fearing the worst, the committee took the unprecedented action of placing a security guard in the auditorium of the Essex high school.

There were no violent episodes from the crowd of three hundred packed into the hall, but there was no doubt as to where its sympathies lay. Carl Hathaway, the first speaker, told the committee about his mother-in-law, an invalid for seventeen years because of an attacker who also killed her daughter. "You live with someone like that in your household and you see that the murderer was allowed to go scot-free," the Essex man said.

"And the state did not so much as apologize.... What does it tell us? It tells us that the basic philosophy about the criminal code at that time, and right down to the present time, has been 'Let us be kind and nice to these murderers, but let's don't do a single thing on behalf of their victims or their potential victims.'"

The audience fell silent when Carl Walbridge, Melissa's uncle, rose to speak. He was brief, simply reminding the committee members that the number of signatures on the petition would soon be over 30,000. Melissa's parents had come to the meeting, but were silent throughout.

Their next-door neighbor, Patty Garvey, however, spoke her mind. She was shocked to hear that Defender General Andrew Crane had reported that although convicted murderers were often sentenced to life imprisonment, the average time they spent in prison was only eight to ten years. "Excuse me for losing my voice," the young mother said, "but I thought a life sentence was a life sentence. To suggest that people like Hamlin will be out in eight years is absurd. It is a gross miscarriage of justice in our system. We are the system, are we not?"

There was applause. Mrs. Garvey, who had lived in Essex since she was a year old, continued, asking whether lowering the age of criminal responsibility to fourteen, as Lorraine Graham's bill asked, was enough. "Next year we could be sitting here contemplating the murder of another child, committed by a twelve- or thirteen-year-old very masculine guy and what are we going to do with him? We will be here next year saying the same thing. He will be out."

There were no surprises in the comments of the local speakers. They were determined that juvenile crimes would no longer go unpunished, that they could still draw moral lines in the miasma of modern values. They were so angry that resident Michael Armstrong vowed that "my single vote and economic support of any party will solely rest on the response to crime in Vermont."

They accused the legislators, as did Joe Purvis, of not having "the guts" to correct the situation. "It surprises me not that we have a situation that prevails today wherein a fifteen-year-old juvenile—commonly referred to as a juvenile, sure—goes free at eighteen years old. Do you think it was a lowly layman that devised that law? Like hell it was!" Purvis exclaimed.

Wes McClellan of Essex was angry that state officials consistently complained they did not have the million and a half dollars needed to construct a juvenile detention facility, using that to excuse their failure to incarcerate dangerous youngsters. "Go from Richmond to Waterbury today," he suggested, "and they are paving the road, the Interstate, so that we can get from here to there faster. I was told that it costs a million dollars a mile. What I am hearing on the radio today is that it takes a million and a half dollars for the juvenile detention center so that my nine-year-old, and my four-year-old when he wants to get to school, can get there safely. It is a matter of values, I guess."

The citizens were sure of themselves, sure about what was right. "One thing the death penalty does very effectively," said Mike Armstrong, "is eliminate repetitive crime." "The purpose of punishment is to protect innocent people," said Madeline Nash, the mother of two daughters. "Punishment may not be a deterrent," said Dennis Spencer, Hope's husband, "but rehabilitation sure as heck is not a deterrent. If we are going to teach our children that crime does not pay, we better have some laws to back up that stand."

In his blunt fashion, State's Attorney Mark Keller also warned the legislators: "Basically you people don't have a choice. We know that, and everybody else in the audience knows that. If you do not pass the juvenile law, you won't be back in the legislature. It is as simple as that."

Keller argued strenuously for the inclusion of a "repeat felony" clause in the list of offenses to be treated in adult court, pointing out that some juvenile criminals repeat their crimes over and over, aware that they cannot be punished. "I know of one person who brags about committing a hundred and fifty B&E's [breaking and entering] before he turned sixteen. When he turned sixteen, we were waiting for him because we could not do anything to prevent him while he was fifteen. I would say there are at least ten kids in Chittenden County who fall in the same category that he did—juveniles who have done in excess of thirty, forty, fifty B&E's. We are just waiting until they turn sixteen."

Keller next addressed a particularly bitter subject: that under juvenile confidentiality, the victim would not know the identity and whereabouts of her attacker. "The victims should be able to know who did it to them," he told the crowd emphatically. "Right now, technically, if the fifteen-year-old is released from detention, we are legally prohibited from telling Meghan O'Rourke or her family about it because we are not allowed to give any information to her."

Keller paused, then announced dramatically, "We will not follow that. I have already planned to violate that law if he is released." Keller's vow to break the law and tell Meghan of Jamie Savage's whereabouts would later bring him censure from his colleagues and a reprimand from the state's highest court, but that night it was greeted with loud cheers from Essex residents.

Within two weeks of the Essex hearing, Governor Snelling issued a proclamation convening an emergency session of the legislature. On a hot Wednesday, July 15, 1981, the state's lawmakers returned to Montpelier. Many were not pleased, grumbling privately that the governor had yielded to public pressure. They complained that they were being rushed; they insisted that the juvenile bill could easily have waited until the next regular session. "They never said that too loudly, however," reported Karvelas of the *Free Press,* "because of the wide support for the session from the people back home."

Once called to order in the spacious, white-pilastered chambers of the capitol, the 180 lawmakers were all business. The Senate and the House quickly passed different measures, and sent the two bills to a conference committee. The only major differences between the bills were a controversial proposal to make the new law retroactive and a disagreement over the age at which a juvenile could be tried as an adult.

Narrowly, the Senate had passed a provision making it possible still to try Jamie Savage as an adult, but the House had rejected it on the grounds that it was probably unconstitutional, a violation of the *ex post facto* tradition. The House had passed a proposal eliminating age as a criterion for homicide, and one that allowed the state to prosecute minors ten years and older for other serious crimes. The Senate had set the minimum age for prosecution at twelve.

The differences were easily reconciled in conference committee, and a compromise bill was written and ready for a full legislative vote the next day.

The major provisions represented one of the harshest reactions to juvenile crime anywhere in the country: If a child between the ages of ten and sixteen commits a serious crime, he or she could be tried and sentenced as if he or she were an adult, including the possibility of a penalty of life imprisonment or death. Those serious crimes were arson causing death, assault and robbery with a dangerous weapon, assault and robbery causing bodily injury, aggravated assault, murder, manslaughter, kidnapping, maiming, sexual assault, aggravated sexual assault, burglary of sleeping apartments at night.

There would be no age criterion at all for the prosecution of murder. This was the guts of the new law, a complete departure from the previous code, in which no one below the age of sixteen could be tried for anything but delinquency. One controversial omission from the laundry list of "serious" crimes was the "double felony" provision offered by State's Attorney Keller.

Other provisions of the new bill included a prohibition against imprisoning a juvenile in an adult penal institution and a provision to tell the victim of a felony the identity of the juvenile criminal.

But the new proposal stopped far short of opening the juvenile court or juvenile criminal records to public scrutiny. Though the new law exempted serious crimes, children judged as delinquents would still be protected from "the taint of criminality." Their records would still be sealed and destroyed when they obtained the age of majority.

When H.1, as it was known, was presented to the legislators gathered around long curving banks of tables that Thursday afternoon, there was little debate. When the speaker called for a voice vote, the chamber filled with yeas. When he asked for nays, the hall was silent. And so "An Act Relating to Juvenile Crime" was unanimously passed into Vermont law.

Governor Snelling rose to address the lawmakers at the close of the emergency session. The stocky three-term governor had lost a battle with two Vermont housewives, but he now recognized what they represented. "In the finest tradition of this citizen legislature," he began, "you have answered the call of the people of Vermont. It is a sad truth that in many parts of the country the events which led to this special legislative session would not even have been front-page news," he continued. "But here in Vermont we have not been so hardened and so accustomed to crime, and we will never accept thoughtless violence as a necessary part of our lives."

It had taken public pressure, mobilized by two Essex women, to change the law that had allowed Jamie Savage to get away with murder. Unlike many other Americans, Vermonters had shown themselves still to have the capacity for public outrage.

CHAPTER 15

A Case of Incest

A FEW MINUTES before seven o'clock on the morning Jamie
Savage and Louie Hamlin were arrested, a procession of police
cruisers, both marked and unmarked, arrived in front of 211
Elmwood Avenue. Inside, Butch Hamlin was eating breakfast
with his fifteen-year-old daughter Lisa when he heard the insistent knock.

Pushing open the screen door, Butch Hamlin calmly greeted
State Trooper Steven Miller and took the proffered search warrant. Plainclothes police were stationed on the porch, the walkway, and in front of their cars. Hamlin expected the visit, ever
since his wife, with reddened eyes, had met him at the Koffee
Kup Bakery at six that morning and explained what had happened with Louie at the State Police barracks. The police, she
told him, were going to search their house sometime that morning.

In silence, the two had walked along deserted Riverside

Avenue, a hillside of well-tended homes on their left and the flat plane of the Intervale below them to the right, back toward the Old North End. It was their last hour together as private citizens, the last moment before their hard-bitten, routine life, with its secret seeds of violence, would be thrown open for public scrutiny.

At the corner of Spring Street and Elmwood, Mary turned toward the Wheeler School. Straining to hold on to the last touch of normalcy, she walked into the gray stone schoolhouse where Louie had been a sometimes bright-eyed, other times mischievous pupil, and where she still worked as a teacher's aide each morning. Before parting, Mary told her husband that they would have to be at the courthouse at nine. Butch frowned and walked solemnly up the block toward their house.

A half hour later, the police were at his door. Hamlin, still wearing the long-sleeved blue work shirt with the oval patch "Butch" on its chest, accepted the search warrant from Miller, glanced at it briefly, then gave it back. He was still furious with Mary for what he believed was her role in implicating Louie. He was convinced that his son was not a killer, and was angered by this violation of the privacy of his home. But the warrant, signed by Judge Costello, gave the police the authority to search for evidence: BBs, blue jeans, a green shirt, a plaid shirt, and a package or box for a BB or pellet gun. Hamlin, silent, stood aside, letting the cops enter.

One of the first inside was Corporal Gregory Mitchell of the South Burlington Police Department. Big Mitch, as his colleagues called him, was in charge of security. He immediately looked around the living room, at the wide-eyed children, then asked that Hamlin and his children stay in the room.

The police worked quickly and methodically, with Miller and Lieutenant Brian Searles of the South Burlington Police Department supervising the tagging of evidence as it was found. Patrolman Robert Bouffard and Sergeant Todd McCabe of Essex were to search Louie's bedroom. Corporal Michael Spernak of the Burlington PD was to photograph every piece of evidence seized. Patrolman Steven Belanus of Essex and Patrolman James Penniman and Sergeant Thomas Stech of Colchester were to search the rest of the house. Outside, Sergeant Edward Madonna and Corporal Larry Soutiere of Burlington waited in police cruisers in case of trouble.

Butch Hamlin directed Bouffard, McCabe, Searles, Miller, and Spernak to his son's bedroom near the kitchen and watched warily as Penniman and Belanus fanned out through the rest of the house with their notebooks, plastic and paper bags, staple guns, and evidence tags.

Louie's small room was cluttered with the paraphernalia of macho adolescence. Clothes were strewn about, posters were pasted on the wall. On the bed the sheets were crumpled and tied together. A large Marine Corps poster was taped on the wall, marked with scribbled writing that appeared to be a phone number and a gun registration number. Stech flashed a photo, then Bouffard and McCabe pulled down the poster and handed it to Miller who rolled it up, put it in one of his bags, and tagged it. Searles, standing in the doorway, noted the time— 0720—and the item as number H-2.

The search proceeded for another thirty minutes. Slowly a large pile of seized items mounted in the hall outside. On his hands and knees, McCabe found five small BBs under a paint-chipped desk and scooped them up, one by one. On the other side of the room Bouffard was in the same position retrieving two silver chains and a gold-colored chain with a cross. He grabbed a pair of denim pants from the tiny couch and another pair of jeans and two green shirts from a dresser drawer.

Searles kept writing as the other two officers picked up a pair of jockey shorts from the floor, a pack of BBs on the desk, an empty box of BBs, more BBs rolling around their feet, two stained and dirty sheets that had been thrown into a corner, a green knapsack on the couch. In the knapsack was a pot pie, a sheath knife, a jackknife, and a whetstone. In a shoebox was a Crossman BB gun warranty card.

In another box were old magazines, two of which caught the policemen's eyes. One, the February issue of *Official Detective*, had splashed across its cover a photograph of a man in dark glasses leering close to a young girl, her mouth twisted in fear, struggling to pull something from around her neck. On the cover of the second magazine, *Master Detective*, another young girl, this one scantily dressed, was cornered against a wall like a frightened deer, a pistol pointed at her head by an unseen figure. The cover story, headlined first in small letters, *Homicide probers grimly set out to solve the,* was followed by an inch-high legend, SEX-TORTURE OF A 5-YEAR-OLD GIRL! The magazines were tagged at 0750 hours.

While the five officers were combing through Louie's bedroom, Penniman and Belanus had wandered downstairs to the basement of the small house, where at the bottom of the stairs they found two large trash barrels against a wall, one overflowing with old papers and magazines. Belanus noticed that many of the papers were photo cutouts of nude women. As the officers rummaged through the barrels, they realized that most of the trash was pornography.

Summoning Mitchell from upstairs, Penniman and Belanus wondered whether the pornographic material might be germane to the case against Hamlin. Mitchell came down the stairs with Butch Hamlin, perused the girlie photos spilling from the trash barrels, then noticed a door nearby. He grabbed the knob to enter, but the door was locked.

"Would you mind unlocking that, Mr. Hamlin?" the policeman asked.

"No," Butch Hamlin responded. "That's my private room and no one's been in there for three months except me." Hamlin was losing the calm he had exhibited during the search. His tone became defensive.

"Sir, we have a court order to search this house," Mitchell said firmly. The police officer, who stood a full head taller than Hamlin, spoke calmly. "If you don't open the door, Mr. Hamlin, we'll have to break it down."

Muttering objections, Butch Hamlin unlocked the door, permitting the officers to peer into a completely dark room that had a harsh chemical smell. Flipping a light switch, they realized the reason for the total darkness. A photographic enlarger sat on a counter against the far wall. There were plastic trays lined up beside it, and a rudimentary sink against another wall. Floodlights were attached to a large wooden chair; nearby was a crudely fashioned homemade couch.

Dozens of photos, most of nude women, were scattered about the room, while others were stuffed into boxes lying on tables and in corners. Mitchell ran back upstairs and told Lieutenant Searles of the find. Although not specifically mentioned in the search warrant, Mitchell suggested that the pornographic material might be pertinent to Louie Hamlin's sexual assault.

Back in the basement, Mitchell and the other officers carefully dug through a large cardboard box that contained nude photos of women, magazine cutouts, and sex manuals. They found a curious combination: a J. C. Penney catalog and an illustrated *Femina Libido Sexualis*. There were notebooks with more nude photo cutouts and assorted girlie magazines.

Butch Hamlin, his secret now revealed, watched in angry silence as the policemen worked through his sex library. When Mitchell asked him to unlock a large wooden trunk resting on the floor, he scowled. "That's my private property," he protested. But again he relinquished the key when Mitchell informed him that he would simply force it open.

Inside the big box the police found several eight-track stereo units, one of which had serial numbers scraped away, rolls of camera film, boxes of negatives, magazine pages ripped from their bindings, a vise grip, an account book with photographs depicting various sexual acts, and hardcover three-ring binders and notebooks with more pornographic photographs.

Butch Hamlin's private life was no longer private. Three strangers, then a fourth and a fifth, were pawing at his secrets, at fantasies he had shared with no one. Or almost no one. Mitchell was opening the flaps of a cardboard box when his eyes focused on a manila folder with the name LISA HAMLIN printed on it. He opened the folder slowly. Inside were two 35mm negatives, too small to indicate anything but a long figure in a prone position. But two glossy 8 × 11 photographs nestled in the folder left little to the imagination: They showed a naked young girl in explicit sexual poses with an unclothed man whose face was turned from the camera. Mitchell recognized the girl in the photos as Butch Hamlin's fifteen-year-old daughter Lisa.

Mitchell closed the folder, placed it back in the trunk, and faced Butch Hamlin. The small man was standing in the doorway, his arms folded across his chest.

"Let's go upstairs, Mr. Hamlin," said Mitchell. The sympathy the cops had once reserved for the father of the suspect was eroding. That small bit of empathy that parents might have for one another, knowing how difficult it was to raise children, was destroyed by Butch Hamlin's dirty little secret. The police now saw a piece of the puzzle, an unmistakable link between the elder Hamlin's personal perversions, his acrid basement cluttered with pornography, and his son's raging act in the woods of Maple Street Park.

Upstairs, Mitchell advised Butch Hamlin of his rights and asked him if he wanted a lawyer. Hamlin seemed confident, and unlike the advice he had given his wife earlier that morning, decided he needed no attorney. Mitchell asked him about the locked room and the pictures, and Butch admitted taking the photos of his daughter.

"That's my photo studio down there and it's my daughter," Hamlin said belligerently. His proprietary instincts, old and misshapen as they were, buoyed his confidence. This was *his* home and *his* daughter. It was a private matter and had nothing to do with the charges against his son or the intrusive police. The police was trespassing.

But the police were not convinced. Officer Miller talked to Susan Via on the phone, explaining what they had found. Legally, it was risky, she said, but finally concluded there were sufficient grounds to take the material. The photographs might reflect on Louie Hamlin's state of mind and therefore be either incriminating or exculpatory. If not seized, they might open the prosecution to charges of misconduct by a defense attorney trying to plead insanity for his client. They might also be evidence of lascivious conduct by Butch Hamlin.

The officers shoved the cardboard boxes, the trash barrels, and the trunk either through a basement window or up the stairs, and carted off the photo enlarger, jars of chemicals, the chair with the lights, and old clothes.

Butch Hamlin waited impatiently upstairs with his daughters and small son, complaining to his silent, gawking children that the police were taking what they had no right to take. But, powerless to intervene, Hamlin could only watch from the front window as the officers carried boxes and bags across the muddy front lawn to the cruisers on the street. Several neighbors wandering along the sidewalks stopped, watched for a few moments, then walked on.

The police left Louie Hamlin's father to contemplate the complexities of the modern law of the land. And gradually, Butch Hamlin would come to realize that there were rules of accountability more complicated than he had ever suspected.

Like other Vermonters driving to work that Thursday morning, Chris Davis, his wife, and a friend heard the news of the arrests of Louie and Jamie on the radio. Unlike most people in the state, Davis and his wife immediately began weighing the odds that they might become involved. "You better not get that case," Mrs. Davis said to her husband. With a chuckle the young defense attorney answered that it would be most unlikely. "The public defender will probably handle it if they don't have attorneys themselves."

Davis stopped off at his sixth-floor office in the downtown Burlington mall to pick up some papers, then walked to the nearby district court building on Pearl Street for a routine court appearance on behalf of a juvenile client. The building was already filled with reporters, police, and court officials arranging the hastily called arraignment of the two murder suspects. "It was a madhouse," Davis recalled. "Everybody was running around going nuts."

The young attorney watched the scene with some bemusement, but he was not surprised. Since arriving in Burlington after graduating an upstate New York law school in 1975, he had never seen such community outrage over a crime. "It was the randomness of the killing and the innocence of the girls that was so shocking," he later explained. "I mean, this was not a family fight where somebody ends up killed. That's the type of murder you get in Vermont, you know, a fight between a bunch of people that have criminal records themselves. But here, the victims were young, nice little girls. They were such outstanding little girls in their own community." Davis thought of the murder case in which a man had stabbed a small baby while raping the baby-sitter, dripping blood all over her. "It was a horrible, horrible crime," recalled Davis. "There was an angry reaction to it, but nothing like Essex Junction."

As Davis talked to friends and colleagues during the week of the manhunt for the killers of Missy Walbridge, the question always came up: Could he defend someone who had committed a crime like that? It had always been the grand theoretical question among criminal lawyers. "Any time I ever talked to anybody who knew I was involved in criminal law, they asked me, 'What if you had to represent somebody that committed a brutal rape and then killed somebody? Would you represent that guy?'" Davis had always responded that he wasn't sure.

After the Essex killing, the question took on real dimensions. "There was talk within the legal community, many people saying 'I hope I don't get assigned to that case if the guys are ever caught,'" Davis recounted. "I'd be over at district court and run into somebody and we would be talking about it. Some lawyers told me, 'I wouldn't ever take it,' or 'No way in hell; they ought to kill the bastards.'"

Finally, that Thursday, Davis inadvertently met the question head-on. While in the courtroom preparing for a hearing, he was approached by a clerk who asked if he could take the case of one of the Essex defendants. Davis said, "Yes."

Within a few moments, the young attorney's life suddenly took a new turn. "I'd already heard that one of them was a juvenile," he remembered, "and I presumed she was talking about the juvenile case. So I said yes, because the juvenile case is normally a lot less work."

The thirty-year-old attorney, who had been a member of the bar for less than six years, had represented a number of young people in delinquency hearings, child neglect, and child abuse cases, and had handled more contested child custody cases than anyone else in Burlington. "I've seen it all. I have dealt repeatedly with families where the parents are the worst of all examples," he explained. "They are drunks, they are child beaters, they commit crimes themselves. And all the children are is a reflection of their parents. I have also seen situations in which decent low-income parents are trying their damnedest to deal with their children but just cannot because of the environment they live in. Other children are doing whatever they want and are going out and committing crimes at night or are into drugs, drinking alcohol, skipping school."

In a few minutes the clerk returned and told Davis that his new client was not a juvenile. It would be sixteen-year-old Louie Hamlin, who would be tried as an adult.

"I just happened to be in the wrong place at the right time," Davis recalled with a laugh. At the time he was not aware that the clerk's office had already tried to contact other attorneys to take the case. Not surprisingly, those attorneys were either not yet at their offices or, as some assumed, had decided to delay their arrivals as soon as they learned about the arrests on their radios. "There were a dozen other criminal lawyers in the county with more experience than me," says Davis. "I wasn't selected because I was supposedly a premier defense attorney. I was selected because I just happened to be there at the time."

So too was Gregory Packan, the executive director of the Advocacy Rights Council for Juveniles, who at that moment was on his way to meet Davis. He was grabbed by the county's public defender in the lobby. "Forget whatever you've got today," John Franco said hurriedly as Packan made his way to the clerk's office, "and get upstairs to Keller's office."

At that point Packan knew that two people had been arrested for the Essex murder, but nothing more. "My fondest prayer that week," he recalled, "was that they turned out to be a nineteen- and twenty-year-old so I would have been dealt right out of the picture. They wouldn't need a guardian." But the young attorney, who had long acted as a court-appointed guardian for juveniles, suspected the worst almost as soon as Franco collared him. The public defender quickly confirmed his suspicions. One of the suspects was only fifteen and was then sitting in the state's attorney's office without a lawyer.

"Just get up there and make sure he doesn't make any damaging statements," Franco told him. As Packan started toward the back stairway, Mark Keller was pushing his way through a throng of reporters and television cameras crowding around his third-floor offices.

A friend of Keller's, Paul Thabault, hailed the prosecutor over a barrage of questions coming at him from the media. "Kells, glad to see yah," Thabault shouted. "What's going on?" Thabault had left town the previous Friday, just after the rape and murder, and had returned only the previous evening. He was one of the few in Vermont who had not heard the news of the arrests. "I brought you a little Stroh's to cheer you up," he told Keller when he managed to sidle up next to him. It was Keller's favorite beer.

The prosecutor motioned his friend to follow him as he fended off the microphones. The two men finally made it through the vestibule door and pushed it closed behind them, closing off the noise from the crowded corridor.

"Ever seen a killer, Paul?" Keller asked abruptly.

Thabault didn't quite understand, but he followed his friend's gaze to the tiny corner waiting area just outside of Keller's private office. There a pimple-faced teenager sat on a small couch by himself, his long legs pressing his knees awkwardly high, his handcuffed wrists pushed hard between his thighs. He had the look of a frightened deer.

"Well, there's a killer sitting right there!" Keller almost shouted, walking quickly into his office. "The son of a bitch!" he muttered as he slammed the door. He then explained to Thabault that he didn't need any cheering up. "We got our killers."

Although Greg Packan, through the Advocacy Rights Council for Juveniles, had been involved with almost every juvenile delinquent in the county, he did not know what to expect when he arrived at the state's attorney's office to meet Jamie Savage. "Everyone was surprised that a crime that violent against children that young would occur. It was even more surprising that local kids did it," Packan would later explain. "I don't think that people were prepared to accept the fact that children born in Chittenden County, educated in Chittenden County, who were in contact with their parents on a daily basis for the last fifteen years, were capable of a crime like this. And I certainly shared that assumption prior to the arrest. I had never even had an armed robbery with somebody under the age of sixteen."

When Packan looked at Jamie Savage sitting desolately on the couch that morning, he saw a teenager who looked little different than most his office had tried to help. "He wasn't overly dirty and wasn't terribly clean, and, certainly, he wasn't well dressed," the attorney recalled. "He didn't show any emotions, but he seemed tired and confused by all the activity in the office at that moment."

Packan introduced himself to Savage and sat down. The young lawyer, long-haired and mustachioed, had been handicapped with cerebral palsy since his own youth. The condition slurred his speech and produced the ticks that affected his limbs. He asked Jamie if he knew whether a lawyer was coming and the youth said he thought so.

On the second floor, attorney Chris Davis was desperately trying to find out what little he could about his new client, Louie Hamlin. He had run up the wide stairs and pushed his way by reporters, knowing he had only fifteen minutes to prepare for the arraignment. In a side hallway next to the courtroom, Davis met a pair of burly sheriffs standing guard outside a double-locked door. Through the clear shatterproof glass windows that sealed off the small detention cell, Davis could see Hamlin, his hands manacled, sitting on the only piece of furniture in the room, a battered metal chair.

As he was escorted in by one of the sheriffs, Davis could see the scarred walls against which the chair had been thrown by violent detainees. But Louie Hamlin was calm. He wore the same clothes he had hurriedly thrown on in the middle of the night nine hours before. His light yellow cardigan hung loosely over a thin T-shirt. His sneakers were dirty. Except for the lack of a belt on his blue pants—removed by police—and the chains around his wrists, Louie Hamlin looked like a kid. He nodded slightly, without expression, as Davis quickly explained what would happen next.

Waiting outside the cell, Mary Hamlin fidgeted. As Chris Davis approached her, she started sobbing. The attorney tried to question her, but it was fruitless. "She was a wreck," said Davis. "Crying and crying. I really couldn't get anything coherent from her." Just as Butch Hamlin appeared, everyone present was summoned into the courtroom.

The hearing lasted little more than ten minutes. Judge David Jenkins assigned Davis as Hamlin's attorney and Butch Hamlin as his son's guardian. Mary Hamlin sat beside Louie at the defense table, struggling against fainting, as Mark Keller recited the long list of reasons to charge her son with murder and sexual assault. On the murder charge alone, conviction could mean life imprisonment. Davis immediately invoked the twenty-four hour rule that allowed Hamlin one day before entering his plea. Judge Jenkins imposed a $100,000 bail on the youth and ordered him to be detained in the Chittenden Community Correctional Center. Davis made no objection. "I didn't want him released anyway," the attorney later confided. Louie Hamlin was safer in prison.

The appointment of Butch Hamlin as his son's guardian was made casually. The irony of it quickly became clear to Mark Keller and his investigators as they sorted through the material seized from Butch's basement room. In the musty cartons and boxes from Hamlin's disorganized sex library were the photographs depicting a sordid part of his family's home life.

"There were notebooks with homemade pictures of him in various sexual positions by himself," Keller related, "and then all the pictures of his daughter Lisa. Butch took the pictures with remote control."

As the investigators began tracking the incest case, they pieced together part of the story behind the obscene pictures. Joseph Safford, Mary Hamlin's brother, who many years before had helped Butch set up his darkroom, told police about a visit he had made to his brother-in-law's house not long after they moved to Elmwood Avenue. "I was sitting down in the front room of his house and he was showing these little pictures to his wife," Safford later recounted. "So I said, 'Let me see.' And he showed them to me. They were pictures he took of himself in the nude."

Mary Hamlin harbored the same sickening suspicions about the sexual activities going on in her home, but kept them to herself. She closeted them in the back of her mind, continuing to teach her catechism classes at church. Her disgust with her husband's sexual perversions—those that she allowed herself to recognize—never reached beyond her once gaining the courage secretly to cancel Butch's subscriptions to his girlie magazines.

"My father raped me in the house we used to live in on Vermont Parkway," Louie Hamlin, accused killer, would later say. Mary Hamlin told Officer Miller that her son John had also reported being abused by his father. "Mrs. Hamlin indicated John advised this occurred when he was approximately seven," Miller noted in his report.

After the many years of denying what she suspected, Mary Hamlin was now helping police officers reconstruct a case against her husband for sexually assaulting their daughter Lisa. She told Miller that her younger daughter, Carol, had noticed something strange. "Carol told her that [her father] asked her to watch Mark Hamlin as he and [Lisa] went to an upstairs bedroom," Miller reported. "Mrs. Hamlin advised that Carol indicated she heard [her father] say, 'Take your pants down' and [Lisa] replying 'Off, no.' Mrs. Hamlin advised she felt this incident occurred in the month of May 1981."

On June 4th, less than two weeks after Louie Hamlin was arrested, police brought Mrs. Hamlin and Lisa to the state's attorney's office to conduct a formal inquest. Unsure of the extent of the incest, Keller ordered the other children brought to the courthouse for an emergency detention hearing. It was a precaution that Keller took to protect them from their father. With her mother waiting in another room with Carol and Mark, young Lisa was frightened and nervous as Mark Keller and Susan Via handed her the photographs to identify.

One by one the girl sorted through them, sobbing, pointing out her father and herself in sexual poses that dated back to the time when Lisa was four years old. Reluctantly, the girl described the sexual relations that her father had forced her to have, threatening to punish her severely if she told anyone. "He told me I would only have to do it until I was eighteen," she sobbed.

Keller left his office after the interview and was walking down the hall toward a deputy's office when an angry Butch Hamlin burst through the reception area doors. "What the hell are you doing with my kids?"

Keller turned and faced him, his own anger beginning to surface. "Mr. Hamlin, you're under arrest."

"For what?"

Receptionists, secretaries, attorneys, and police officers watched intently as Keller pressed his face to within inches of Hamlin's. The prosecutor stared directly into the man's eyes and shouted, "For screwing your daughter!" Butch Hamlin was suddenly quiet, the anger drained from his face. "Book him," said Keller, then walked away.

As he returned to his office, a woman came up behind him. "Are you Mark Keller?" she asked.

Keller recognized Mary Hamlin, even though he had never spoken to her. Staring now at the short, heavy woman, her eyes red from crying, he did not know what to expect. "I was waiting for her to put me through the wall or something," Keller said later. "We'd destroyed her family. First Louie. Then we had picked John up for parole violation. Now the father was being arrested and the other kids put, at least temporarily, into foster homes."

Instead of berating Keller, Mary Hamlin suddenly reached out and hugged him. "Thank you for helping my daughter," she cried.

CHAPTER 16

No Deal

THE ATTACKS ON Melissa Walbridge and Meghan O'Rourke
and the arrests of Louie Hamlin and Jamie Savage had quickly
drawn the state of Vermont into an imbroglio not soon resolved.

In late June, the Burlington *Free Press* dropped its mantle
of journalistic objectivity and filed a lawsuit demanding that
the doors to Savage's juvenile hearing be opened to the public.
Surprising those who expected him to offer only a token defense, Savage's attorney, Stephen Blodgett, objected strenuously and vowed to take the case to the state's highest court.

A week later, he filed a motion of his own, asking that Mark
Keller and his office be thrown off the case. Keller, he claimed,
had made prejudicial remarks at the public hearing in Essex.
At the same time Blodgett was receiving death threats for defending Savage, and Chris Davis was trying to convince his
wife to ignore the abusive anonymous calls coming to their
house.

The death threats, the angry letters to editors, the petition drive, and public hearings were proof that revenge was still a powerful human motivator, even in tranquil Vermont. But there was more at stake than a need to exact retribution from two teenagers. In the courts, at the legislature, in the press, on the street, in bars and living rooms all over the state, dozens of important issues hung in the balance.

Feminists marched in Essex to protest the continued violence against women. School officials huddled in Burlington to discuss what was wrong with the educational system. Community groups urged their members to begin talking openly about incest. Essex citizens began organizing neighborhood watch groups to patrol their streets. Legislative committees argued the merits of constructing a new juvenile jail, of giving the state greater powers to remove children from their homes, of allowing teachers to spank their students.

Everyone wanted to know how to protect their daughters, how the future could be safeguarded. As Hope Spencer and Carol Hathaway had stated in their petition to the governor, "Not only one girl will be fearing for her life when [Jamie Savage] is set free, but any one of our daughters or wives could be the next victim."

The rapes and killings touched a myriad of community nerves, all at once. Yet, however disparate and complex these issues were, the fulcrum upon which they seemed to balance was the legal proceedings against the two youths. Savage and Hamlin were symbols of a threat to a way of life; what happened to them would be the test of the state's resolve to protect itself.

On July 8th Vermont District Court Judge Alden Bryan gave the proponents of discipline their first legal victory by ordering the juvenile court doors unlocked. While it pleased the public, the decision was unprecedented. Nowhere in the nation were juvenile proceedings completely open. But Bryan reasoned that the charges against "said juvenile" were also unprecedented; he would not accept Blodgett's contention that a "delinquent" act was never a crime and therefore not subject to constitutional requirements for an open public trial.

"It would be difficult to convince any rational person that the delinquent acts alleged in this case were not crimes," Bryan wrote. "For the purpose of the First Amendment, this is a criminal proceeding which the press and public are entitled to attend."

The young Burlington attorney appealed the ruling, but two weeks later Judge Bryan handed Blodgett his second defeat, refusing to disqualify Keller from the case. Again, Blodgett appealed to the Vermont Supreme Court. Meanwhile, the proceedings against Savage ground to a halt.

In the middle of August the state's highest court took action. In a three-to-two vote, it supported Savage's lawyer and threw Keller's office off the case. So sensitive were the justices to the question of juvenile confidentiality that they refused even to mention the supposedly prejudicial remarks made by Keller.

Mark Keller was angry. "Their opinion stinks," he said. "Susan Via finished the argument in Montpelier and drove directly back to Burlington. Before she even got here, the decision was handed down. It was decided in twenty minutes. It is two pages long and has no legal cases to support it. It skirts all the facts by saying they weren't going to even mention what was said because they didn't want to hurt Savage's case any more. And that was it."

Keller was sorry he had been thrown off Savage's case, but he had no apologies for promising to divulge Savage's whereabouts. He would do it again, he said. "I told them that I was going to do it whether they liked it or not. Meghan O'Rourke had already talked to us and asked, 'Is he going to come back and kill me when he gets out?' With that question, and seeing the other little girl and knowing what Meghan had gone through herself, I'd be damned if I wasn't going to tell her when Savage got out."

Keller was later vindicated when the special session changed the law, but the state's attorney general's office now had to take over the prosecution of the Savage case. The question of whether the hearings would be public or private remained unresolved until December 1, 1981, when the Vermont Supreme Court issued a blistering, unanimous denunciation of Judge Bryan's decision to open Savage's juvenile hearings.

Appropriately, the opinion was titled "In re J. S." Not once did the justices mention Savage's name. They also felt compelled not to name Louie Hamlin, referring to him only as "the sixteen-year-old." The court rejected Judge Bryan's opinion that the charges against Savage were too serious to be considered "delinquent," and refused to make Savage an exception to the juvenile law.

"Juvenile proceedings are not criminal prosecutions," the court said, then quoted from a 1979 United States Supreme Court decision. "This insistence on confidentiality is born of a tender concern for the welfare of the child, to hide his youthful errors and 'bury them in the graveyard of the forgotten past.'"

It was like a red flag to an outraged public that had just finished waging a furious statewide campaign against the juvenile code. They knew all too well the purposes of the old law. It had been their goal to redraft it so that no longer could murder and rape be treated as "youthful errors."

Though disappointed, Keller's office viewed the decisions as the product of an absurd legal code. "We sort of figured that the Savage case would get bargained away anyway," Susan Via pointed out. "What was the use of going through the trials on it? Nothing was going to happen to Jamie Savage whether he was convicted of disorderly conduct or murder. So give him some deal and end it. Why screw around? Besides, we felt that Hamlin was the big fish. Not only because he was the one you could prosecute, but also because we felt that he was the murderer, in the traditional sense of the word—that he was the one who used the knife."

It would not be an easy assertion to prove. Defense attorney Chris Davis was not totally immersed in Hamlin's case. "Most people felt that my role was simply to play dead and let the state roll over me, let them get a quick and easy conviction," Davis later commented. This was far from his reaction, however.

Davis convinced the court to let him hire a research firm and a private investigator. By early September, the court had also permitted him to hire another attorney, Rusty Valsangiacomo, a young Barre attorney, as co-counsel. Davis and Valsangiacomo, both of whom eventually came to believe that

Louie was innocent of the murder, made a financial sacrifice
in order to represent Hamlin, working up to eighty hours a
week to make up for lost income.

"It was a joke," Davis said. "The state paid fifteen dollars
an hour plus expenses. And I have to charge twenty-five an
hour just to run my office. I was working on Hamlin an average
of twenty hours a week for fourteen months. Some weeks I
worked only on Hamlin. But you figure it out."

Oblivious to the public mood, the two defense attorneys
took advantage of every possible legal maneuver. Considering
the insanity defense, they asked the court to pay for an independent psychiatrist. They then filed motions asking that the
case be moved to the juvenile court, that the venue be changed
to another part of the state, that evidence obtained in the Hamlin
house search on May 21st be suppressed, that the statement
Louis Hamlin made to police be held inadmissible in court.

"If the person walks out of the court having committed a
heinous crime and goes scot-free, you feel sick about it inside,"
Davis would later say. "But that personal feeling cannot affect
my role as an attorney. My obligation is to the client. I do not,
when defending a client, have a duty to society other than the
duty not to allow a fraud on the court and basic ethical con-
siderations like that."

On a personal level, Davis also began to feel a responsibility
to Hamlin. "I had a good rapport with him," he said. "I liked
Louie. As I got to know him, I found that he was an intelligent
person who had a number of good qualities."

Davis's concern for Hamlin was more than many people
could understand. "I would have turned in my license before
I defended Louie Hamlin," said Susan Via. "I wouldn't be able
to live with myself. I don't know what kind of machinations
you'd have to go through to do such a thing. You can't ask
somebody who went to the scene and dealt with what I and
other attorneys dealt with to defend someone like that. You'd
be asking them to be schizophrenic."

Via had herself once been in Davis's position. As a young
radical bent on fighting what she saw as a discriminatory system, she had become a public defender in Colorado directly
out of law school. But the experience quickly soured her. On

her first case, she realized that not all criminal justice turned on racial prejudice. "I spent the majority of the summer," she recalled, "helping some four-time rapist get off. I swore that I would never again use my skills, my intelligence, gifts, whatever, so that somebody like that could prey on people again.

"This was a black guy who raped little black girls and it was suddenly clear to me that this wasn't a racial issue. He told me and the investigator that he couldn't wait to get out and find 'another fine little fox.' And his idea of a fine little fox was an eleven-year-old. My research helped get this guy off on what is commonly called a technicality, and I swore that I would never do it again. I might not do anything to make people's lives better, but I certainly was not going to affirmatively make them worse. Here I was helping this disgusting pervert to get out when he ought to be taken out and have his brains blown out."

Angered by the viciousness of the Essex attack, Susan Via was now determined to use her legal talents to convict the killer of Melissa Walbridge.

On January 7, 1982, Jamie Savage was ushered into the Chittenden County Courthouse through a basement parking lot wearing handcuffs and surrounded by attorneys and guards. To protect his identity as a juvenile, he was given a ski mask to wear over his face. Though no one would talk for the record, it was known that Savage's case was over. He had been adjudicated a "delinquent" and was to be sent, it was reported, to a Pennsylvania psychiatric institution for evaluation. Before he could leave, however, he had to testify at his partner's trial. And Louie Hamlin's defense attorneys would have the right to question him.

In the courthouse that morning, Jamie saw Louie for the first time since his arrest. The former friends barely looked at one another. Word had leaked out from the St. Albans Correctional Facility that Hamlin had threatened to kill Jamie if he got hold of him. County sheriffs guarded both youths as they sat at opposite ends of the room.

Rusty Valsangiacomo, sitting across from Savage at the long polished table, began the questioning. Within minutes, he had established that Jamie Savage was lying. To a routine query about how far he had gotten in school, Savage said he had completed the ninth grade; school records showed he had dropped out after only two months of high school. Asked if he had ever been in trouble with the police, he answered "No." A few moments later he admitted stealing money from his mother and stepfather and food and money from the Lincoln Inn on a number of occasions, but he denied taking the rolls of nickels and dimes from the Inn on May 15th, the day of the murder.

"Do you know what the word perjury means?" asked Valsangiacomo. Mark Keller had explained to Savage a number of times what a deposition meant: that he was under oath, that he could be prosecuted for perjury if he lied.

"I can't remember," Savage responded.

For the next two days, Rusty Valsangiacomo and Jamie Savage contested in this manner. Savage changed his statements almost as quickly as he uttered them. When the three long court depositions were complete, the headline in the Burlington newspaper exclaimed SAVAGE NOW ADMITS KILLING. Suddenly, unexpectedly, Savage had altered his story and claimed to be the one who thrust the knife into Melissa's heart.

Louie Hamlin now had a reasonable chance of avoiding a first-degree murder charge, and Savage could not be prosecuted. But as dramatic as was Savage's new admission, it was so clouded by misstatements and contradictions that, except for Hamlin's counsel, close observers felt no nearer to the truth.

"We knew that parts of his confession were true," Via explained. "And we knew that parts of it were lies. Like in his statement to police, where he said he never had oral sex. And it took about eighty-five pages of deposition to get that out of him. Whether he admitted it because he finally understood or whether he was just tired of being badgered, I don't know. We figured that he had some hangup about oral sex. I mean, as crazy as it is, he admitted to stabbing and choking but he couldn't admit to that."

Many in Burlington believed that Savage had decided to confess to the killing only when he realized that it would not affect him as a juvenile offender. "He might have been thinking, 'No matter what I say, they can't do anything to me,'" said

Robbie Yandow. "'At eighteen, I am going to boogie outta here, but Louie is going to do some time depending on the outcome of the trial.' He could very well have changed his story in the hope that they would not be able to prove a first degree murder case against Louie."

The more police and lawyers talked to Jamie Savage, the less they were sure that his "lies" were intended as such. "This guy lies like most people breathe," Susan Via concluded. "I firmly believe in my heart that this man-child cannot tell the difference between truth and lying. You ask him, 'Jamie, what color are your shoes?' And he looks down and he knows they are blue and he says 'Green.' And you say, 'Jamie, but they look blue to me.' And you press him a bit and he says, 'Well, they are blue.' 'Why did you lie?' 'I don't know.' There is no value attached to telling the truth. I think if you sat down with him in a room for three days, and grilled him, you would still not know what the truth was."

After the depositions were finished, at the urging of Chris Davis, Jamie Savage was given a polygraph test. The results suggested that his claim to have killed Melissa was true. Hamlin's defense attorneys were elated, and for a few days Davis believed it would be a major break in the case against Louie.

"The day they polygraphed Savage, Mark called me up and he was very upset," reported the defense attorney. "I honestly think he knew that at that time Savage was telling the truth. And he said, 'We gotta do something here. I have a duty as a prosecutor not to obtain a conviction but to ascertain the truth.' He said that to me. And he said, 'Maybe we could work something out.'"

The hopeful defense attorney suggested informally to Keller that they could send Savage to jail and quell the public outcry that he was getting away "scot-free." Since Savage was now sixteen, his conflicting statements under oath could be the basis of a perjury charge. Davis offered to let Hamlin testify at a perjury trial if Keller reduced the murder charges against their client. To Hamlin's attorneys, it looked like a perfect solution, a way to place both teenagers behind bars, at least for a few years.

"Then," Davis recalled, "a few days later when I talked to Mark again, he said, 'No deals. Nothing. Louie did it.'" I said, 'Why the change?' but he wouldn't tell me. I suspect that he talked to Susan and Susan said, 'No way.' I believe that had this case been handled solely by Mark there never would have been a trial. Savage would have been convicted of perjury and Hamlin would have entered into a plea agreement."

Susan Via laughed at the charge that she influenced Keller not to take a plea. "I can't figure out those guys. They must think I'm some kind of Svengali or something. I sit around and do mind control. They give me credit for a lot more power than I ever thought that I had. I mean, Mark talked about their offer with the people at the office. And everybody thought it was crazy."

Keller, who was taken aback by the polygraph tests, admitted having second thoughts about the case after he got the results. "I said to myself, 'Wait a second, I'm going to stop and rethink the whole thing.'" He then talked with Via and Simpson. "They were saying everybody is going to be real upset and I said, 'Well, I have a job to do. I'm not going to worry about what people are saying. I just can't screw the guy because everybody expects us to. So we'll worry about the press after we make the decision.'"

Keller decided to enter into a full review of the case. He sat down with his own attorneys and those from the state attorney general's office, but by the end of the week he had come back to his original conclusion: Hamlin was responsible for Melissa's death. Though the polygraph had touched off some rethinking, Keller finally dismissed the test results as inconsequential. He was not going to negotiate a plea bargain based on them.

David theorized that Keller and Via could not back down because they had made too many public statements regarding Hamlin. "They shouldn't have been talking to the press constantly," the defense attorney maintained. "They made representations to the public that Louie was the killer. And they got so far out on a limb that they had to keep going."

David remained convinced that the prosecution, especially

Mark Keller, had simply refused to follow its own instincts. "They're going to deny it until they're blue in the face," Davis later said, "but I believe that deep down Keller's going to have doubts the rest of his life. Ask them how many people pass the polygraph. Ask them how often they use it and how often they ignore the polygraph."

"That polygraph exam isn't worth beans," Keller retorted. "The whole thing with the polygraph is that you're supposed to get nervous when you lie and that sets the machine off. It doesn't work with pathological liars. And Jamie lies all the time. Savage himself didn't know if he was lying."

The prosecutors were developing a fallback strategy that would show that even if Hamlin did not make the fatal stab wound, he was equally responsible for Melissa's death. According to the law of Vermont, as in most states, an accomplice to murder is subject to the same sentence as the actual murderer. "Meghan told us that Hamlin was in charge," Via explained. "Based on everything I had been told by Meghan, based on the psychiatrists who interviewed them and everything we knew about their lives, Louie was the leader, Jamie was a little puppy dog following Louie. Who cares who actually did the stabbing? It had to be one of the two. It doesn't matter, under the law, which one did it. They are accomplices."

By now Davis and Valsangiacomo were confident that it had been Jamie Savage, not Hamlin, who actually killed Melissa. "I'm convinced that this is what truly occurred," Davis insisted. "It all makes sense. According to Savage, what happened is that Melissa started to fight. And that is Meghan's memory as well. Melissa ran and that's when Jamie lost it. He shot her in the back and dragged her back and just went into a rage because she wouldn't obey. And so he started cutting her up. It certainly was his knife. And because he was ignorant and couldn't figure out how to kill her, he kept doing things like shooting her with the BB gun and things that you'd see on television. It wasn't torture as much as it was just an ignorant person in a rage not knowing how to kill somebody."

Davis did not deny that Hamlin made the remark about the pig slaughter. "That was to scare them," he would claim. "And that threat was made during the course of the rape, before they got to the place where Melissa was killed."

Jamie's confession had made the insanity and diminished-capacity defenses for Hamlin less vital, Davis thought. In addition, Dr. William Woodruff, the state's most respected forensic psychiatrist, had virtually destroyed the case for an insanity plea. "The court should realize," Woodruff stated in his court-requested report, "that this is probably one of the most harrowing and disgusting cases that I have ever had to deal with. It has been necessary for me to listen to confessions by two young men about a particularly heinous, sadistic, and degrading sexual assault and murder." Woodruff concluded his thirteen-page analysis of Hamlin by stating that an insanity plea could not be supported by the psychiatric evidence.

Defense attorney Davis immediately consulted an independent child psychiatrist, Australian-born Barry Nurcombe, a University of Vermont clinician. But a month later, after Nurcombe had interviewed Hamlin, some of his friends, and family members, the psychiatrist reported equally discouraging news for the defense. "There is no evidence that he was suffering from a mental disorder of such a nature, or degree, that he was unable to understand what he was doing, or that what he was doing was wrong," Nurcombe concluded. "I do not think that his behavior was the result of irresistible impulse. The offense was premeditated, planned, and took place in an emotional atmosphere of anger, the need for vengeance, and a fear of being found out."

On the last day of April 1982, Davis and Valsangiacomo sent Mark Keller a letter formally asking for a deal in return for reduced charges. "We offered accessory-after-the-fact, which only carries seven years; but we were willing to have it run consecutively with the assault charge," Davis said. "And we also asked them to come back with a counterproposal."

"That letter was made into a paper airplane and flown around the room," Keller remembered with a laugh. "I'm sure they probably believed what they were saying. But it really didn't make a damn bit of difference. Both guys were guilty. The defense's whole routine was that Savage is going to walk away

in two years and we were killing Hamlin. They wanted a plea
to aggravated sexual assault and accessory after the fact. The
sexual assault carries a maximum of twenty-five and the accessory a maximum of seven years. And with minimums it
could have been something like ten to twelve years. I wasn't
going to buy anything at that price."

Via was in the office when Keller received the crucial letter.
"Mark never for even two seconds considered that," she recalled. "He laughed out loud. He called up Davis and said,
'What, are you crazy? I want to live in Chittenden County. I
want to live in Vermont, Davis. If I took a plea to accessory
after the fact, they would burn my house down.' He was kid-
ding; that wasn't the reason, but he was trying to tell him that
it was so preposterous. I mean, this was the tightest first-degree
murder case, rape, torture, death, a baby—Jesus! If he took a
plea of accessory after the fact, he *should* be lynched. And that
was his feeling too."

Up until the last moment Keller weighed the possibility of
still prosecuting Savage for perjury, but he was forced to balance it against Savage's value as a prosecution witness at Hamlin's trial. If he wanted Savage to testify he would have to
grant him immunity on the perjury charge. The price seemed
too high to pay. Besides, as Susan Via argued, who would
believe Savage anyway?

Keller required little convincing about Savage's credibility,
but he knew that without him, the only eyewitness was Meghan
O'Rourke. "I didn't know whether or not I could get him for
perjury, but I really wanted to get him. And so I said to myself,
'Forget it. I can't give him immunity.' And I put all my money
on Meghan O'Rourke."

CHAPTER 17

Meghan's Test

IT WAS UNCLEAR whether Jamie Savage's confession that he did the actual stabbing would benefit Louie Hamlin's defense. But it *was* clear that the sudden turnabout had made twelve-year-old Meghan O'Rourke the fulcrum of the case. The outcome of Louie Hamlin's murder trial would rest on her testimony.

Meghan had left the hospital on May 24, 1981, only nine days after the brutal attack, proof of her resilience. On July 4th, she had recovered enough to return to Maple Street Park for a celebration honoring the police officers who had participated in the manhunt. Seated only a few hundred yards from the spot where she and Melissa had been attacked, Meghan applauded with other Essex citizens as the governor presented citations to thirty-eight men and women from throughout the state.

Hamlin's trial had finally been scheduled for May of 1982,

but no one was sure that Meghan would be able to meet the demands made upon her. Although healing, Meghan still had some difficult emotional obstacles to overcome. During the first days after the attack, she worried constantly about what the Walbridges would say; she had survived and their daughter was dead. Compounding this guilt was Meghan's fear that the men who attacked her would threaten her again. "Will I have to see them sometime?" she asked Via plaintively.

"I explained the court process to her," Via related. "I told her what the deposition was, and that Hamlin would be there. But no one would be able to hurt her. She would be guarded by police. I also explained that she might have to go to a police station and see a whole group of men and maybe pick them out."

Meghan was actually confronting a larger emotional ordeal. Not only would she have to see her attackers again, she would have to repeat, perhaps over and over, in public, what they had done to her.

Meghan's first encounter came less than two weeks after she left the hospital, when she was required to attend a deposition conducted by Jamie's defense attorney. In a conference room at the Burlington courthouse, she sat ill at ease among unfamiliar adults. Solicitous of the girl, Savage's attorney, Stephen Blodgett, queried Meghan about her photo identification of the teenagers at the hospital. He wanted to see if she had been influenced in any way by Via or the police. But despite her shyness, Meghan displayed amazing self-assurance. When shown the photographs again she told Blodgett she had no doubt about the identification.

"And do you think you would recognize him again in court or on the street if you saw him?" Blodgett asked.

"Yes," Meghan responded confidently.

Blodgett asked Meghan if at any time during the assault the blond-haired man [Jamie] showed that he was afraid of the dark-haired man [Louis]. Meghan stuttered in her tiny, throaty voice, "Well, sort of—he sort of seemed to be—sort of going under him."

"When you say 'going under,' what do you mean?"

Meghan struggled to find the right words. "Well, he sort of

seemed like—well, maybe he wasn't really afraid of him but he seemed sort of like—like the dark-haired guy was sort of more the boss."

The defense attorney asked Meghan what gave her that impression. "Well, he was more aggressive, the dark-haired man," she answered with candid innocence. "He was more mean; like, he would, you know, he would hurt us more."

But that was as open as Meghan could be. As Blodgett queried her about the rape, she could manage only soft yeses and nos, and frightened nods of her head. Finally, Via, who was determined to shield Meghan, objected that the line of questioning had gone too far. "I'm going to ask for a recess," the state's attorney interrupted. "I think we've gone over what she remembers about the specific sexual activity—what she saw happen to her and Melissa, who did what. If you have a new question, fine." Blodgett retreated, asked Meghan one more question, and ended the deposition.

Because Savage was a juvenile, Meghan had been spared the ferocious cross-examination of a determined defense attorney. But more was at stake for Louie Hamlin, who, if convicted of first-degree murder, faced the possibility of a life behind bars. However guilty the public believed Hamlin to be, his attorneys were planning to fight for at least a lighter sentence.

"Our job is to ask the questions from the other side of the coin," said Chris Davis. "No matter how heinous the crime, in our system there are gradations of guilt, and even if there is some culpability, I would have no reservations at all about fighting as hard as possible."

If it was Hamlin's fate to face life in prison, and Davis's role to prevent that sentence, it was Meghan O'Rourke's unfortunate role to stand in the center of this battle for justice.

On a Saturday morning in mid-November, James and Stephanie O'Rourke drove their daughter to the State Police barracks in Colchester for a crucial test.

With little hope for a successful insanity plea, Davis and Valsangiacomo had to meet the prosecution head-on. Davis's first move was to ask for a live lineup session in which Meghan would have to identify her attacker in the flesh. Since Davis was allowed to make the selections of the lineup subjects, the advantage was his. Seven months after an attack, any witness, especially a young child, might be confused looking at several men who resembled one another. But if Meghan could not identify Hamlin in the live lineup, a conviction would be difficult, perhaps impossible.

A little after nine-thirty, Sergeant Horton and two sheriffs escorted five young men into a viewing room. He gave them numbered placards and instructed them to stand against a metal bookcase with their feet on a faded white line painted on the floor. All of them, including Hamlin—who was now clean-shaven—looked like typical teenagers.

Standing on the far left, Hamlin held a large white card marked 5. Next to him, out of numerical order with card number 3, was a youthful-looking twenty-two-year-old with a mustache. The other three men were all nineteen, all born in the month of January 1962. Louie, who had just turned seventeen, was the youngest, but looked somewhat older than his years, though the age differences among the five were not apparent.

All the subjects were within an inch of each other in height. All had dark hair, all weighed within ten or twenty pounds of the others, all had slightly pudgy, adolescent faces. They stared blankly at an opaque one-way window, unable to see the people gathering behind it. For this vital confrontation, Meghan was accompanied by her parents, Mark Keller, and Susan Via. Chris Davis joined the group behind the one-way mirror.

With a telephone in hand, Jay Fish relayed instructions to Horton in the lineup room to begin with number 4 on the right. Fish had already explained to Meghan that the man who assaulted her might or might not be in the lineup. He had also stressed that the hair on his face and head might be different from that at the time of the attack.

Subject number 4 stepped forward into the middle of the room, looked right, then left, then straight ahead. Meghan showed no expression as he, followed by numbers 1, 2, and 3, moved forward, then back. When Fish called out number 5, the burly, dark-haired man on the left paced ahead and stopped just a few feet away from the glass. For the first time

Meghan reacted. Fish immediately noticed the change. "Ms. O'Rourke, for lack of a better term," he later recounted, "swallowed hard and her facial expression changed and tears built up in her eyes."

But, as she was instructed, Meghan said nothing until Hamlin stepped back into line. Fish asked her if she recognized any of the subjects.

"Yes," she answered quickly.

"What is his number?" asked the police officer.

"Number 5," said Meghan.

"Are you sure?"

"Yes."

Meghan's next test came just a few days later, on November 20th, when she had to face Hamlin's defense attorneys for what promised to be a grueling interrogation. Davis and Valsangiacomo had the right to question all witnesses that the prosecution planned to call at the trial.

The morning session began at 8:45 in a courthouse conference room in Burlington and quickly developed into a clash between Via and Valsangiacomo over the defense attorney's tactics. In this small room, surrounded by adults—police officers, defense attorneys, the court reporter—Meghan would have to describe the awful sexual and physical events of May 15th. She would, for the first time, have to personally confront Louie Hamlin, who, guarded by two sheriffs, was placed at the opposite end of the room. Sitting with her mother and Susan Via, Meghan kept her eyes averted from him.

Davis had already decided that his colleague would question Meghan. As the session began, Valsangiacomo rose, walked toward Meghan, and stood before her. He asked perfunctory questions: her name, date of birth, the school she attended. Even in the small room Meghan's voice could barely be heard. As Valsangiacomo paced back and forth towering over the little girl, Via interrupted.

"Rusty, is there any reason why you can't sit?"

"I think I'd feel uncomfortable sitting in the middle of the room," he replied.

"Well, there's plenty of tables," said Via.

"I prefer to do it this way." Valsangiacomo was determined to stand.

Via was perturbed. "I'm going to object," she said coolly. "I think it's intimidating to have it done this way, a few feet from someone. It's a deposition. And it's not a courtroom. And it's not a cross-examination. And I'll be perfectly happy to let you rearrange the tables and take the time. But this is the only deposition which either you or Mr. Davis has conducted standing. And you have conducted over twenty-five depositions in this case. And I think it's inappropriate to select this one to do differently."

"Well, that's—"

Via continued, "I'm going to ask that it be stopped and we'll go to a judge unless you take some time—"

"I suggest you go to a judge then."

As quickly as the questioning of Meghan began, it ended. Via was livid, convinced that Valsangiacomo's tactics were purposefully intimidating. "He gave me some bullshit—and that is exactly what it was—about trying to make her feel more comfortable. I knew that that child was being intimidated and wanted him to sit down. I asked Meghan about it afterward and that was the case. I just was not going to allow him to badger her that way. Don't get me wrong. I think she should be tested as to her recollection. But there is a way to do that without causing her unnecessary pain."

Chris Davis was equally angry, rejecting the validity of Via's charge. "That was a bunch of hogwash. He wasn't *standing over her*. That's typical Susan, putting on a show. He was standing about six to ten feet away from her. He was just trying to be really pleasant to her and accommodating. That was just one of Susan's tactics to show the family that the state was going to protect Meghan."

The youthful-looking defense attorney raised his voice in exasperation as he recalled that clash. "We walked out of there and right in front of Mrs. O'Rourke and Meghan, Susan had the audacity to say to Rusty and me that it was our fault for the mental damage that Meghan was going to be suffering. She

knew that she had the power to work out a plea argument and
to get this matter resolved and get Savage convicted and Louie
convicted.

"The most miserable aspect of this case was putting Meghan
through the whole thing, but it was our job. Via knew that.
We let Meghan speak to her mother and tried in every way to
make it as pleasant an experience as possible. We even agreed
to have Louie hidden off to the side. Susan had no right to say
that in front of Meghan and Mrs. O'Rourke. We were outraged.
That's one of my most bitter memories of the case."

Meghan had become a fragile crucible of legal morality in
the contest between prosecution and defense. Was it possible
to hold her in the iron vise of the adversary system without
emotional injury?

Because of the bitter argument, the deposition was moved
from Burlington to Woodstock, Vermont, some one hundred
miles to the south, where Judge Thomas Hayes waited in his
chambers in case he was needed to referee. The deposition was
continued the next morning at ten-thirty and lasted past four-
thirty in the afternoon, with only two short breaks. Meghan
sat with her mother at a table just in front of the bench. This
time Valsangiacomo interrogated Meghan while seated, but it
was still a stormy session. As he plied Meghan with complicated questions, Susan Via interjected frequently.

Attempting to straddle the difficult line between tough defense attorney and solicitous father, Valsangiacomo often tired
and angered Meghan and, sometimes, only confused her. At
one point, trying to determine if Via had rehearsed the witness,
he asked: "Now, what I'm trying to ask you—to see if you
can remember in your mind whether or not you had a discussion
with Susan Via when you went through what had happened to
you before you started giving Susan a statement that was going
to be recorded and typed. Do you understand what I said to
you?"

"No," said Meghan tersely.

Other times Valsangiacomo tried, unsuccessfully, to be pa-
ternal. He asked Meghan if she was embarrassed by talking

about having to take her clothes off. Meghan said she was.

"I'm embarrassed too," said Valsangiacomo. "Does that make you feel better?"

Meghan only shook her head.

"No? I didn't think so." Valsangiacomo knew he was mired in a no-win situation: trying to fight for his client and simultaneously not offend his client's accuser. It was obvious that the Vermont community would not countenance any verbal abuse of the child.

"All right," he continued, seeking to convince Meghan of his decent intentions. "Does it make you feel any better to know that I've got a little girl also, and I kind of understand what you're going through?"

"What do you mean?" Meghan responded uncomprehendingly.

There was no easy way out. Susan Via listened with increasing consternation. "There was a lot of talk at the beginning about wanting to be nice and 'If you need a break we'll take one,'" Via recalled. "It was extremely patronizing and Meghan knew it. She may have been small and tiny and weak, but she is a smart little cookie. And she certainly knew that this guy was being condescending."

Throughout the session Louie Hamlin sat at a table in the well of the courtroom looking bored. Occasionally he stared at Meghan or watched Via or Keller. A few times he appeared to doze. Meghan, except when asked to identify him, never looked at Hamlin.

The tension in the spacious, empty room rose when Valsangiacomo started to question Meghan about the rape. Meghan fidgeted, her voice dropped, she hesitated, she demurred, she didn't remember. When Valsangiacomo asked what Jamie Savage had said to her after she had taken her clothes off, Meghan became flustered. "Don't know how to put it," Meghan said softly. "I don't know how to put it. I don't know."

"Just say it," Susan Via prompted. "Close your eyes if it helps."

Meghan continued to sit silently.

"You can't be nice about it," said Mark Keller. "You just have to say it."

"I don't know," Meghan repeated.

Finally, after Mrs. O'Rourke and Via went over to console the child, Meghan answered the question in a barely audible voice. "He said, 'Suck me.'" Meghan then bravely described the sexual abuse forced on her by both teenagers.

"Next thing I remember is I was down on the ground and I'm tied up with gags," Meghan said, then described what she remembered up to the point that she passed out. When she regained consciousness, the gag was out of her mouth, and Meghan saw blood all around her.

"I thought I was at home watching TV but then I realized that I wasn't," Meghan told the attorneys. "And I got up from the foam mattress."

Meghan related how, while only semiconscious, she looked around for Melissa, but could not see her. Bleeding profusely from the knife wound in her chest, she pushed her way through the brush and back onto the path where they had first been attacked. "I didn't run. I staggered," Meghan recounted. "I fell over and then I got back up again. I walked to the railroad tracks and I saw somebody there. I yelled to him, but he didn't hear me. Then I yelled again and he heard me."

When asked about the murder weapon, the knife, Meghan remembered seeing it but could not tell exactly when. Valsangiacomo implied that perhaps she didn't really see it, but Meghan protested vociferously: "I know I saw it. I know I saw it." As the attorney mildly prodded her about the things she could not remember, Meghan became annoyed.

She paused, then told the defense attorney what she did remember. She recalled seeing the dark-haired man with the knife, but could not say where he stuck it. She remembered that Hamlin had stepped on Missy's back as she lay on the ground, then had raised his pistol and shot her. The recollection was clear, but it was different from the account of the crime she had given in the hospital. At that time, Meghan had said that it was the blond-haired man who had "stomped" on Missy.

Valsangiacomo pointed out the discrepancy, but Meghan, who had now regained some of her assurance, said she had been wrong in the hospital. She reminded the attorney that she had later changed that statement, for the record, when Via and

Robin Hollwedel came to her house prior to Hamlin's arraignment. Valsangiacomo probed Meghan about why she changed her story, trying to shake her memory of the event. But Meghan was sure; suddenly she was finding a bigger voice.

"Do you have a hard time remembering whether or not you were remembering what happened or what somebody told you or what you've read?" The defense attorney was pushing the witness, again implying that she might have been rehearsed.

"What do you mean?" Meghan responded.

"Well," said Valsangiacomo, "would you agree with me that you appear to have been having a hard time remembering what happened, right?"

"Okay," said Meghan. "Yes."

"And is it possible that through listening to other people, that some of the things you're telling us are from what they've said and not necessarily from what you remember?"

But Meghan would not let herself be intimidated.

"No," she said quietly but firmly.

"It's not?"

"No."

During Meghan's testimony Keller walked around the large room, occasionally sitting in the empty jury box, evaluating the projection of her small voice. "I can't hear you," he called out to Meghan. "This is where the jury's going to sit."

Late in the day-long proceedings, Susan Via rose and walked over to a bench at the side of the room and lay down. "I have a weak back and those chairs were wooden and very uncomfortable," she later explained. "I just couldn't take it anymore. I mean, there was no end to the questioning."

Via was angry at what Meghan had to endure. "I think it was unnecessary," she remarked. "It served no purpose except to harass and intimidate a child who is about as pure and guiltless as a person can be. It was obvious that the child was incapable of lying and was not lying about anything. If we would have done that to a defendant, they would have cried coercion. Just because he has a legal right to do it doesn't mean he has a moral right."

The deposition yielded mixed results for both the prosecution and the defense. Meghan had been a good witness against

Hamlin, but Valsangiacomo and Davis believed that they had discovered gaps in her story. Meghan "has had a tremendous lapse of memory," Davis told reporters.

Keller and Via knew that Meghan had held up well in the closed pretrial hearings, but they were still worried. Could she tell the full story of her rape in a courtroom filled with strangers? She had been courageous during her long deposition, but at important moments, she had frozen. She couldn't get the words out. Even with Keller, who by now was a friend, Meghan could not talk openly about the attack.

One Sunday in April 1982, two weeks before the trial, Keller and Via went to the O'Rourke home in Essex and subjected Meghan to as intensive an interrogation as she would have on the witness stand. But the young woman stubbornly refused to talk about the assault, frustrating the two prosecutors. Finally, groping for an idea that would break Meghan's resistance, Keller and Via decided on shock treatment—they would all go to the park and walk through the attack. Her parents looked to their daughter for her reaction, and Meghan, surprisingly, registered no objection. Ever since that day, she had walked home from school on the street, always accompanied by friends. Meghan had never returned to the woods.

With her parents and the two prosecutors, Meghan went to Maple Street Park and walked down the same path that she and Missy had taken on May 15th. The experience proved to be more traumatic than Via or Keller anticipated. As they retraced the steps that had led to her friend's death, the girl turned inward, growing quieter. The attorneys and her parents all tried to coax Meghan, but they were unsuccessful. "She just withdrew like I had never seen her do before," recalled Via. "Just refused to answer anything."

Leaving the woods but still in the park, Via and Keller asked Meghan to sit at a picnic table and pretend that she was on the witness stand. The two fired questions at her, but Meghan still refused to talk. "Missy's dead!" Via shouted. "She can't do it for you! She can't convict Hamlin! You have to do it for her!" But Meghan only glared back in silence, then placed her head disconsolately down in her hands.

"It was all very unpleasant," Via recalled. "Especially for Mark and me. I felt rotten and so did Mark. Frustration was part of it. I just felt like a ghoul doing something like that."

At the O'Rourke home, the exhausted child lay down on the couch as Via and Keller exhorted her to try again, but Meghan continued her silence. Meghan had yet to tell her parents the details of the attack, and she refused to talk as long as they were in the room. When they left, Via coaxed her to tell what Jamie Savage had made her do. "Get Mark out of here," Meghan insisted. It was as if she wanted to tell her, but could not in front of a man.

"How about if Mark stays and you just cover yourself up?" Via suggested.

Meghan agreed. She dragged the blanket off the back of the couch and completely covered herself with it. Keller and Via moved up to within inches of the child so they could hear. Slowly, tentatively, Meghan began to speak of that horrid day, but even hiding under the blanket in her own living room, only two weeks away from the trial, she could not repeat the details of the sexual assault. "She just couldn't get the words out," Via related. The attorneys gave up and left.

That night Meghan's older sister, Jennifer, went to Meghan's room to massage her back. She pleaded with her to try to talk about the attack. But again, Meghan refused. What she had been able to say in those first days now seemed shut away behind a wall of confusion and shame.

But a half hour after Jennifer left Meghan, the young girl knocked on her sister's door. "Okay, here's what happened," Meghan said. And slowly, with Jennifer's patient help, Meghan reconstructed her story in full. "I had to help her learn to use words that thirteen-year-olds just don't say or think about," Jennifer recalled.

CHAPTER 18

Hamlin's Trial

THE 126-YEAR-OLD COURTHOUSE, surrounded by massive broadleaf maples and lush expanses of lawn, was an anachronism. The staircase leading to the second-floor courtroom groaned as the fifty Windsor County residents climbed it slowly. Wide wooden doors swung open to a large, light room lined with old spindle-back benches and wicker chairs that made quiet, comforting sounds as the potential jurors took their seats on this Monday morning in May. Through the tall arched windows the midmorning spring sun rolled into the room. It was a place for civilized jousting over property lines and water rights, an occasional ruckus spilling from a Saturday night bar, or a boutique burglary. It hardly seemed a likely stage for a reenactment of a murder and rape.

The ancient courthouse was at the center of the sleepy village of Woodstock, hidden in the Green Mountains, 260 miles from New York City, protected from all but the most civilized intrusions of the twentieth century. Tourists touted Woodstock as "a Currier & Ives gem of a town," with numerous church steeples, four Paul Revere bells, covered bridges, and 3200 residents, at least fifty of them millionaires.

The village turned up regularly in the travel section of the *New York Times* or the *Philadelphia Inquirer* or even the *Los Angeles Times,* always with such headlines as WOODSTOCK: STILL A WISTFUL DREAM. It was not to be confused with the Woodstock, New York, of rock music fame. Rather, it was so quiet and pretty that, according to the National Historic Trust, it is "one of the five most architecturally beautiful villages in the United States."

Because Laurence Rockefeller was reputed to own ten percent of Woodstock and was fond of restoration, it was sometimes referred to as The Town That Rocky Rebuilt. The millionaire imported a covered bridge from New Hampshire to span a little river on Union Street and tore down the eighty-year-old Woodstock Inn in the village center to build a new three-million-dollar, 120-room inn designed to look more colonial and more opulent than the mansions tucked away on the town's small side streets.

"Woodstock," said the *New York Times*, "with its covered bridges, graceful Georgian mansions and elliptical village green, emerges out of the backwoods like a stage set: a fusion of 18th-century elegance and naiveté gently spiked with contemporary sophistication."

The trial venue had been moved to this quaint village in order to free it, as much as possible, from the local anger directed at the defendant.

"Ladies and gentlemen of the jury panel," Judge Thomas Hayes intoned from the high seat in the front of the courtroom, "I welcome you to membership in the organization of this court. You are now a part of our judicial process." Hayes was a large, dark-haired man with a reputation for fairness, legal acumen, and good humor.

As if preparing the prospective jurors for the task of judging an unpopular defendant, Hayes recounted the story of William Henry Seward's defense of a black man in 1846. "A horrible crime had been committed without any provocation," Judge

Hayes told the prospective jurors. "Freeman was an emancipated slave, deaf, and obviously insane," Hayes recounted. "The sheriff had the greatest difficulty in preventing him from being lynched. Clergymen railed from the pulpit against anyone who would defend this man. In the crowded courthouse, when the judge asked, 'Will anyone defend this man?' Seward rose and said he would be counsel for the accused.

"Seward's friends told him of the unpopularity of the cause and of the adverse effect that his advocacy might have on a promising political career," Hayes continued. "But Seward let his sense of duty prevail over the cries of the mob and the protest of friends, and he gave the black man Freeman the full measure of his strength and advocacy. He told the jury that the most degraded human being in a civilized state is entitled to a fair hearing."

Hayes had chosen a relevant tale, for in few Vermont trials had the public been so ready to suspend the presumption of innocence. Most, in fact, truly believed there were few humans more degraded than sixteen-year-old accused murderer Louie Hamlin. No one anticipated lynch mobs swarming across the Woodstock green, but security was tighter at the courthouse that day than it had ever been. Sheriffs were posted at the door to search every handbag and briefcase.

Jane Norman, the veteran Windsor court clerk, worked nights to prepare for the press, the spectators, and the prospective jurors. "I never had anything so difficult to handle," said the spunky, gray-haired clerk. "Back in the late twenties there was the John Winter case, a rape-murder, and I guess that attracted a lot of attention. Clarence Darrow even came to Vermont to help on the appeal, though he lost. But in my time here I had never seen any case get as much attention as the Hamlin one. And I hope I never have something like it again."

Norman's prime headache was to find a pool of potential jurors from which twelve impartial ones could be selected. The clerk mounted a monumental search. In that mountainous and forested mid-state county, there were twenty-four towns, 50,000 residents, and almost 26,000 people on the voting rolls. From the latter Norman had amassed a master jury list of about 2,000 people, from whom she would normally call in two or three dozen for jury duty. But for the Hamlin trial, Norman was taking no chances. She drew a lot of 350 names and sent a questionnaire to each. From the responses she selected 150 names, asking that they pack a suitcase and report for jury duty. Their appearances were staggered: fifty on Monday, fifty on Tuesday, and fifty on Wednesday.

Even though the trial location had been shifted, Susan Via estimated that it could take as long as ten days to find twelve people impartial enough to judge the case. On Monday morning, the first fifty, along with reporters and a few spectators, arranged themselves on the old benches of the second-floor courtroom. Despite Judge Hayes's admonition that the republic demanded a fair trial for the most despicable of men, everyone's worst expectations began to unfold. After Jane Norman announced the designation of the case: "State of Vermont versus Louis Hamlin III," Judge Hayes asked, "If there is anyone who has not—repeat, not—read or heard anything about this case, if there is anyone who has no knowledge from any source concerning the case before us, would you please stand."

Only six of the fifty in the room stood.

Judge Hayes then asked who had "deep-seated feelings about the crime and the defendant charged."

Thirteen of the fifty potential jurors rose.

After the inauspicious beginning, the potential jurors were summoned, one by one, into the judge's chambers to be questioned further by both the prosecution and defense. Few of these ordinary Vermont citizens had ever been selected for jury duty. "The Vermont character is live and let live," Jane Norman later explained. "Most of the people in the county have never been in the courthouse."

They entered the judge's chambers warily. Two side judges, laymen elected by the local community to assist the regular judge, sat next to Hayes. From the far side of the room, reporters took notes. Susan Via and Mark Keller were there as well as Chris Davis, Rusty Valsangiacomo, and Sheldon Keitel, Hamlin's newly appointed guardian. (Keitel, a law student, was given the guardianship after Butch Hamlin's sexual assault arrest.) Louie slouched on a green couch next to Davis and Valsangiacomo, his arms folded on his chest. He fixed his eyes on each person being questioned for the jury, but showed no emotion. Even when the attorneys described the rape and murder and asked if the potential juror could stomach the gruesome details, Hamlin failed to react.

It was an ordeal for many of those ushered into the chambers. The attorneys tried to calm them, assuring them that "they weren't on a hot seat." "Mrs. Kibble, how you doin' today?" Mark Keller asked a woman furtively glancing about the room. "You look a little nervous."

Keller then asked if she could give the defendant the presumption of innocence and not make up her mind until after the facts had been presented. "No," she said. "I just feel he's guilty. He'd have to prove it the other way to me."

"There's nothing the judge could tell you to change you around?" asked the prosecutor.

"No."

Nervous or not, the men and women who paraded in and out of the room behind the main courtroom during the next two days did not leave behind their frankness. They were a representative cross-section of the rural state. They came from Ascutney and Ludlow and Wilder and Cavendish and Chester, small villages and farm towns. They were sheep farmers and worm farmers, mailmen and housewives. One man was the brother of a state legislator, another was "a pick and shovel man," and one woman was a writer of historical fiction. They were open, honest, good-humored, and, as Judge Hayes had admonished them that first day, they brought their common sense with them.

"Do you think you have common sense?" Keller asked one man.

"I think so," he responded. "But I don't know if anybody else does or not."

The most candid among the panel readily admitted that they would be poor choices for a jury assigned to judge Louie Hamlin. An elderly grandmother told the court: "I will be honest and say that I had read quite a bit about the case in the paper. The only thing I can say honestly is that I don't know if I could be an impartial juror or not. I have three granddaughters and one is nine and two are eleven."

One mother of a thirteen-year-old daughter was perturbed by Keller's description of what had happened to Meghan and Melissa. She was asked if having a daughter would prevent her from judging the case objectively.

"Well," the woman began, "the thing is, if it was my daughter..." She stopped. "I'm going to cry, I know I am, because I'm nervous."

"Just relax," Keller said patiently.

"If it was my daughter, I'd probably want—the most, whatever could be done to the guy done, you know."

Chris Davis nodded toward Hamlin and asked her if she thought he had done something wrong.

"Yes," said the woman.

"Why is that?" Davis asked.

"Because he's here."

It was a common reaction. Louie Hamlin would not have been brought to trial if he had not done something wrong. More disturbing to many prospective jurors was Chris Davis's forewarning that Hamlin himself would not testify at his trial. If he were truly innocent, others said, why would he not take the stand?

When Susan Via asked another man whether he believed in the presumption of innocence, he said yes, but...

"I think sometimes it's taken a little bit extreme."

"Can you explain what you mean?" Via asked.

"Well, for instance, in referring to the Hinckley thing, it's on black and white on your screen and you're seeing it. How can he be presumed innocent even though, you know, by the law he is? To me that's ridiculous."

One grandfather had no opinion about Hamlin's guilt or innocence but he did not believe he could sit through Meghan O'Rourke's testimony. "I think her emotions would upset my emotions very much," he complained.

Many of the potential jurors were from the town of Springfield, which posed a special problem: Just two months after Melissa Walbridge was killed, twelve-year-old Theresa Fenton was murdered in Springfield. As in Essex, the town had reacted with profound shock, and her killer had never been found. In the judge's chambers one man dourly reported that he would have problems sitting on the Hamlin jury because he had a twelve-year-old daughter who had been in Theresa Fenton's class. Could he put that out of his mind if he sat with this jury? Keller asked.

"Can try," he said. "Could be difficult. It's changed our life a lot. My daughter doesn't go out alone anymore. She has to be with a friend and even that doesn't help. She goes to Head-start to work with little kids, but now I have to wait for her to come home on the bus and take her in the car. . . . I don't sleep good."

Other prospective jurors were insistent that they could be objective about the case, if properly directed. One woman remembered seeing something about the killing on television, but, as she said, "as soon as they caught them, that's when I stopped following it." Did she believe in the presumption of innocence? "I haven't thought about it. I presumed they were guilty when they were caught. I don't like to think about things that don't concern me." What if the judge told her that the defendant had to be considered innocent until proven guilty? "If rules are laid down for me to observe, I will observe them. That's what I can say."

Beyond the basic problem of finding jurors able to accept the presumption of innocence, the prosecution and defense attorneys had their own particular interests to protect. Keller and Via wanted to know if the juror might give Hamlin a psychological break because he was only sixteen at the time of his arrest. They also asked each candidate whether he or she could accept the "accomplice liability" law. They wanted everyone to understand that being an accomplice to the murder carried the same legal liability as that imposed on the murderer.

To each potential juror Keller and Via set out the case in its grisliest details; they asked each person if hearing about and seeing photographs of those details would disturb them. They wanted to know if the person had children, if he or she could afford to be sequestered, away from family, for up to four weeks of a trial.

Chris Davis and Rusty Valsangiacomo had other concerns. How much had the person heard about the case? Had he or she already formed an opinion about Hamlin's guilt? Hamlin's attorneys had no illusions about the difficulty of their task. "We started off with a case that appeared, on its face, to be a loser," Davis recalled. The most they could hope for was a jury that would listen to what they had to say before finally judging their client.

Surprisingly, for all the publicity on the case, the jury selection progressed at a much quicker pace than expected. By Wednesday afternoon, only three days after the selection began, the full complement of twelve jurors and two alternates was seated. "I was amazed that it went so quickly and smoothly," said Clerk Jane Norman. "You'd have to be a person of stone not to be affected by the case. But I don't think there's anywhere else he could have had a fairer trial."

Of the eight men and four women chosen, almost all had children, which somewhat disturbed the defense. Four of the jurors lived in Springfield, the largest town near Woodstock. William Fogg, father of two, was a business manager and had spent a year in Vietnam; Victor Mazzella was a forty-one-year-old father of a six-year-old daughter; Patricia Graham, mother of five, worked part-time in the grade-school cafeteria; Edward Peck was a consulting engineer with one young child.

While everyone was still in the judge's chambers congratulating each other on a speedy jury selection, Lois Webby, a reporter for the Rutland *Herald*, walked in and told Judge Hayes that she had heard two court officers, within hearing distance of two jurors, discussing Hamlin's "lack of remorse."

Hayes was furious. "What good does it do us to sequester the jury?" he moaned. This was the most important trial in the state, and no one wanted the slightest suggestion of irregularity.

Hayes called Greg Mitchell, who was now an investigator with Keller's office, and Deputy Sheriff Paul Alexander to his chambers, separately. Both men admitted that a remark was made about Hamlin, but firmly denied they were talking loud enough for a juror to overhear them. Hayes called in the two jurors who had been in the jury box when the conversation took place. Both said they had heard nothing, but Hayes was not mollified. He reprimanded Mitchell and Alexander for making the statement at all.

Finally, at six-thirty that night, the jury was sworn in. "I have never been associated with a criminal case that took so little time to draw the jury in," Hayes told them. "We're all very happy. Everyone said that it would take us a week or two to select the jury, and we've done it in record time. I think we've got a good jury. So have a good night tonight, and our work will start tomorrow."

Susan Via was keeping a promise she had made to Meghan O'Rourke. Though she had quit her job with the state's attorney's office in April to become a deputy commissioner of the Vermont Health Department, she stayed on to help prosecute Louie Hamlin. On Thursday afternoon the curly-haired, thirty-year-old attorney rose to deliver the opening statement in the murder and sexual assault trial of Louie Hamlin.

Dressed in a crisp off-white suit, she walked back and forth in front of the jury box, her voice sailing through the old courtroom like a stone across a flat lake. "It's May 15, 1981, Essex Junction Town, Chittenden County, suburb of Burlington," Via said in a slow ominous cadence. "It's about four o'clock in the afternoon, four-fifteen. Two girls go to the Albert Lawton School. One has to stay late to give a report to the music teacher, so they leave school just a bit late. Melissa Walbridge and Meghan O'Rourke are the best of friends, and they leave that school together, and they do what hundreds of schoolchildren do when they walk home. They take a short-cut."

As she spoke, telling of that fateful day, Via pointed to a large, 6 foot by 4 foot aerial-view drawing set up on an easel in front of the jury. It showed the school, the park, the woods, the railroad, tracks, and the path that Melissa and Meghan took.

The jury members watched Via closely as she led them through the rape, the gagging, the stomping, and stabbing. "When you hear the evidence from Meghan O'Rourke, when you hear her testify," Via said, her voice rising, "you will not only have no reasonable doubt, you will have no doubt whatsoever in your minds that she was the victim of a vicious, brutal, aggravated sexual assault. And likewise, you will have absolutely no doubt in your minds whatsoever that the murder of Missy Walbridge was willful and premeditated and that it was done with deliberation and certainly with malice aforethought. So the question for you is: Who did it? Did the defendant do it? Is he an accomplice?"

Via then repeated the story of the attack, this time making clear her accusations against the two teenagers. "Hamlin and Savage," she announced, enunciating the two names as if she were chiseling them into the courtroom wall. "They were there, the two of them, together. And that horrible Friday last year, the two of them were waiting there to ambush children, those little girls. The two of them grabbed them off the path. The two of them put hands over their mouths. The two of them said don't move or we'll shoot you. The two of them ordered the girls to strip."

Via then switched from her description of the "two of them" to only Louie. "Hamlin himself shot Meghan in the neck," she continued. "Hamlin himself shot Melissa Walbridge in the back. Hamlin himself stabbed Meghan O'Rourke in the back."

From the long wooden table on the left of the courtroom Louie Hamlin watched Via intently, but impassively. Members of the press, seated to his left, watched for a reaction to this accusation, but saw none.

Within a few minutes Via had finished, and Chris Davis began his opening statement. Louie Hamlin's sober-speaking attorney, with his round, fair-skinned face and sandy blond hair, looked at least five years younger than his youthful thirty years. He had an innocent mien, but it was a natural disguise for a tenacious trial lawyer.

Davis wasted no time placing his case before the jury. "There's no dispute that there was a horrible tragedy last year on May 15th," he began. Davis's strategy was to accept that his client was involved, but to deny that Louie Hamlin was the actual murderer. "There's no dispute about the sex acts," he continued. "And we, as the defense, are not going to try and minimize the tragedy, the terrible acts that happened on May 15th. If that's the case, then why are we here?

"In our system of justice," he continued, "we have different types of crimes, different types of offenses with different elements, different punishments. We ask people like yourselves, the jurors, in cases like this to determine what crimes, if any, were committed. As I say, we have no dispute with the results here. But there is a dispute as to who did what to whom."

Davis and Valsangiacomo were retreating to what they considered the only safe harbor. They firmly believed that the evidence was not available to prove that Hamlin delivered the fatal wound to Melissa's heart. Even in her dramatic opening statement Susan Via had not actually accused Hamlin of killing Melissa.

Their theory was simple. There were only four witnesses to the attack. Missy Walbridge was dead and could testify only indirectly through the medical examiner. Louie was there, but his testimony would be rejected as self-serving. In any case the defense attorneys could not risk putting him on the stand and permitting the prosecution to pull him apart.

That left only two witnesses—Jamie Savage and Meghan O'Rourke. Jamie had changed his story at least once. Though his credibility was suspect, in his final version he appeared to accept blame for the murder. Meghan could reconstruct a good deal of what happened, but the defense was hoping she did not actually see which of the teenagers killed Melissa. If she could not remember, and if Jamie Savage confessed to the killing, then, Davis and Valsangiacomo would argue, there was sufficient doubt to absolve their client of the murder charge.

As a counterpoint to the inhumanity Susan Via had described, Davis tried to picture the defense in human terms. He interrupted his opening statement to the jury to introduce himself and the people who were sitting at the defense table. His partner for the trial was "the gentleman with the red hair sitting at the defense table." Then, sitting next to him, was "the tall gentleman with the glasses and the tan jacket," Sheldon Keitel.

"Mr. Keitel is a third-year law student at the Vermont Law School nearby here and he's been appointed what the court calls a guardian *ad litem*," Davis stated, casually nodding toward the table. "Let me just briefly explain to you what that is. It's a person who's been appointed to be, in effect, a parent, if you will, for the purpose of some sort of legal proceeding for a minor, somebody under seventeen years old." It was a small point, but one perhaps worth noting. Louie Hamlin, Davis was intimating, was just a kid. He needed a guardian, even one appointed by the court.

Davis now looked toward his client. "And then finally, the most important person is the defendant, the gentleman sitting with the dark hair and the glasses, Louis Hamlin." Hamlin sat upright, his hands folded together on the desk in front of him, as passive as a stone. He was no longer the scruffy "Hulk" of the Old North End neighborhood. He was now a "gentleman." Davis and Valsangiacomo had cleaned Louie up in a virtual cosmetic remake. The space between his eyes where his two brows had perpetually grown together was shaved clean. His hair had been trimmed and he was outfitted with a long-sleeve dress shirt and conservative tortoiseshell glasses.

He was now, as Davis spoke of him, the more respectable "Louis," with the *s* pronounced, not the rangy, roving "Louie." To help breathe a sense of humanity into his client, the defense attorney introduced him, as a native Vermonter with a family, a place in the life of the world.

"Mr. Hamlin is now seventeen years old," Davis said. "He's from Burlington, Vermont, was born and raised there. At the time of these charges, he was sixteen years old, was a junior in high school at Burlington High School, was living at home with his mother and father. His father worked in town. He had an older brother, two younger sisters, and a younger brother. He was on the wrestling team, had interests in writing some poetry, and also interests in drawing and draftsmanship."

Trying to prepare the jurors for the crucial test, his cross-examination of Meghan O'Rourke, Davis warned them that it would be necessary for the defense to question certain people for inconsistencies. Davis knew he would be facing a little girl who would evoke sympathy in everyone in the courtroom. "Nobody questions whether Meghan O'Rourke is lying," Davis said. "Obviously she's not lying. But I want it clear in everybody's mind that when you hear the state's witnesses and you hear both their direct and their cross that there may be many reasons, many purposes, for the questions being posed. I want you to keep those purposes in mind."

During the next several days, most of the prosecution witnesses called by Keller and Via—police officers, doctors, the medical examiner—described what they knew of the crime but were given little or no cross-examination. The defense attorneys listened without a word of protest to trainman Alton Bruso describe how he found a bloodied Meghan wandering down the railroad tracks. They had no questions for Officer Michael Bolduc after he told the jurors how he had discovered the body of Melissa Walbridge. They asked Officer Gary Taylor, who told jurors how he had gotten sick after seeing the body, only about his returning to the scene with Jamie Savage to find the girls' belongings and search unsuccessfully for the guns.

Rusty Valsangiacomo did, however, grill Lieutenant Robbie Yandow about the statement that Jamie Savage made to police the night of the arrests. Why, Valsangiacomo asked, wasn't Savage challenged when he denied any knowledge about the knife used to kill Melissa? "You knew with respect to what he was telling you about that murder weapon that he was not being truthful?" the defense attorney questioned.

"Yes," replied Yandow.

Valsangiacomo was trying to suggest that if Savage was obviously lying about the murder weapon, he could also have been lying about seeing Hamlin stab Melissa. "I assume at that point in your investigation that you, as an investigator, would certainly like to know who it was that stabbed Melissa Walbridge. Right?" pressed the attorney.

"Right," Yandow assented.

Susan Via, rising to question Yandow again, went directly to the prosecution's backup theory of complicity. "Lieutenant Yandow, did it matter to you for purposes of probable cause which of the two persons stabbed Melissa Walbridge in the heart?" she asked.

"No."

"Why is that?"

"Because," replied Yandow, "the accomplice would be just as guilty as the one that actually did the stabbing."

The first surprise for the defense came at the end of the first day of the trial when Mark Keller announced he would be calling Marie Walbridge, mother of the dead child, as a witness the next day. Valsangiacomo and Davis, fearing the emotional power of her presence, objected, arguing that her testimony would be inflammatory. Judge Hayes was equally unnerved by the prospect. "What if, despite your confidence, she shrieks, 'There is the man that killed my daughter'?" the judge asked Keller.

"Then we are in trouble, Your Honor," the prosecutor responded candidly. Keller knew that if Mrs. Walbridge were to lunge, verbally or otherwise, at Hamlin, the trial might very well be over. But he was also willing to take that risk. "I sat with her for two hours one day," he explained to Hayes "described every single injury her daughter received, with diagrams and pictures. And she was able to go through that. She wanted to know how her daughter died. I have all the confidence in the world that she will conduct herself properly on the witness stand."

Judge Hayes reluctantly permitted Keller to call Mrs. Walbridge to the stand on Friday morning, the second day of the trial. The small, dark-haired woman who took the stand testified with a voice that displayed the strain of determined self-control. Eric Walbridge sat ashen-faced in the front row, his arm around their son. Mrs. Walbridge's mouth tensed slightly as Mark Keller showed her, one by one, the things that Melissa was carrying as she walked home from school on May 15th. "That's Melissa's notebook," Marie Walbridge said in a firm, barely audible voice. "She's a doodler. She made cute little bugs and things."

With each small item, the mother reported a memory that made the killing more vivid, and thus more tragic, than any autopsy report. "That's the *Baby-sitter's Guide* by Dennis the Menace," she continued. "Melissa had just started baby-sitting with great enthusiasm and excitement. And she ran into Dennis the Menace types. I wanted to give her this to support her." Keller showed her the other books, a pair of Eric's sweat socks, her Le Team shirt, and her knapsack. Even the small pair of boots touched her memory. "She had just learned to lace those up with one hand. I don't know how she ever figured that out."

When Keller showed Mrs. Walbridge a picture of her daughter, taken on a sunny day in front of a boat on the lake, he asked if she looked like that the last time she saw her.

"Very much like that," she replied. "Unscarred, unblemished, happy, looking forward to a wonderful weekend."

There was nothing that the defense could do to minimize the emotional impact of her testimony.

Later that day, the defense faced another obstacle in the person of the medical examiner, Dr. Eleanor McQuillen. Though they had tried repeatedly to block her testimony in out-of-court motions, finally Davis and Valsangiacomo could not stop the jury from looking at numerous color slides of Melissa Walbridge's battered and bloodied corpse.

"Ladies and gentlemen, if you feel uneasy watching these, may I suggest that you take some deep breaths," Medical Examiner McQuillen told the jurors as the courtroom lights dimmed so that she could project the slides of the body of the dead girl. "It helps to oxygenate and if you really feel uncomfortable, please put your head down and we will shut the slides off."

"Is there water available?" asked Mrs. Edwards from juror seat number two.

"I think it might be a good idea if everybody had a cup," suggested Dr. McQuillen.

As the medical examiner projected the color slides of Melissa's mutilated body onto a screen, the jury reacted with fixed gazes of disbelief. Dr. McQuillen explained that there were three major stab wounds in the young woman's left chest. "One of them, the fatal wound, was the lowest and it penetrated the chest wall and entered the ventricle of the heart, the lower portion of the heart," she told the court.

"This is the lethal stab wound," the medical examiner continued as the white screen in the darkened courtroom lit with the picture of Melissa's terribly damaged chest. "It is much more a conventional stab wound with a small fishtail appearance that is due to the fact that the blade is drawn out at a slightly different angle than it was put in due to either motion of the body or motion of the hand holding the instrument."

Meghan's injuries were also described to the jury by Dr. Thomas Montag, a resident in gynecology, who had first examined her when she was brought into the hospital. "Most significantly, there was blood on her chest, her abdomen, her external genitalia and in the area of the rectum," he testified.

His findings, he explained, were consistent with "forcible intercourse."

Meghan was treated at the hospital by Dr. Richard Mellish, chairman of pediatric surgery at the Medical Center of Vermont, who described the opening in her chest. "I considered it a very serious injury. . . . A knife inserted into a person's chest in this region is clearly going to endanger the major vessels in the thorax. If the knife reaches it, it will reach her aorta, which is just beneath the left chest, and if the aorta is opened you would not survive for more than a few seconds. . . . She could well have died from such an injury."

Piece by piece the prosecution built its case against Louie Hamlin. Witnesses were brought to the stand to reconstruct the teenagers' actions prior to and after the attack. Hamlin's uncle, Joseph Safford, told the jury about the pig slaughter; Cathy Bailey described how Louie and Jamie came home from the park Friday afternoon; Mary Hamlin told the jury that Louie had showed her a gun that morning, and that the next day she washed his wet and sandy clothes; a schoolmate of Melissa and Meghan identified Hamlin as one of the two "scummy" men who were in the woods with guns on the day before the killing.

Barbara Parker testified that after the killing Louie had said, "Actually, we did it." An old neighbor of Hamlin's, who was in prison with him prior to the trial, testified that he heard Louie admit to stabbing Melissa. Hamlin also threatened to kill Savage "for ratting him out" as well as the "little girl that picked him out of the lineup." A former prison guard recounted hearing Hamlin say, "I killed the girl, I figure I owe ten years."

It took less than three days for the prosecution to present two dozen witnesses to the jury. Not all were articulate or persuasive, but together they drew a portrait of Louie Hamlin as a sadistic criminal. The defense could only try persistently to chip away at the witnesses' powers of recall. They suggested that they misheard Hamlin, or implied that they were lying. But they failed to impeach any of Hamlin's accusers convincingly; nor could they unravel the threads of circumstantial evidence that placed Hamlin in the woods on May 15th.

• • •

On Tuesday morning, the fourth day of the trial, the state was finally ready to call Meghan O'Rourke to the stand. Jennifer escorted her younger sister into the courtroom and slowly up to the witness box. An embarrassed Meghan had asked that her parents not be in the courtroom, but James and Stephanie O'Rourke were permitted to wait in a lawyers' anteroom with the door slightly ajar. They could not see Meghan but were able to listen to their daughter's crucial testimony. From the front row of the spectator's section, Jennifer smiled at her sister supportively.

As Susan Via began the questioning, Meghan squirmed in her chair and fidgeted with the ribbon on her dress. Her voice was tiny, but raspy, and she seemed to be gulping for air as she spoke. Via ran Meghan through a quick series of biographical questions about Melissa and herself, then asked: "Are you a little nervous?"

"Yeah."

"Just try to relax. Take a deep breath," coaxed the prosecutor. Via had not proceeded much farther when she interrupted herself. "Your Honor, it's very difficult—members of the press are squeaking in those chairs. And I'm not sure the jurors are able to hear the answers. Is the jury having a hard time hearing?"

A number of jurors nodded affirmatively. The dozen reporters in the courtroom had already seated themselves as quietly as they could in their old straw- and spindle-back chairs. Judge Hayes asked that the volume for the loudspeaker system be turned up and the tall windows running along the street side of the second-floor room be closed.

Susan Via now concentrated on the business at hand, and little Meghan followed her lead. Before the trial the deputy prosecutor had drilled her: She was to listen to each question and wait until it was over before answering; she should not guess at what was said; if she did not understand, she was to say so even if it was the judge who asked the question.

Meghan sat very straight and bit her lip as she listened to Via pose the questions. The young girl determinedly moved herself up to the microphone. When the loudspeakers hummed or she had to cough, Meghan reached up and flicked off the microphone switch. "Only a child would do those things," Via later remarked. "She was trying her darnedest to be as mature as she could and give this her fullest attention. I have seen witnesses in a fog on the stand. But Meghan was paying attention very hard to what she had to be doing. She was determined to get through this."

Meghan told the jury how she had been frightened by two men on the Wednesday before the attack; on Friday these same men had grabbed her and Melissa and pushed them deep into the woods. At the moment Meghan was to describe the rape she began to twist in her seat.

"And then what did he do, Meghan?" Via asked firmly.

There was a long, tense silence as Meghan held back the profane words. When she finally whispered that the blond-haired man forced her to take his penis in her mouth, the courtroom reacted with the same revulsion that the child had felt.

"How did he do that?" Via asked immediately.

"He pushed down on my head," said Meghan.

"Did you want to do that?"

"No."

"Did you tell him you didn't want to do that?"

"Yes."

"Were you crying?"

"Yes."

"He made you do it anyway?"

"Yes."

Meghan continued without interruption, telling the court that after finishing with her, Savage "pushed me over to the dark-haired man." Hamlin then forced her down on the ground, on her back, and without taking his pants down, tried to have intercourse with her.

The next series of questions proffered by Via might have been shockingly embarrassing for Meghan and the court but for the fact that the prosecutor faced the sensitive issue directly. She steered Meghan, who sat in the witness box for two and a half hours, through the painful memory expertly, eliciting both the emotion and the facts of Meghan's ordeal without exploiting the child. Meghan was nervous throughout, but steeled herself, knowing the importance of her answers.

"What did the dark-haired man try to do to you?"

"He tried to have sexual intercourse."

"Was he successful when he did that?"

"No."

"Did he try to put his penis into your vagina?"

"Yes."

"Do you know what a vagina is?"

"Yes," Meghan answered.

"He couldn't get it in?" Via prompted Meghan.

"No."

"Did it hurt?"

"Yes," said Meghan.

"Did you tell him to stop?"

"Yes."

"Did he stop?"

"No."

"Were you crying?" asked Via.

"Yes."

"While he was doing that, where was Missy?"

"She was with the blond-haired man."

"And what was the blond-haired man doing with Missy while the dark-haired man was doing that to you?"

"The same thing."

"Making Missy suck his penis?"

"Yes," Meghan answered.

"What happened after the dark-haired man tried to put his penis into your vagina?"

"He stood me up," Meghan answered.

"Did he try to do anything else to you?" Via asked.

"Yes."

"What did he try to do to you—the dark-haired man?"

"He tried to put his penis in my rear end."

"In your rectum?"

"Yes."

"Did he get it in?"

"Just a little bit."

"Did it hurt?"

"Yes."

"Did you tell him to stop?"

"Yes."

"Were you crying?"

"Yes."

"Did he eventually stop?"

"Yes."

"Meghan," Via asked, "do you know what it means when a man ejaculates?"

"Yes."

"Did the dark-haired man ejaculate?"

"Yes."

"How do you know that?"

"Because I saw it," Meghan responded.

"After the dark-haired man took his penis out of your rectum, what did he say to you?"

"He told me to lick it off."

"Did you do that?"

"No."

"Did he say anything else?"

"He said, 'Oh, forget it.'"

With Via's careful prompting, Meghan recounted one ugly fact after another. She astonished the court with her recall, but what Meghan could not remember—and what Via did not ask her—was how Missy received her fatal wounds. It would be Chris Davis's challenge, when he rose to cross-examine Meghan, to turn that absence of memory to his advantage. And, given the age and innocence of his subject, it would be a formidable task.

The defense attorney trod gingerly. After a pretrial hearing, Rusty Valsangiacomo had suggested to Mark Keller that Meghan was not telling the whole truth. It could not be true, he told the prosecutor, that the twelve-year-old did not remember who did the actual stabbing. Keller screwed up his eyes and looked at the defense attorney, as if to say "You gotta be crazy!" When Keller later told Via about Valsangiacomo's charge, he added: "I hope that he gets up and says that in front of the jury."

Via and Keller believed that the defense had learned their lesson. As Davis walked toward the stand, it was now obvious that the defense would not risk letting Rusty Valsangiacomo, who had so shaken Meghan at the deposition, repeat that performance. Instead, Davis was now questioning the young girl.

Davis stood a few feet from Meghan and very patiently questioned her.

"Do you remember absolutely everything that happened on May 15th?"

"Not everything."

"If you get upset or you want to stop, just tell me," Davis said politely.

Davis was too shrewd to suggest that Meghan was lying, but he firmly believed that the girl had seen more than she claimed to remember. "What she has in her memory are flashes of certain events," Davis later explained. "If you read Jamie's corrected version of the deposition, his scenario makes sense. Meghan has just fragments of what happened and I don't even think they are necessarily in order. We agonized over this whole thing, because we were convinced that Meghan saw her friend killed, and we were very fearful about beating her up on the stand, so to speak, in order to bring back her memory. Jamie said that Meghan was watching as he killed Melissa and that after he killed her he jumped over and stabbed Meghan in the back and chest so there wouldn't be a witness. I'm concerned that she saw him and has blocked it out of her mind."

Davis continued his cross-examination of Meghan, trying to shake the girl's testimony. "As you sit here today, are you able to recall all of the things that you just talked about with Miss Via?" he asked.

But Meghan knew the difference between remembering everything and remembering what she remembered. "Yes," she said.

"Do you have trouble remembering certain things about what happened that day?" Davis persisted.

"I have trouble remembering what order they went in and stuff," Meghan responded stubbornly.

The thirteen-year-old remained composed as Davis brought up the question of the murder knife. She saw the knife only once? Yes. Did you see the dark-haired man strike anyone with it. No. Did she see him use it in any way? No. Did she remember the dark-haired man stabbing her with the knife? No.

Davis then quickly changed subjects, challenging Meghan's memory about who stomped Melissa on the back.

"All you remember is that you saw a foot coming down on her back, is that right?" Davis asked.

"It was a boot," Meghan said confidently.

"You didn't see the face of the person?" the attorney continued.

"No," rasped Meghan, "but the dark-haired man was wearing the boots."

"But you felt that the dark-haired man was wearing the boots, right?"

"I knew," the girl challenged.

Meghan saw clearly through Davis's strategy. As the defense attorney became less solicitous of her age and more demanding of her memory, she seemed to dismiss his questions as unimportant.

"Referring to your deposition," Davis asked, handing Meghan the bulky sheaf of papers. "Specifically, page ninety-eight, line twelve, do you remember Mr. Valsangiacomo asking you, 'You say that on Friday you saw the blond-haired man choking Melissa?' And do you remember your answer was yes?"

"I guess so." Meghan shrugged as if to say "Who cares?"

"Are you saying there's anything wrong with the deposition the way it was—"

"No," Meghan interrupted.

"Never mind," said Davis, frustrated. "Do you remember Mr. Valsangiacomo then asking you—line fifteen, the same page—'Did you ever see the dark-haired man choke Melissa?' And do you remember your answer, 'Not that I know of'?"

"I guess so," she repeated.

Over and over Davis tried to force Meghan to admit that she changed her testimony, to admit that she had trouble remembering what happened. It was difficult to gauge whether the jury, watching the brave girl testifying, was intent on matching the statements Davis was alluding to. Could they follow the long excerpts from the depositions, compare them with Meghan's hospital interviews, and still keep track of what it was that the dark-haired and the blond-haired men did or didn't do?

As Davis increased the pressure, Meghan grimaced and looked at her sister for encouragement. Jennifer later admitted that she "felt like strangling" the attorney.

Davis tried to finish his long cross-examination with an allusion to Hamlin's supposed moderation.

"At some point in time you asked the dark-haired man not to hurt you, right?"

"Yes," Meghan replied.

"And he promised that he wouldn't do that, right? That he would not hurt you?"

"Yes."

"I have nothing further," said the attorney as he started toward the defense table.

Susan Via moved quickly to her feet, and before Davis could sit down, the acerbic prosecutor was lacing her first question across the well of the courtroom.

"Meghan," she almost shouted, "the dark-haired man lied when he said he wouldn't hurt you, right?"

"Yes."

"What hurt you that the dark-haired man did?"

"Everything."

"Everything?"

"Yes."

"How about getting shot in the neck?"

"Yeah."

"Did that hurt?"

"Yeah."

In moments Via succeeded in destroying what Davis had tried to build in forty-five minutes.

"Mr. Davis asked you a lot of questions and asked you whether you were confused or had a bad memory about what happened," she said. "And I think you said something about you were not sure about the order things happened in?"

"Yes."

"You are not sure about the order that some things happened in, but what actually happened to you, are you sure about that?"

"Yes."

"Are you confused about who grabbed Missy off the path?"

"No."

"Who did that?"

"The dark-haired man."

"Are you confused about who choked Missy when she refused to take her clothes off?"

"No."

"Who did that?"

"The dark-haired man."

"Are you confused about who tried to push his penis into your vagina and then your rectum?"

"No."

"Who did that?"

"The dark-haired man."

"Are you confused about who said, 'Lick it off'?"

"No."

"Who said that?"

"The dark-haired man."

"Are you confused about whether or not you were gagged with a knee sock?"

"No."

"You are sure about that?"

"Yeah."

"Who did it?"

"The dark-haired man."

Via continued, with the beat of a metronome, methodically leading Meghan back through Hamlin's attack.

As Meghan finished and left the witness stand, Jennifer rose from her front-row seat and put her arm around her sister. Both smiled with relief as they walked from the courtroom.

Chris Davis was dejected. "Her testimony was incredibly damaging," he later said. "Statements like Louie saying, 'You're going to die like a pig.' I mean, that was just devastating."

When the court had recessed for the day, the jurors were escorted across the street to their plush retreat at the Woodstock Inn. They hardly noticed the small groups of people waiting in front of the courthouse hoping to catch sight of the suspected killer. "Ordinarily, the people in this area have never turned a hair about what's going on in this courthouse," said County Clerk Jane Norman.

The first day of the trial a rumor had raced through the town: Judge Hayes, it was said, had ordered Hamlin to stay away from the Woodstock Inn. Doors and shutters were bolted tight as residents, who now believed that Hamlin was free between court appearances, braced themselves, fearful that the young criminal would be wandering through the rest of the town. Apprised of the furor, Hayes quickly explained he intended only to make sure that sheriffs guarding the subject would not take him out of the courthouse for lunch. The judge assured the townspeople that Hamlin was being kept behind bars at all times; even when he was brought to the courthouse he was handcuffed and guarded.

There were no demonstrations by irate mothers as some had predicted, but local teenagers leaned against the iron fence surrounding the green and shouted insults at Hamlin as sheriffs escorted him out to a waiting police cruiser. One little girl remarked, "I felt scared, weird, as if I shouldn't be here." Said another, "I came to see the monster."

Despite the efforts to make Hamlin presentable, he looked self-conscious as he entered the court, walking stoop-shouldered, arms dangling, apelike. His only words throughout the trial were confined to "Yes, Your Honor," and "No, Your Honor." Courtroom spectators watched the defendant closely as he drummed his fingers nervously on the table when the slides of Melissa's body were being shown. They craned to see how Hamlin would react to Meghan O'Rourke, tried to read some meaning into his vacant face.

"I have a daughter that age and I came one day just to see him with my own eyes," exclaimed one Woodstock woman. "I made a point of looking in his eyes and it was a pretty awful sight. It was a steely, eerie look. And his weird body carriage. There was no remorse there at all."

As the trial progressed, Hamlin could be seen consulting with Valsangiacomo or Davis or Keitel, resting an arm on one of their shoulders, a touch of humanity greeted with mixed reactions by those who witnessed it. Other times, as the court recessed for the day, Chris Davis could be seen stopping in the defendant's room to say good night to Hamlin. During lunch breaks, passersby on the lawn below could see, framed in the

second-floor window, Hamlin's silhouetted presence silently
gazing out.

When the defense attorneys decided not to plead their defendant insane, they had effectively closed the door to a view
of Louie Hamlin's interior life. Without an insanity defense
the jurors would know nothing about Louie except that he was
charged with committing the heinous act.

But Hamlin had his defenders, few as they were. "I am a
volunteer going to St. Albans Correctional Facility weekly to
visit various individuals on a one-to-one basis," a woman had
written to Chris Davis. "I have seen Louis since July 16, 1981,
a total of 36 times, many of them for an hour or more. After
the first few weeks of struggling with my own feelings of
revulsion of the crime itself, I found a real person inside Louis:
a person who knows right from wrong, and ultimately wants
to do right; a very immature boy who is having a hard time
growing up but is doing so; a young man with more intelligence
and potential than he has been given credit for."

Susan Craighead, Louie's Paradise Project friend, corre-
sponded with him as she prepared to enter Princeton University.
Shaken by the killing, Craighead wrote an essay, eventually
published in the *Daily Princetonian*, about what it felt like to
be Louie's friend. From Agatha Christie she borrowed her
theme: "Every murderer is probably somebody's old friend."

In her account, Craighead recalled the morning she first
read of the killing. "Even as I sighed with relief that my twelve-
year-old sister was securely tuned in to cartoons that morning,
a tide of rage dampened my breakfast." She remembered a note
passed to her in French class stating that someone from Burlington High School had been arrested for the murder. "Maintaining a facade of disinterest, it was not until the end of class
that I discovered the identities of the accused. To my horror,
one was an old friend."

During the months following the arrest, Craighead argued
on behalf of Louie's constitutional right to a presumption of
innocence. "No one seemed to agree with me," she wrote. "To
most people Louie remained an abhorrent phantom criminal.
So he would have remained to me as well, but for his special

status in my memories. I owed him a minimum of confidence.

"As co-workers on a student literary magazine, Louie was to me a poet whose stanzas had graced my editorial desk," she continued. "In my memories, Louie was featured as a child, not a rapist nor a murderer. . . . Behind his gruff manner and mysterious, dark eyes Louie was the gentlest of boys. From our meeting at the age of twelve, I trusted him . . . To me Louie wasn't a murderer. But neither was he a poet or comrade to the community. It was as though we were judging two different boys. . . . As the conflict divided my conscience, my mind cleaved Louie. There are two Louies now."

If Louie Hamlin was a poet, there was no opportunity for verse at his trial. The only refrain was a sordid stanza barely disguised as a question: Who raped two innocent girls, and stabbed, choked, and killed one of them?

After Meghan's testimony, Davis and Valsangiacomo were left with but a single avenue of defense, the word of sixteen-year-old Jamie Savage.

The defense attorneys, piecing together the teenager's account, concluded that Savage and Hamlin planned to rape the two girls, but not to kill them. It was Savage who said he wanted to eliminate the witness, who killed Melissa. Louie, they claimed, neither participated in the planning of a murder nor in the killing itself. He could not therefore even be considered an accomplice to that crime.

It was a difficult theory for the defense to prove. It rested first on doubts about Meghan's memory; second, on Jamie's credibility. Davis and Valsangiacomo felt they could avoid much of the confusion if they could question Savage on the witness stand, but the prosecution refused to grant Savage immunity for his testimony. Instead, they threatened the youth with a perjury charge. Without that immunity his attorneys would not let him testify. Hamlin's defense lawyers would have to explain the crimes of Jamie Savage to the jury without Jamie's presence.

On Tuesday afternoon, the defense called as their first witness Greg Packan, Savage's court-appointed guardian *ad litem*.

Packan had been with Savage at the Waterbury detention center when the youth changed his story and took the blame for killing Melissa.

On the stand, Packan explained that Savage's plea agreement with the state, made in November of 1981, included a promise that, in return for testifying at Hamlin's trial, Savage would have the right of approval of the facility he would be lodged in until his eighteenth birthday. There was no promise, said Packan, that Savage would have to testify for the prosecution, only that he would tell the truth.

"And did you at some point in time in January or earlier inform Mr. Savage that he was now or could be considered now as an adult for the purpose of the criminal laws of the State of Vermont?" asked Valsangiacomo. He was leading up to his theory that Savage, who was now sixteen, and legally an adult in criminal court, had changed his account only when he realized that he could be prosecuted for not telling the truth. "Yes," said Packan, "we apprised him of that many times."

To support his case that Savage, not Hamlin, was truly the killer, Valsangiacomo suggested it would have made more sense for Savage to take the blame for the crime while he was still a juvenile and not subject to a perjury prosecution. If Savage changed his testimony only to protect his friend, the attorney implied, he would have done that when he had nothing to lose—while he was still a juvenile.

But prosecutor Mark Keller was determined to show the jury that Savage was merely a pathological liar, that nothing he said could be trusted.

"During the depositions," Keller asked Packan, "Mr. Savage was constantly changing his testimony?"

"There were inconsistencies on the three dates, yes," he replied. "And sometimes inconsistencies within a day's testimony."

"Sometimes the inconsistencies were within minutes?"

"Such things were known to happen."

"And didn't it happen that during recesses he'd be asked the same question two or three times and would give two different answers?"

"That did happen," Packan admitted.

"And even though he was warned, 'If you lie, you're going to commit perjury,' ask him the question, he gives one answer; ask him the same question, he gives another answer?"

"That did happen."

"As a matter of fact, if he was going to testify today, you wouldn't know what he was going to testify to?"

"I would not be certain."

The next morning, and for almost two full days, the jury would have a chance to judge for itself the meaning of Jamie Savage's statements.

There was a moment of excitement in the courtroom as Jamie himself was called to the witness stand. It was the first time the public had an opportunity to see the young criminal since the arrest. Jurors watched closely as the gangly youth walked up the center aisle of the courtroom to the platform. Hamlin turned in his seat to see his former friend. Savage's appearance had changed little after almost a year in the Waterbury detention center. He wore a navy blue cardigan sweater, brown corduroy pants, and yellow and orange striped sneakers.

Savage's lawyers had already told the court that because the prosecution would not grant him immunity from perjury Savage would refuse to talk. Savage had been called to the stand only to help the jury associate a face with the words that were to be read to them for eight hours over the next day and a half. The teenager first stated his name and address, then said he would invoke his Fifth Amendment right against self-incrimination if asked any question about the attack. Within a few minutes of walking into the witness docket, he stepped down and left.

Taking his place was Harry Ames, friend of Judge Hayes, father of two, Dartmouth College graduate, and now volunteer stand-in for Jamie Savage. Court Clerk Jane Norman would ordinarily have done the reading, but Hayes decided that the language in Savage's deposition was "too rough" for her. Ames, who happened to stop by the courthouse one night to invite the judge to a spaghetti dinner, had been enlisted.

It was a long, tedious process. Harry Ames sat in the witness stand, playing the part of Savage. Rusty Valsangiacomo played himself, sometimes with great emotion. Every hour Hayes called for a fifteen-minute break to give the jury an opportunity to stretch and clear their heads.

Because Savage had changed many of his answers after the deposition, Ames first read the youth's original version, then read his penciled changes on the typed transcript. Whenever there was a reference to the stabbing Savage had crossed out Hamlin's name and inserted "I" or "me."

"He told me that he was going to kill them and I said 'What for?' and he said 'So we don't have a witness.'" In an instant this accusation became a confession: "I told Louie that I was going to kill them and he said 'What for?' and I said 'So we don't have a witness.'"

Many jurors appeared as distraught over the reading, littered with Savage's four-letter-word descriptions of the rape, as with viewing the graphic autopsy slides of Melissa's wounds.

"She said, 'Why are you doing this?' I told her to shut up. . . . Then I told her to suck on my dong. . . . So she did it. Then I told her to turn around. . . . I tried to fuck her in the ass. . . . Then it didn't fit so I told her to give me another head. Then I went back up to the mouth because it didn't fit. . . . Then I asked Louie if he was done."

At this point in the deposition, Valsangiacomo had asked Savage: "You didn't know what else to say but 'fuck,' did you?"

"No," Harry Ames read from Savage's deposition. "Still don't."

As they listened, the jurors wiped their eyes as if drying tears. Some glared at Hamlin, who sat impassively at the defense table throughout the eight hours. The jurors could hear Savage say that he decided to kill Melissa after she had run away because he got "mad." Through the deposition, they heard him admit that he lost control and explain the BB gun wounds by saying that he believed "enough pain will kill somebody."

It was May 14, 1982, when Mark Keller rose to offer the prosecution's closing statement to the eight men and four women in the jury box. It was one day short of a year since Keller first saw the body of the twelve-year-old girl sprawled naked and bloody in the woods of Maple Street Park. He still could not forget it. Keller slowly repeated for the jurors what he had been telling them through witnesses and photographs for the previous six days of Hamlin's murder trial: that Missy died slowly, painfully.

"Think of a boy who pulls one wing off a fly," he said. "Then he pulls the other wing off, and then one leg, so all the fly can do is buzz around in a circle." The attorney paused. "He pulls off the last leg, and what do you have? You have a little body twitching. And the boy watches until he's bored. And then he crushes it."

Meghan O'Rourke survived, Keller told the jury, only because she passed out. His voice peppered with sarcasm, Keller exclaimed, "Meghan O'Rourke wasn't fun to play with. Meghan O'Rourke wasn't fun to torture because she kept passing out. . . . This wasn't a case in which somebody got mad and started stabbing. This is a case in which they started to slowly inflict pain, one step at a time, until they finally got bored with it and decided to kill."

Keller's closing remarks took ten minutes. After that, Rusty Valsangiacomo made his last plea to the jury. The prosecution, he argued, had not proved beyond a reasonable doubt that Hamlin had killed Melissa Walbridge. He insisted that Hamlin's only plan was to rape the girls, tie them up, and flee. It was Jamie who actually plunged the knife into Melissa's heart, he claimed. "Mr. Savage got upset. Mr Savage, who has mistreated members of his own family, had difficulty controlling himself. . . . He got an impulse to kill Melissa, but he didn't tell Louis."

Valsangiacomo's closing statement was a long one, but when he had finished, Mark Keller said he wanted to offer a rebuttal. The prosecutor felt there was more at stake in this case than any he had ever tried. Keller and Susan Via had decided that Via would make the prosecution's opening statement because of her more emotional style. Keller, calmer and more measured, would close the case. But as the state's attorney warmed to his last attack on the defense, his voice rose with scorn. "We did a very unusual thing in this case, very unusual," he exclaimed.

"We don't often do that in criminal cases. We proved the defense attorney was wrong and we proved the defendant was right."

The tension in the courtroom mounted as Keller started slowly toward the suspect seated at the defense table. "The reason I say that is because Louie, as he sits here, knows he's guilty," Keller said as he tapped his finger down on the defense table. "He's sitting right here, and he knows he's guilty! And the reason why Louie knows he's guilty is because he said it. When Barbara and Jeanie Parker were there on the bridge, what did Louie say? 'Actually, we did it,' and he laughed."

Keller, now only a few feet from the defendant, pointed his finger directly at Hamlin. And looking at the youth, he almost shouted, taunting the burly teenager, "Right, Louie?"

Hamlin did not flinch. But his attorneys were immediately shouting their objections. When Judge Hayes ruled the remark out of order, Keller apologized, but the trial was now all but over.

Keller still regrets his unfortunate outburst. "I got mad for an instant, but as soon as I said it, I knew I had made a mistake. I've never forgiven myself for that."

At 6:30 P.M. Judge Hayes sent the jury out for dinner and to begin its deliberations. There hours later, the jurors asked that part of Meghan's testimony be read back. At 10:23 P.M., less than four hours after the jury had retired to deliberate, the bell atop the Windsor County courthouse rang to signal the news that a verdict had been reached.

The jurors took their places in front of the courtroom and were polled by the county clerk. One by one they announced their decision. Some made a point of looking directly at Louie Hamlin as unanimously they called out in strong, clear tones the verdict: "Guilty."

CHAPTER 19

Epilogue

RESIDENTS OF ESSEX still talk about the crime with angry revulsion and watch over their children with fearful eyes. Parents still drive their young children to school, almost as a reflex. Residents still lock their doors.

At 10:00 P.M. curfew was hastily clamped on Maple Street Park. "There's nowhere to hang out anymore," explained an annoyed local teenager, "because the adults here have gotten so strict."

Louie Hamlin and Jamie Savage have added a new anxiety to an entire state's attitude toward crime. At a neighborhood meeting, worried residents of Burlington's far North End complained to police officers about an unprotected wooded area that children pass through on their way to school. "We're afraid that something might happen to our kids," said one mother, adding with the shorthand expression that needed no explanation, "We don't want another Essex."

The most dramatic result of the Essex killing has been the enactment of a new juvenile code. Advocates of that emergency legislation felt justified when a fifteen-year-old girl robbed and tried to assault her partially paralyzed great-grandmother. Quickly apprehended, the girl was charged under the new law in adult court, though she spent only fifteen days in jail and had the remainder of her one-year sentence suspended.

The new law was used again, this time to stronger effect, in the case of a fifteen-year-old boy who knocked on a woman's door in Shelburne, a suburb of Burlington, and after asking to borrow an egg beat, stabbed, and raped the woman. It was the teenager's second rape offense. The first time he had been quickly released by juvenile court. Now tried as an adult under the new law, he was sentenced to jail for fifteen to twenty years, a draconian punishment compared to what he would have received only a few months before. "If the new law were not in effect, I'd be willing to bet another woman would be assaulted—possibly killed," says Mark Keller. "The chance of rehabilitation for this guy is zero."

A dozen other juveniles have already been prosecuted under the new law, including two youths who escaped from the Benson Wilderness Camp and returned to rape a staff member and steal her car. But, while the law has proven effective in removing dangerous juvenile criminals from the street, will it *prevent* other crimes from occurring? No one in Vermont can be sure, and argument continues. Some believe the new juvenile code does not go far enough. Mark Keller still complains that there is no mechanism for stopping the repeat offenders.

Others, fewer in number, only grudgingly accept the new statute, arguing that throwing eleven- and twelve-year-olds into adult court is not the solution. "I think the more people focus on punishment, the less likely that something is going to happen that will help kids before the crimes occur," remarks Althea Kroger, the Essex Junction legislator who can see the Savage home from her living room. "What we've done so far isn't going to make a difference."

No matter which side of the ideological spectrum Vermonters have lined up on, all agree that they need to do more to stop juvenile violence. "The law change was a good one," says

Niel Christiansen, Louie Hamlin's former probation officer. "But the hard part is what you do with them after that. Officially, we don't even have a maximum security prison. So if you prosecute and convict a fifteen-year-old as an adult, what the hell do you do with him?"

States receiving federal law enforcement grants are prohibited from incarcerating persons under eighteen in the same prison facility as adults. Vermont's own special session ordered much the same prohibition, but this legal problem produced a practical one: Vermont still had no juvenile jail.

The small town of Waterbury, a half hour east of Burlington by way of the Interstate and already the site of the state's mental hospital, was a logical choice for a juvenile jail. Young violent criminals—including Jamie Savage—were already being housed on a temporary basis in the hospital, but the townsfolk were opposed to the idea of a jail. Waterbury's peaceful tree-lined Main Street, with its white colonial church, was quickly traversed by a large red and white banner: NO JUVENILE DETENTION FACILITY IN WATERBURY! NO!

After a year of argument over the site location, construction of a new thirty-bed juvenile jail finally began in the fall of 1983. In the end, the ground-breaking was sadly ironic, even poignant. The bulldozers began uprooting trees on land given the state by the federal government, a wooded area along the Winooski River in the town of Essex Junction. Louie Hamlin and Jamie Savage had hunted their squirrels in the same spot; Meghan O'Rourke lives just upriver; and Melissa Walbridge is buried only a few miles away.

Regardless of the ultimate effect of the new state law, Vermonters remain anxious about their children's safety. The attack on Melissa and Meghan was followed that September by the murder of twelve-year-old Theresa Fenton in the town of Springfield. Then, with the Fenton murder still unsolved, another Springfield girl was abducted and brutally killed. "It brought more rage," wrote the Burlington *Free Press*. "It brought fresh rage. Rage that a girl, a 4-H'er, a Sunday school student, a ballet dancer, a player with dolls, was the second girl slain here in less than two years."

• • •

There are few places in this tiny, familial state not touched by the Essex killing. It is rare to meet someone who has not heard of the crime, and it is common to encounter those who personally know one of the principals. On a remote stretch of the Interstate highway, a Vermont state trooper told me that he had worked on the Hamlin and Savage manhunt. In a little coffee shop in the southwestern part of the state, a man recalls being in the same prison as Louie Hamlin. A cab driver in Burlington, when asked if he remembered the killing in Essex, replies, "Yeah, I'm related to Jamie Savage."

For more than a year the Walbridges continued to live less than a mile from the Lefebvres' Gaines Court home. The O'Rourkes are in the same home and the Lefebvre children still go to Lawton School. Cathy Bailey has moved out of the Lefebvre house, but only to another home two doors down Gaines Court.

Though Vermonters reacted angrily to the crime, it never drained them of their fairness and common sense. They could condemn the sons without punishing the parents. "Yeah, Mary Hamlin told me that she was getting threatening calls," recalls a neighbor who believes that the death penalty would not be enough for Louie Hamlin. "But the only people I know of that went over there was mainly to see if there was anything to do for Mrs. Hamlin and the other kids—like bringing dishes of food over. Everybody sympathized with her, but didn't give a hang about Louie or the father."

Even Marie Walbridge could sympathize with Savage's brothers. "One of the boys was still going to the junior high school," she recalls, "and was getting a lot of flack for what his brother had done. He announced that he was not his brother and not his brother's keeper. He is himself and will be judged for what he is."

Many of those personally touched by the tragedy wanted to forget; a few needed to remember; and all bear the scars. The Walbridges and O'Rourkes, though inextricably bound by the same crime, are forever separated by the crime's outcome: Meghan survived and Melissa did not.

Meghan O'Rourke has made an extraordinary recovery. After the Hamlin trial, more than a year after the attack, *Life* magazine writer Christopher Whipple noted that Meghan "hangs pictures of horses on her bedroom walls, leaves her clothes scattered on the floor, cannot decide whether to become a great actress or a great photographer, has temporary crushes on boys, doodles constantly and has been known to plunge into a pool fully clothed on a dare. She does not stop to think that these wonderfully ordinary reflections of early adolescence might be unusual after such an ordeal."

But Meghan still does not talk about her friend Melissa. "Meghan is not able to discuss it," says Marie Walbridge. "It is, I think, her claim to sanity. She has put it behind her and the fact that she's been able to come back and join the real world is commendable."

Dr. William Woodruff, who helped treat Meghan, does not believe that she will be scarred for life. He explains her psychic and emotional injury as "a sort of exaggeration of a war trauma, of a battle injury. We found in warfare that people who were seriously injured could say, 'I wasn't a coward. I was badly hurt. I couldn't do a thing about it.' And, therefore, guilt and the problems of surviving do not exist."

For the Walbridges the aftermath of the crime has been excruciating. It has meant adjusting to the greatest and most irretrievable loss. "We've had a very shattered life," says Marie Walbridge. "And now we have to pick up the pieces. It's not easy." Immediately after the killing, Missy's parents—both of whom are religious—had an instinctive reaction of compassion for the killers. But as the pain of their daughter's loss grew, their anger about Melissa's senseless death increased, as did their frustration with the legal system. "It's nice to be protected," said Eric Walbridge. "I wish somebody would protect us."

"I really came to realize that our laws aren't adequate," adds Marie. "They're not firm, they're not just. They are convenient. Because if they had been more firm when Hamlin first started getting into trouble, this might not have happened. The results are that Melissa is dead and Meghan will be affected by her experience the rest of her life."

Eric Walbridge had to take a leave of absence from his job and Marie was forced to give up her painting business and take a steady job to help pay the bills. Living in Essex, they were constantly reminded of their daughter in some way. "Everything reminds me of Melissa," Mrs. Walbridge commented the night of a local fair. "The fair reminds me of Melissa."

Sitting in the Lincoln Inn a few weeks after the killing, Eric saw a group of high school students come in dressed in party clothes for the prom. In that instant he realized he would never see his daughter go to a prom or give her hand in marriage. "Those are the two things that really hit me," he said. "She was my only daughter," he would say, "the only daughter I'll ever have, and she was very important to me. And that's never going to change."

"I saw the Walbridges come into the restaurant quite a few times since this thing happened," recalls Betty Colby, a waitress at the Inn. "Eric would sit by himself and she and the boy would sit in the other seat. By the way they were acting—it seemed to me that they thought there was a fourth person there. It was just a strange feeling you get . . . like he didn't move his elbow because he was afraid he was going to poke her with it."

The Walbridges have sold the ranch-style house that they loved in Essex and moved into a four-family house in Burlington's south end, not far from the G. E. plant where Eric still works. Pictures of Missy are all around. Despite their sense of loss, the family talks proudly about their daughter. "We like to talk about Melissa," says Marie Walbridge. "But we don't get much of a chance to talk about her because everyone we know feels uncomfortable listening. We're so sorry that Melissa had to leave this world in that way, but we have to accept that, and we have to pick up the pieces and make sense of what's left for us."

The Hamlin and Savage families, and some of their relatives, have also had to put their lives back together. Ernest Hoffman sold his interest in the pig farm where Louie had witnessed the fateful slaughter. Joseph Safford, a year after the killing, had only slaughtered one pig on his farm. "It bothers me now, for some reason, you know," he said. Emery Hamlin, another uncle, was angered at even being questioned about his nephew. "I don't want to have anything to do with them. Louie disgraced the family and I shut him right out."

Almost overnight Mary Hamlin had lost her family. First Louie went to jail; then her husband. Lisa was quickly removed from the house and placed in a local home for girls. John Hamlin, in a foster home for his delinquent behavior at the time of the killing, was subsequently admitted to Brattleboro Retreat in the southeastern part of the state. As a psychiatrist noted, he was suffering from "depression and suicidal ideation. John is apparently quite guilty about Louis."

Mary Hamlin continues to hope that everything will be all right, her life buttressed by seeing a psychiatrist and recommitting herself to religion, to the faith that has guided her through her travail. She has lost most of her excess weight and has become a firmer person, which surprises those who remembered her as "wishy-washy" and defenseless. There is now an earnestness about her. One cold winter day in 1983 she stood on the front porch of her home, a worn cardigan sweater her only protection, looking down the street banked by snow. "I really enjoy the changing of the seasons," she exclaimed almost wistfully. "It shows that there is renovation in the world." In her folded arms she carried a paperback book for "born-again Catholics."

"The neighborhood is different than it used to be. There are more people and," Mary adds without hesitation, "more crime." It doesn't bother her to talk about crime as she edges close to *the* crime. She has formed some very definite opinions on the subject. "Pornography is at the root of it," says Mrs. Hamlin. "There's too much of it, and it's too easy for the kids to get a hold of it. They should ban it. If adults quit making it, the world would be a better place."

She learned too late, Mary Hamlin continues, that kids need love *and* discipline. "I lost my two older boys because I didn't learn that." But she also complains that the government authorities did not help her out, that they failed to recognize Louie's problems and did not discipline him. "They just slapped him on the wrist and let him go. He was on parole and they weren't watching him, didn't make him go to counseling."

Nevertheless, she believes the agencies are too tough on parents who *are* disciplinarians. "The kids know exactly what the laws are. They tell their parents that they can't touch them—that they'll get in trouble for child abuse and will be taken away." She tells of a friend who had that happen to her. "She tried to spank her child and the state came in and took him away. So what's a parent to do?"

Butch Hamlin received a six-to-fifteen-year jail term and has asked to be enrolled in an experimental program for sex offenders. In a telephone interview from a state correctional center near the New Hampshire border, the senior Hamlin expressed bitterness about the treatment given him and his family by the press. "It's all a bunch of lies," he exclaimed, but would not comment further.

The Savage family has been no less affected by the crime. Rene Savage, Sr., hounded by the press about a son he rarely saw, temporarily moved out of the state, confused by the killing. "I was hurt," he told a reporter. "How do you feel when you find out your son's in for murder?" Jodie Savage, Jamie's eldest brother, left town to work on a farm elsewhere in the state. "I'm having my own life," he said. But he was soon back in Essex, working on another farm and joining the National Guard.

Rene Jr. felt the wrath that some townsfolk wished on his younger brother. A number of times after the killing of Melissa Walbridge, Rene was accosted on the street in the Old North End and had to fight to defend himself. He then left town "to make a new start," as he said, but was soon back on Church Street in downtown Burlington, hanging out on street corners and in Upton's electronic arcade, boasting to reporters that he could tell "some stories."

Rene would never get to make his new start; and the final story was one he would never be able to tell. In September of 1984, as if unable to escape the shadow of anger left by his brother, Rene Savage was murdered.

Bernie and Janet Lefebvre remain confused and disturbed. They are bewildered by the publicity suddenly thrust upon them and angry that they will not be left alone. As much as possible, they withdraw into their Gaines Court home and lock the door to strangers. Among friends, the name of Jamie rarely comes up.

Candy Hackett, the college student who had eluded Louie Hamlin's knife just five months before the Essex killing, reacted strongly to the news of his crime. "I was very upset. I was more than upset. I was emotionally out of control. Like, 'God! Why didn't they do something for that guy? Why did they let him go?' Why did it take a tragedy?"

Immediately after his arrest, Jamie was sent to the Waterbury State Hospital, where he spent most of his time watching television and listening to a stereo in the common room, mopping floors, and washing dishes. He was allowed visits only from his immediate family and lawyers. If what his brother Jodie recalled is correct, Jamie continued his storytelling. "He said he got a kick out of it when he was drunk," Jodie reported, "but after he was sober and everything, he realized what he had done."

Once his case was secretly adjudicated in juvenile court, Jamie was sent out of state for rehabilitation. To where, no one but the authorities knew for sure. The newspapers could say only that Savage was "reportedly" sent to Pennsylvania, "reportedly" transferred to Texas.

A little more than a year after Louie Hamlin's trial, his accomplice in rape and murder was eligible to be free. Jamie Savage turned eighteen on September 20, 1983, officially terminating his punishment, his rehabilitation, his service to the society he had harmed. It was rumored that he had agreed to stay on at the privately run Brown School in Austin, Texas, at state expense. But no Vermont juvenile authority or anyone at the Brown School would confirm that, or even acknowledge knowing a Jamie Savage.

Then, at the end of May 1984, there was a surprise. An Arizona newspaper ran a story titled, "You can rape, and you can kill, and then you can move to Arizona and change your name."

Jamie Savage had surfaced. It was the first confirmed report of the youth's whereabouts since his aborted appearance at Louie Hamlin's murder trial two years before. A few days later, the Burlington *Free Press*, in yet another front-page story about the case, gave the news to Vermonters: JAMIE SAVAGE CHANGES NAME IN ARIZONA.

According to Maricopa County Superior Court records, the youth had asked to have his name changed in December of 1983. Citing "poor family background," he had told the court, "I would like to get a new head start in life with a new name." He put a checkmark in the box of the petition form stating he had "not been convicted of a criminal proceeding amounting to a felony in a state court or federal court." He was not lying. Because of his age, his participation in Melissa Walbridge's killing was not a felony. And, in January of 1984, his name-change request was granted. Jamie Savage was gone. For his "new head start in life" he would be known as John W. Barber.

And so the search continued; now, for John Barber.

Journalist Michael Tulumello, who discovered the name-change records and wrote the May 1984 *New Times* story, was a month behind Savage/Barber. By the time the reporter arrived at the Mesa address Savage had given as his home, the teenager had moved.

"An employee at the apartment complex says the youth's parents (or perhaps social workers representing themselves as parents) moved back East, but is not aware if the youth moved with them," Tulumello recounted.

Vermont's Department of Social and Rehabilitation Services was no help in the search. A caseworker told Tulumello that the youth had "received extensive and intensive treatment at more than one facility," but would say no more. "Vermont officials steadfastly refused to discuss the case further," Tulumello said, "even sidestepping questions as to whether Savage is still being supervised."

With the recent rape-murder of a Tempe, Arizona, thirteen-year-old girl still unsolved, sidestepping was not what the reporter wanted to hear.

"Is James Savage—now John W. Barber—still in Arizona?" he concluded. "And if so, is he now on his own? Has he been rehabilitated to the extent that he no longer presents the dangers remembered so graphically in Vermont?

"Nobody in Arizona seems to know."

In September of 1984 I received a telephone call from Bill Richardson, a detective with the Mesa, Arizona, police department. "Would you have any idea where James Savage is?" he asked.

Richardson said he had been searching for Savage for six months. "If some ole lady gets butchered in the next town, I just want to know where this guy is," the detective explained. "And if he isn't in my town, I want to let the next city know where he is."

Richardson had discovered that Savage had lived in Mesa with a caseworker for Vermont's Social and Rehabilitative Services Department. Rent on the apartment had been paid by a local counseling center—which was reimbursed by the state of Vermont—until the arrangement was "terminated due to bad faith on Vermont's part," according to Richardson.

When Barber and his counselor/companion vacated their Mesa apartment, the detective found, they left a forwarding address: it was in St. Albans, Vermont.

It is doubtful that Jamie Savage will find his "new head start"—with Barber or any other name. In Burlington, a few people still talk quietly about seeking retribution should he ever return.

For Louie Hamlin, the calendar dictated a different fate. On July 15, 1982, he stood before a three-judge panel in the Woodstock courthouse to receive his prison sentence. He had already made a short speech asking the court and the room of three dozen spectators—who included Jim and Stephanie O'Rourke and Marie Walbridge—for leniency. He was sorry for what he did, he said, and claimed to have already changed his life for the better. "Three weeks ago," Louie continued in a clear but hesitant teenage voice, "I found Jesus. Now I'm a born-again Christian." The voice was not hollow, but the person uttering the words had already forfeited any claim to credibility.

The three judges gave Louie the most severe sentence handed to any convicted killer in Vermont since the state abolished its mandatory life sentence statute in 1978. He was sentenced to forty-five years to life for murder and fifteen to twenty-five years for sexual assault. Allowing for good behavior time,

Louie will be past fifty before he ever walks the streets again.

Louie was taken to the St. Albans Correctional Center, the state's closest approximation to a maximum security prison. His lawyers began an appeal, of both the conviction and the sentence, an automatic right in cases of criminal crimes.

At first, Hamlin's main goal—for someone who was a "kid killer"—was survival. Death threats from his fellow prisoners and harassment by guards had become his lot, and officials finally put him in isolation for his own protection. From the St. Albans Correctional Center he wrote his aunt Joyce Hoffman:

> I'm doing fine and am exercising. It's pretty boring up here and what's worse is that all the inmates want to kill me and I don't doubt that they will if they get a chance to. But I'm staying under protected custody until all of this is over. Tell little Ernie that it's not nice up here at all and to stay out of trouble and be good because this place is hell.

In September 1982, Judge Hayes ruled that the sentence was justified. In early November, Hamlin was secreted out of the state at 3:00 A.M. by prison officials who gave neither Hamlin nor his attorneys any warning. Stating that they did not have the facilities to guarantee his safety, he was flown to a federal penitentiary in Springfield, Missouri, to be processed into the federal prison system. After a month in Springfield, Hamlin was transferred to the Federal Correctional Institution in Oxford, Wisconsin.

Had Louie Hamlin, convicted child killer, really changed in prison? Did he now realize the gravity of his act? Was he repentant?

In a series of six telephone interviews from federal prisons in Missouri and Wisconsin, Hamlin opened the door on his private life a crack while refusing to talk about the events of May 15, 1981.

That Hamlin agreed to speak at all was surprising. His attorney, Chris Davis, repeatedly rejected requests to interview his client, explaining that he had advised Louie not to talk to the press about anything until the appeal process was complete. Deciding to circumvent Davis, I telephoned the federal penitentiary in Springfield in late November 1982, and asked about visiting privileges. The response was a curious one: Bureau of Prisons' policy allows "contact" interviews with inmates only by members of the press who work for newspapers, television or radio stations, or magazines. Authors do not qualify, said the prison spokesman, who added that "the inmate is free to make collect phone calls to anyone during the appropriate hours."

"Please ask Mr. Hamlin to call me collect." It was said without any hope that Hamlin would respond to a writer against the advice of his attorney.

But that night the telephone rang. A distant operator asked if I would accept a collect call from Louis (pronounced "Lewis") Hamlin. That was November 30, 1982. The phone rang again the next four evenings, and again on December 9th. The logistics of my conversations with Hamlin were hardly the most convenient: The long-distance connection was often plagued by static, and background noise from other prisoners was annoying. If Hamlin and I talked past ten o'clock, the line was disconnected by prison authorities. I could not call Hamlin directly; he had to call me.

Nevertheless, I had some five hours of interviews with Hamlin in which he spoke about everything from the sexual abuse he suffered at the hands of his father to his admission that he intended to rape Candy Hackett when he assaulted her on Super Bowl Sunday, four months before Melissa Walbridge's killing.

Then, as abruptly as they began, the telephone calls from Louie Hamlin ceased. In March of 1983 I wrote Hamlin at the Wisconsin penitentiary. A week later I received another collect call, the first in almost four months.

Hamlin explained the reason for the long silence. He had been speaking with some of the other inmates. "They tell me that I shouldn't be saying anything for nothing."

"Why is that?" I asked.

"Well," he began hesitantly, "I know one guy who was down at Springfield and he made some money off some paper in Boston for his story. And I was wonderin' if I could get a little somethin' myself."

I told Hamlin that it was "tricky." I was not sure whether the New York State law prohibiting such payments to prisoners was applicable in this case. (In fact, I doubted that New York would have any jurisdiction over a federal prisoner who had committed a crime in another state, but I didn't want to jeopardize my relationship with Hamlin at this point by telling him that, regardless of any law, I would not pay him anything.) I reaffirmed my desire to continue our interviews until the issue of money was resolved. Appealing to a law seemed to work. Hamlin now seemed less confident about his demand.

"Well, what you'll have to let me do is you'll have to let me get a hold of my lawyer first. I'll talk to Chris and get back to you then."

But if Louie consulted an attorney, it was most likely one in an adjacent cell. The day after our phone conversation, he wrote a letter that bore the traits of jailhouse lawyering. Hamlin was to the point, in language that was unsophisticated but aspired to be legal and formal. The page was topped by his full name, inmate number, and address, centered and underlined to approximate a letterhead. It was dated March 24, 1983, was single-spaced, had numerous spelling and grammatical errors, and was signed Louis A. Hamlin III.

The letter was typewritten. Louie seemed to have gained some rudimentary knowledge about the book publishing business, mentioning "up front" money and percentages on sales:

> Sir:
>   In answer to your question on March 23, 1983 I would say yes but for one minor problem. You see I am but a poor man and am in need of some financial help. . . . Now if you did make a contract lets say for about $4,000 up front and maybe 10% on the amount you get on the books well then I think you could get the information you want and maybe even a little more.

I wrote Hamlin immediately, explaining my refusal, concluding: "I guess I can be brief. The answer is no."

The same night that I mailed the letter Hamlin called, wanting to know if I had received his letter. After telling him what

I had just written, the teenager responded bluntly, "Well, I guess we ain't got nothin' to talk about then. Bye."

Louie Hamlin called once more, unexpectedly, in August 1983. He made no mention of his financial demands, but instead, it seemed, wanted simply to talk. He said he had been reading some detective magazines and it made him wonder how my book was doing. He was obviously curious about how he would appear on the printed page.

"A guy tried to kill me the other day," said Louie. His comment came without introduction. It was a departure from the usual flow of our conversations. I would normally have to lead the teenager to a topic, but tonight Hamlin was more voluble. He seemed to want to portray himself as the tough guy of his fantasies, the hero of his detective magazines. The dispute with the prisoner who tried to kill him, he said, involved "extortion." The other guy "was tryin' to shake me down for cigarettes, crap like that." When Louie balked, the man threatened to kill him, but it never resulted in a physical attack. "He backed down as soon as he found out I had a shank on me," Louie added nonchalantly.

Louie Hamlin remains an elusive individual. I asked him about his "rebirth" into Christianity, but it is hard to evaluate the sincerity of his response. The husband of a third cousin, a Christian, came to visit him in prison, Hamlin explained. "He came down to see me and talk with me and he asked me one night to accept the Lord and I did."

"And what's that like?" I asked. "What does that mean?"

"It's a little hard to describe, really. After I accepted the Lord, I felt a calmness. I was calm and peaceful."

"But how do you do it? How do you prepare for it?"

"All you do is just say, 'Lord, I repent for all my sins and I would like you to come into my life.' That's about it. All you have to do is be sincere."

"Did you think that doing that would make you feel better?"

"I don't know exactly why. I just left things up to the Lord. I do feel a lot better now than I used to."

"How's that?"

"Things just seem a little easier."

"Does that mean that you pray?"

"I don't pray as often as I should. I try to do it at least once a week, but sometimes more or sometimes less. Whenever a problem comes up I just pray. Like when they brought me here [to Springfield] and we went in the plane. That was the first time I'd been in a plane and I was scared at first because I'd never been in a plane before. And I said, 'Lord, I know you'll protect me and you'll see that I get there safely.' I just felt better after. Usually if I have a difficulty or I'm scared of something I just pray."

I wondered if his attitude toward prayer would shed some light on his feelings about his crime.

"Do you ever pray for the Walbridges?" I asked. "Or for the O'Rourkes?"

"Ya," he whispered.

"And how does that work?"

"I just pray that they wouldn't feel so much hatred and contempt for me or for my co-defendant. It ain't right. Not in front of the Lord. It shouldn't be there."

"What shouldn't be there?"

"The hate towards me. The contempt. I don't know if they were Christians, but I was told that they were religious people and then after they were telling the court that they agreed with the sentence that the state offered [life imprisonment], and that right there proves that they ain't as religious as they might profess."

"So you think that a religious person would forgive you?"

"I don't ask forgiveness from nobody. If the Lord forgives me that's all I care about. He forgives me for anything I've ever done. All I really want is for people to stop hating. All they got to do is try to work and help me. It's no sense in hating the person."

"Even for what you were convicted of doing?"

"Yup. There are people in prison who are in for a lot worse than what I am in for."

"Like what?"

"You got these mass murderers that go around cutting people up, things like that."

"What do you think the Walbridges or O'Rourkes could do to help you?"

"I don't really have nothing in mind. I just figure that if they really thought all this bad stuff about me, then they would try to see if there was anything they could do to help. Instead of hating like they are. I think the best thing would be to try to help the younger people, kids who have problems or something, before they go out and rob somebody or kill somebody or something. I've always helped myself and I'll continue to do it. But if there's anybody who really wants to help, all they got to do is help some other people. I'm not talking about the older people, I'm talking about teenagers."

Susan Craighead receives poems from Louie regularly, and was especially struck by one of them. "He is stuck behind those walls," she recounts, "and then he has a dream in which the walls fall away and he is free. One of my friends at school asked me to read *In the Belly of the Beast* [the best-selling book by prisoner Jack Abbott, who, after his release, killed a waiter in a Manhattan restaurant], and I was really struck by the similarity between Abbott's ideas and Louie's. Abbott is certainly more articulate, but Louie's ideas are very much the same in terms of dealing with captivity. It was definitely very frightening, considering what happened to Abbott when he got out."

It was Craighead who initiated the correspondence. "I wrote to him first. It took me a long time to compose the first letter because I didn't know exactly what to say. So I ended up just reminiscing about our trip to Boston and things like that. Then he wrote right back and I have been writing to him all along."

Louie's letters soon began to express his love for Susan. "He was sort of writing amorous things," she explains. "He sent me some love poems. I mean the allusions to me were very, very clear. When the only person in the world who cares about you is someone your age who's got blond hair and is running off to Princeton, you can just imagine that he had some confused feelings."

The day that Susan was leaving for Princeton, in the fall following the trial, Louie asked her to come visit him. "You can just imagine how I felt going off for my freshman year and I get this letter the morning right before we were leaving.

And it was about 'Oh, Susan, I love you, and you have got to tell me how you feel about me.' Well, I didn't say anything to my parents because I didn't think there was anything they could do.

"As soon as I got to school, I found some people who were working in a prison counseling service out of Princeton and talked to them about what I should say. Essentially, I wrote to him and I said that I feel that I am too young to discuss love with anyone. I'm sorry, but it sort of makes me feel uncomfortable. And the next letter he wrote back, 'Well, Susan, I'm sorry I made you feel uncomfortable. The matter is hereby forgotten,' and he went on with the rest of his letter. So far, it has been forgotten."

From prison Hamlin confided to Craighead the story of his childhood. That, combined with her remembrance of their friendship, has made the Princeton student doubt Hamlin's guilt. "According to his letters he was sexually abused since he was five. When you think about the anger that must build up in a person and where the outlet has to come, the killing makes more sense. I think maybe the poems he was writing then were his way of trying to resolve it. You can be angry, but you cannot kill. Maybe that is what happened in those woods. He got angry but did not kill. Emotionally, that is sort of how I feel about it."

From the beginning of their correspondence, Louie told Susan that he did not kill Melissa. "The first letter he wrote to me, he said, 'Before you judge me, Susan, I want you to know what happened to me when I was five years old.' And he told me. 'So I really know what that girl who is living feels right now.' He never said that he didn't rape anybody. But over and over again, he said, 'I didn't kill anyone.' He was adamant—and he still is adamant—about not being guilty."

Craighead admits that her belief that Hamlin did not do the actual killing may be splitting hairs, that it rests on no more than her belief that he could not do such a thing. It is a distinction that she maintains nevertheless. "I can't be quite so disloyal as to assume that he did it."

• • •

Hamlin apparently still holds his unique concept of honor. After the killing, reported a psychiatrist who interviewed him, Hamlin said that "he considers that the appropriate way for him to be handled now is for him to be released into the woods. There, the dead girl's father would be free to pursue him and, if he could, to kill him. He considers the matter something between the girl's father and himself."

Louie confided to the psychiatrist that he felt little guilt for his crime. "It just happened," said Louie. "He is sorry that it happened because he is in prison," the psychiatrist noted. "He only feels guilty about it if he talks; otherwise, he puts it out of his head. As he spoke about the issue of guilt, he became more emotionally involved and self-justified. 'I didn't really feel it was wrong. I am only in prison because it is the law. That's all. They have no right to prosecute me. Nobody has any right to put me away; they should mind their own business.'"

The psychiatrist concluded that Louie's conscience is so primitive that he "does not exhibit any embarrassment or guilt over breaking rules of society. . . . Both Hamlin's goals and his definition of what is 'right' seem to be based upon hedonism, that which is needed or desired by the subject. He does not think that he would hurt anybody in the future," noted the psychiatrist, "but admits that 'it could happen again.'"

Steve Galyean, Louie's boyhood friend, saw Louie in jail, as a fellow inmate at the St. Albans Correctional Facility, where Louie's father, Butch, was also incarcerated. "I used to sit by Louie's cell door and chat with him and stuff. Everybody else used to call him raper and shit like that, you know. I didn't care, you know. 'Cuz I know him and stuff."

In prison, according to Galyean, Louie wavered between bragging about the attack and denying the murder. "He used to talk about it, saying to people that he thought it was pretty decent and explain a coupla things," says Galyean. "That's why people would always give him a hard time. If he would've kept his mouth shut, people wouldn't a gave him a hard time as they did. But he used to sit there, 'Yeah, yeah, it was pretty decent,' and explain how he fucked the shit outta her and stuff like that. Another thing that really surprised me is it seemed like he never felt no guilt or nothin'. Like he was innocent all the way—like this never happened."

A psychiatrist who interviewed both Hamlin and Savage during the summer following the killing described Hamlin's lack of guilt.

This young man shares few of the common feelings of human beings. He is entirely selfish, sees himself as an isolated person, feels no qualms of conscience about any of his behavior, has an extremely unpredictable and destructive undercurrent of rage.

Diagnostically, he fits the category of a pathological personality, of the antisocial type.

The attack on Meghan O'Rourke and Melissa Walbridge was perpetrated in secret. The exact truth of what happened that day in the dark woods of Maple Street Park may never be known. But enough has been reconstructed to condemn both teenagers for a brutal crime beyond normal comprehension.

Little Melissa, in her insistence on maintaining the innocence of both childhood and her community, had said, "That wouldn't happen in Vermont." We know now that it can happen there, and apparently anywhere where the excesses of violent youth are either condoned or not understood.

CHAPTER 20

The Violent Juvenile Mind

OF ALL THE QUESTIONS asked in the aftermath of the killing of Melissa Walbridge, none seemed more important but less answerable than "Why?" The crime was without sense. When Louie Hamlin and Jamie Savage—themselves only a few years older than the children they attacked—were arrested, reason was pushed even farther into the shadows. How could such viciousness stalk the minds of those youths? What possible motive could they have had?

"People often describe such human cruelty as 'bestial,'" Dostoevski's Ivan Karamazov says to his younger brother Alyosha about soldiers who nailed their prisoners to fences by the ears, "but that's, of course, unfair to animals, for no beast could ever be as cruel as man, I mean as refinedly and artistically cruel. The tiger simply gnaws and tears his victim to pieces because that's all he knows. It would never occur to a tiger to nail people to fences by their ears, even if he were able to do it."

The young breed of killers upsets our image of childhood innocence, of how young people should act. How is it, one might ask, that children have risen from their cribs to nail people to fences by their ears?

The thousands of murders, rapes, robberies, and assaults committed by youngsters every year have raised the issue of juvenile delinquency from a question of thwarting adolescent pranks to that of saving lives. Increasingly, criminologists, sociologists, and psychiatrists want to know not just what makes young people tick, but what makes them kill.

"We have an idealized version of childhood," suggests Dr. Theodore Petti, a child psychiatrist at the University of Pittsburgh School of Medicine. "We find child murderers so disturbing because we can't possibly believe that children are so desperate that they would kill." Yet Jamie Savage and Louie Hamlin and thousands of other youngsters were indeed "so desperate." Did they grow up too fast? Or not fast enough? Or not at all?

There is still much to be learned about what happens to a human mind between the time that an infant is ushered into the world, defenseless, screaming, and crying, and the time— often so few years later—that he rapes, tortures, robs, or kills.

Despite the gaps in knowledge about the making of a murderous mind, one thing seems certain at the outset: By the time a teenager like Jamie Savage or Louie Hamlin picks up a knife or a gun and kills, the chances are that he is already well versed in the ways of violence. More than likely, he has a supporting history of aggression and antisocial behavior in the neighborhood, at school, and is a participant in a chaotic life at home. Parents, neighbors, friends, teachers, or police have already had a taste of his tantrums and arguments, petty thefts, school truancies, runaways, assaults, and vandalisms.

Despite the fictional image of the good-boy-turned-violent, there are very few sudden metamorphoses, few altar boys who overnight are transformed into monsters. Murder has roots, and they stretch deep into violent soil. By the time a Louie Hamlin or Jamie Savage kills, though barely pubescent, his mind is already woven into an intricate pattern of deviance.

New York University psychiatrist Dorothy Otnow-Lewis believes that a careful observer can begin to notice the differences between delinquent and nondelinquent children emerging "before the age of four." In one of her studies of pre-teenage children in a psychiatric institution, Dr. Otnow-Lewis discovered that almost half of her fifty-five subjects were "homicidally aggressive":

• A ten-year-old "tried to stab brother 3 or 4 times with knife and fork";

• A nine-year-old "threatened to kill mother; threatened brother with butcher's knife twice; threatened to poke out teacher's eyes; hit teacher with rubber bat";

• Another nine-year-old "tried to immolate a classmate; tried to hit another boy over head with heavy equipment; threatens brothers with screwdrivers; hides knives under bed; tried to break teacher's glasses and pulled hair from her head; wanted to hurt father with knives; set fire to house."

As a young child Louie Hamlin displayed the kind of uncontrolled behavior that often leads to more serious deviance. "When Louie was only two," his aunt would recall, "he would throw himself on the floor, hit his head on the wall. Whenever he was in bed he would rock back and forth all the time. He completely destroyed a crib."

"He'd get angry and destroy things in his room, things that were his," Mary Hamlin remembered. "He's taken his bed apart many times."

At the Oregon Social Learning Center in Eugene, Gerald Patterson works directly with problem children in their homes, meticulously monitoring what he calls their "rotten behavior." One thing the Oregon therapists have discovered, reported Harvard professor James Q. Wilson, is that troublesome kids are *chronically* troublesome. Six-year-old Don held the "record."

"Nearly four times a *minute* while in his home," Wilson recounted, "Don would whine, yell, disobey, hit, or shove.

"When he was not at home, telephone calls from teachers and merchants would mark his progress through the neighborhood. 'He left school two hours early, stole candy from a store, and appropriated a toy from a neighborhood child.'" Persistent aggression like Don's is not an uncommon story in the biographies of youthful killers, says Wilson.

Whether one starts with a violent adult or a violent adolescent, there is usually a trail of antisocial behavior leading back to childhood. Innumerable studies have shown both the early origins and the stubbornness of such traits:

• Half of the delinquent boys in Sheldon and Eleanor Glueck's classic 1940s study had committed their first crime at the age of eight.

• Some 20 percent of the adult sexual offenders that clinical psychologist Nicholas Groth studied in Connecticut had a history of juvenile sexual assault, and, Groth observed, "an even larger number [almost three-quarters of the cases] admitted to having committed a sexual assault in their early teenage years for which they were never apprehended."

Such continuity often skews crime statistics. A small group of "hard core" criminals commit a disproportionate amount of crime. It is a career that often begins at puberty or before. A Rand Corporation study of forty-nine adult armed robbers discovered that not only had these men committed their first serious crime at an early age—the average age was fourteen—but that they claimed responsibility for more than 10,500 crimes over a twenty-year period, an average of more than 10 crimes a year per person.

Jamie Savage and Louie Hamlin were apprentices in violence from an early age. By the time they wandered into Maple Street Park on May 15, 1981, they already had impressive resumés of delinquent and violent credentials. Hamlin frequently attacked his older brother and admitted that he had

broken into thirty homes and stolen some one hundred cars in
the five years after his eleventh birthday. Savage was a chronic
thief from boyhood on; he often slapped his younger brothers
and sister and threatened his siblings and friends with knives.
Together they had slaughtered dozens of animals.

Dr. William Woodruff, a Vermont psychiatrist who interviewed both teenagers, believes that such brutality develops in
stages. "Getting pleasure in causing pain to others is a peculiar
personal idiosyncracy that isn't achieved overnight. It is a process. You get there by pulling the wings off flies, then getting
back at people by causing pain to them. I thought it was of
some significance that they went around shooting squirrels.
They obviously enjoyed hurting things, both of them. It is a
crescendo of activity that builds."

To those who knew them, Hamlin and Savage did not seem
to be all bad, all the time. As Mary Hamlin said of her son,
"He had a dual personality. There was a lot of good in Louie.
People don't know that part of him." Like most violent juvenile
criminals, Hamlin and Savage did not kill or rape or rob every
day. They had in the past chosen other things to do. Like other
youngsters, they went roller-skating, bought presents for their
siblings, paid back debts. Why, then, did they go to Maple
Street Park and attack two little girls while others their age
went roller-skating that day?

"What is it which leads to the development in some individuals of kindness, tolerance, and a capacity to retain these
attitudes despite adverse circumstances," asks British psychiatrist Arthur Hyatt Williams, "and in other individuals the opposite process seems to take place so that every adversity
increases their sense of aggrievedness, resentment, and wish
for revenge?"

The question is more difficult to answer the younger the
person is. Almost by definition, children enjoy a certain presumption of innocence about their lives. Adults who murder
are generally classified as either immoral—they knowingly
chose to kill—or insane. But children who murder are not as
easily classified. From both the layman's and professional's
perspective, these young killers call attention to themselves in
much the same way as the mentally disturbed. Ostensibly, they

are not yet sufficiently developed to appreciate the gravity and consequences of their act.

That was how Vermont psychiatrist Barry Nurcombe described sixteen-year-old Louie Hamlin. Nurcombe interviewed Hamlin on a number of occasions after the murder of Melissa Walbridge and concluded that "he is amoral rather than immoral, a-responsible rather than irresponsible. In other words, I conclude that he has never acquired the preliminary social relationship and conventions imposed by society, rather than knowingly rebelling against them."

Some researchers believe that the difference between violent juveniles and other youths lies in the existence of brain damage or psychosis. Though Hamlin was not diagnosed as psychotic, there are indications that many aggressive and violent youth are, in a clinical sense, disturbed. When Dr. Otnow-Lewis established a juvenile court psychiatric clinic in New Haven, Connecticut, in the early 1970s, she was surprised to find that of the first forty delinquents she saw, ten of them had symptoms of psychosis.

"One child attempted to throw a sibling out the window in response to a hallucinated voice," she recalled. "Another heard the voice of a dead friend and followed it to the roof of a building; and several children felt continually under attack by imagined people or forces and felt the need to carry weapons ranging from razors to .22 caliber guns."

Violent crimes committed by juveniles are perhaps most similar to what in an adult would be called a "crime of passion." Their acts are impulsive, representing a complete victory of emotion over reason. As Barry Nurcombe described Louie Hamlin, the assault against the two little girls took place "in an emotional setting of smoldering rage." This, in conjunction with a failure to contain the rage, led to the killing.

In 1946 Fritz Redl and David Wineman, authors of *Children Who Hate*, established a group therapy home in Detroit and they found that their subjects—who were only eight, nine, and ten years old—had the same persistent lack of emotional control. Nine-year-old Andy, for instance, "released all of his hostility against his siblings. At times he was sadistic and tried to burn them with a woodburning set. His jealousy was chronic and on every possible occasion he tried to inflict injury upon them in whatever way possible."

Since then, there have been few changes in the research results, except for the increased severity of the offenses. Paul Strasburg, conducting a recent study for the Vera Institute of Justice in New York City, found that violent juveniles lived in an isolated world of internal emotional conflict—one that was resolved only with an emotional outburst.

In the end, violent juveniles, rather than resembling adults, are, in fact, kids with an unredeeming twist. They differ from their nonviolent, nondelinquent contemporaries not so much in the way in which their mind operates but in the violent manner in which it expresses itself. "The impulsive, dangerous act," Dr. Otnow-Lewis says of homicidal children, "seemed to precede the thought and then require some post-event rationale to explain the behavior."

Testing the limits of authority has long been the hallmark of adolescence, the source of great conflict as well as a force for creativity and change. America was tamed by youth. The average age of the immigrant settling Vermont was just nineteen, and he usually came accompanied by a seventeen-year-old wife. At age nineteen Galileo discovered the principle of the isochronism of the pendulum. Jean-Jacques Rousseau became a vagabond at the age of sixteen. Bob Dylan, who left home as a young teenager, ushered in an era of youthful rebellion that would become a celebration of a "youth culture," with, as James Q. Wilson of Harvard has said, "it's attendant emphasis on unfettered self-expression."

Adolescence has always been a time of exuberance, testing of authority, and carelessness. In 1829, William Cobbett reminisced about his youth:

> Every man, and especially every Englishman, . . . will recollect how many mad pranks he has played; how many wild and ridiculous things he has said and done between the age of sixteen and that of twenty-two.

• • •

The difference between the last quarter of the twentieth century and that period is that the "mad prank" now involves death and disfigurement. The FBI reported that in 1982 the rate of homicides for Americans was 9.8 for every 100,000, while the homicide rate among seventeen-year-olds was 22.6, more than double the rate for all ages. It is as if adolescents have abandoned nothing of their wildness, only added murder to the list of pranks.

When the judge presiding over Louie Hamlin's simple assault case asked Louie what made him so angry, he shrugged. "I don't know. It's just events that lead up to things. Just things in my everyday life. I just get mad."

The normal mind, already repelled by the cruel act, reels at the thought that adolescence could have taken such a turn. Homicide committed by children, said *The New York Times*, is "one of the most perplexing of all crimes."

There are dark corners and sinister impulses lurking in everyone's mind, but in the case of the youthful criminal, he has acted it out. Sociologist Howard Becker observes that "there is no reason to assume that only those who finally commit a deviant act usually have the impulse to do so. It is much more likely that most people experience deviant impulses frequently. At least in fantasy, people are much more deviant than they appear."

Dr. Otnow-Lewis, in a study of delinquent youths, found that two groups of subjects, the Less Violent and More Violent, had almost the same overall intelligence test scores, but that the more violent ones scored "markedly" lower on verbal sections of the test. The more violent the children, she observed, the more difficulty they had in putting their thoughts and feelings into words.

The researchers concluded that their subjects lacked one of the fundamental traits of normal children, the ability to fantasize. "At times it was as though the magical thinking of childhood, the cognitive stage in which a thought is said to seem tantamount to an action, has been reversed," they explained.

Such "magical thinking," fantasizing, daydreaming, ruminating, though often dismissed as "childish" or a waste of time, frequently appears missing in violent juveniles. It is thought to be one factor that prevents angry impulses from becoming aggressive action.

In addition to a lack of verbal skills, these violent adolescents also seem to lack what English analyst Arthur Williams calls an "intrapsychic braking mechanism," which would ordinarily contain "violent and criminal impulses."

Behavioral scientists claim to have found evidence of this braking mechanism, and have advanced theories about why some children seem to learn how to "behave" better, and quicker, than others. A number of studies indicate that psychopaths and criminals are limited in their ability to inhibit aggression because of "defective avoidance learning" systems. Sarnoff A. Mednick, a professor of psychology at the University of Southern California, believes it may be a result of a poorly functioning autonomic nervous system—the control center for such automatic bodily functions as heartbeat. This prevents certain individuals from learning the "anticipatory fear" necessary to inhibit their violent behavior.

Children are introduced to the moral process, says Mednick, by parents or other adult authorities, through punishment and reward. The child then learns to fear the consequences of his contemplated act *before* committing it. Then, as a result of the "anticipatory fear" of punishment, the child decides not to commit the act. His fear is reduced and the inhibition receives a positive reinforcement. However, if the system recovers slowly from the fear, there will be little if any reinforcement. "The slower the recovery, the more serious and repetitive the asocial behavior predicted."

Behaviorists see the problem as one of a quasi-biological system of failed "feedback," while more "dynamic" oriented psychologists and psychiatrists speak about such things as the violent juvenile's failure to "internalize" values, the "voice within" which doesn't speak, a "primitive" sense of morality, the inability to "empathize" with others, the "pauperized" ego or "sick" conscience.

Although most psychologists, including Jean Piaget, the

famous Swiss explorer of the mind of the child, doubt that children much below the age of seven are capable of empathizing with others to the degree required for truly ethical behavior, the capacity for such bonding is there from the very beginning. However, it takes time and the right environment in which to blossom.

Vermont psychiatrist Woodruff notes that, for whatever reason, the ability to empathize exists in some persons from a very early age and is absent in others. "You will see children playing together and one gets hurt," he explains. "One of them will laugh uproariously. Another will go over, even as a tiny child, and clasp that child and act tenderly toward him. Another kid will get away from the situation and ignore it, incapable of understanding that the kid is hurt. This kind of kid doesn't seem to have the capacity for appreciating pain in others. That is true of Hamlin. He doesn't understand that other people hurt."

It is that failure to understand other people's pain, according to Woodruff, that lies at the bottom of a person's capacity to inflict pain on others. Louie Hamlin himself explained it best when asked why he fought with his schoolmates. "I did it so that somebody else could be hurting like I do."

Somewhere along the way the violent child failed to acquire the ability to control his impulses, to feel guilty about his actions, feel empathy toward others. Somehow he acquired the anger and rage and desperation sufficient to rape and kill. But how? From where? And why at twelve or fourteen years of age instead of twenty or twenty-two? And if the persistence of this violent, aggressive behavior is so obvious, why is it so resistant to change?

Theories about what causes this aggression in a child, and why it persists, have been almost as numerous as the cases of juvenile violence. They have ranged from extreme "naturists" to extreme "nurturists," from the genetic to the aesthetic, from "bad blood" to "bad neighborhoods," from the constitutional to the institutional, junk food diets to brain dysfunctions to chemical disorders.

The environmental explanation has been the most prevalent

in the last forty years. It has focused on the failure of warm, loving, bonding relationships, particularly in the immediate family. "If nobody in the world has ever indicated to you that you are cared for or, in fact, if they have indicated to you that you were worthless, then it's inconceivable that a conscience would develop," says Dr. Nurcombe. "Because a conscience depends on seeing other people as worthy of emulating, identifying with, of pleasing, of being praised by. If no one feels empathy for you, how do you develop empathy for others?"

Sociologist Travis Hirschi, in his study of several thousand high school students in California, championed the importance of this early bonding. Hirschi believes that it is in forming a "bond" to society—to parents, friends, goals, aspirations, school—that we become nondelinquent. The stronger that bond, the more likely we are to conform; the weaker the bond, the more likely we are to act on our antisocial impulses.

From the psychiatric viewpoint, the failure to form strong bonds with people and the harboring of intense rage is a volatile combination. Dr. Nurcombe believed it no coincidence that Louie Hamlin's knife assault on Candy Hackett and the attack on Melissa Walbridge and Meghan O'Rourke were both preceded by arguments with his mother.

Calling Hamlin "a moral imbecile," Nurcombe adds that Hamlin's "stunted moral development is a consequence of his having been raised in a family with chaotic child-rearing patterns, corrupt and brutalized patterns of sexuality, little affection, and little capacity to appreciate the depth of his alienation and distance."

Adult abuse of children, both physical and sexual, may be a prime factor in the creation of later juvenile violence. "Juvenile crime results from a combination of our society generally becoming more violent and a rise in family breakdown," says Alfred Regnery, director of the U.S. Office of Juvenile Justice and Delinquency Prevention. "Many of these kids are inner city kids and are probably from welfare mothers with no father around. There is often a series of boyfriends or men in the house to whom the children really mean nothing. So the children are often abused. In probably 80 percent of the cases you will find that the violent juveniles were abused as children."

The most emotionally damaging form of assault against children is sexual abuse, a trauma many believe is closely tied to violence by the victimized juvenile. These victims often suffer from a stress disorder similar to that which can afflict war veterans. "They have severe nightmares and become hysterical in situations that remind them of the molestation—changing at bedtime, for instance, or taking a bath," reports writer Katie Leishman.

In New York State in 1982, 3,887 cases of child sexual abuse were reported. In the borough of the Bronx, New York City, there were 134 cases reported in the first six months of 1983. In Westchester County, New York, the Domestic Violence Prosecution unit screens some 200 reports of child abuse each month and 40 of those reports involve sexual abuse; 60 percent of the sexually abused children are under the age of twelve.

Many believe that television is another prime villain, as a model of violence that juveniles act out. Modern television programming has made innocence seem obsolete, even to an eight-year-old mind. Increasingly, it offers sex and violence, beautiful women, fast cars, wealth, and greed.

According to Drs. Linda and Robert Lichter's study for the Media Institute, just six weeks of "prime-time" television programming in 1981 showed 250 criminals committing 417 crimes, an average of 1.7 per show. Every fourth crime committed was a murder, an average of one killing every two and one half programs. Young television viewers may not be aware of it, but that is not reality—at least not yet. Television crime is over a hundred times more likely to involve murder than real-life crime.

U.S. Surgeon General Everett C. Koop cites a 1981 report by the California Commission on Crime Control and Violence Prevention. "I don't know how many times the government has to come out with yet another study of television violence to make the point that it is harmful to children. Children spend at least two hours and a half in front of a TV set each day; many of today's high school graduates will have spent more of their lives in front of a TV set than in the classroom; by the age of eighteen a young person could have witnessed over 18,000 murders on television."

There is no doubt, according to Koop, as to the causal relationship between media violence and juvenile crime. "We begin to believe that violence is a socially acceptable and credible way of responding to frustration or insult or some other direct, personal hurt," he says. "Children especially become 'desensitized' to violent interpersonal conflict and, when seeing another child being hurt, will tend not to do the thing that civilization requires be done—step in and protect the victim. Instead, they will watch, as if this too were dramatized entertainment." It is telling that little Meghan O'Rourke, awakening to the bloody scene in which she was stabbed and raped and her friend murdered, at first thought she was "watching TV."

Historically, criminal behavior was explained with idiosyncratic, sometimes fanciful, theories. Late nineteenth-century explanations were dominated by the pseudo-genetic theories of an Italian psychiatrist and professor of legal medicine, Cesare Lombroso, who believed that the criminal represented a reversion to a more primitive period of human development and could be recognized predominantly by his physical characteristics.

Arthur MacDonald, an employee of the U.S. Bureau of Education, was the most vigorous Lombrosian advocate in the United States. In 1890, he offered this description of "children who seem to be vicious by nature" to the U.S. Congress:

> There is a certain animality in the face, the eyes are without expression, the forehead is low or depressed, the jaws are very large, the edges of the ears are rough, the ears extend out prominently from the head.

"Craniology" was taken so far by some of its adherents that they believed the only remedy was to operate on delinquent children in order to change the shape of their head, jaws, and palates.

At the time, others believed that social and moral attitudes were also inherited. "What right have we today to allow men and women who are diseased and vicious to reproduce their kind, and bring into the world beings whose existence must be one long misery to themselves and others?" asked a nineteenth-century observer. Such deterministic beliefs have by now been mainly relegated to the closets of moral prejudice.

However, biological and chemical explanations for criminal behavior have continued to enjoy the serious interest of scientists, one that is growing. Twenty years ago Sheldon Glueck prophesied that "it is possible that the causes of emotional malaise—whether such illness rests in delinquency or not—will ultimately be traced to disturbances of bodily chemical function and that cures will come not from the psychoanalytical couch but from the physical and chemical laboratories."

The failure to prove conclusive causal links between violence and poverty, social class, and peer association has stimulated the increased interest in biological theories. But the closer one looks at violent youth, the dimmer are the hopes for any single, bold explanation.

Dr. Otnow-Lewis, who discovered physiological abnormalities in violent youths that did not appear in less violent ones, developed a violence rating system ranging from One to Four, Nonviolent to Most Violent. In her study of 97 incarcerated delinquents in Connecticut, she rated only eight of them as One. Eleven of the boys were rated Two, having "some indication of a potential for violence (e.g., isolated episodes of fire setting, isolated episodes of threatening with unloaded weapons)."

Most of the boys, 55 of the 97, were given a Three rating because they had actually committed such serious offenses as murder, rape, multiple arsons, armed robberies, and assaults. Finally, 23 of the boys, almost one-fourth of the total, were rated Four because they had committed "extraordinarily brutal acts." For example, says Dr. Otnow-Lewis, one boy stomped on his victim's face, while another raped and beat one woman and raped and stabbed another.

She discovered significant differences between the boys given ratings of One and Two and those given ratings of Three and Four. She found the violent boys were more likely to be "loose, rambling, and illogical in their thought processes" and were more likely to show signs of "paranoid ideations and of major and minor neurological dysfunction." Significantly, there was a high prevalence of brain damage—electroencephalogram abnormalities—among the more violent juveniles. They had "extreme difficulty remembering even four digits backward," and often could not master the rudimentary skill of skipping, a sign of impaired motor and coordination controls. The more violent youths were much more likely to have suffered some physical injury to the head or face as infants than were the less violent. Most of the violent children—some 75 percent of them—but only a third of the less violent ones had been physically abused while they were growing up.

Jonathan Pincus, professor of neurology at Yale University, believes that the typical violent young person exhibits three basic symptoms: (1) a pervasive view of the world as an unfriendly place, what some label "paranoia"; (2) the experience of having been physically or sexually abused as a child; and (3) neurological abnormality.

About half the more violent delinquents he studied with Dr. Otnow-Lewis had all three symptoms; none of the less violent youngsters had all three. In fact, about half of the latter children had none of the three factors. In contrast, all of the violent children had at least one of the factors.

Pincus believes an argument could be made that brain damage alone is a major factor in youthful criminality. He cites a follow-up study of children who were diagnosed as having "attention deficit disorder," a modern term for minimal brain damage. The author of the study compared 110 of these youngsters with 88 children without behavior disorders and found that almost 30 percent of the brain-damaged children had become seriously delinquent, as against only a small percentage of the others.

Some researchers believe that a poor diet, particularly the teenage addiction to soda pop, can contribute to violent behavior in youngsters. Alexander Schauss, director of the American Institute for Biosocial Research, claims to have amassed evidence that suggests that "diet, toxic metals, food additives, insufficient nutrients, food allergy, and lack of exercise can all contribute to criminal behavior." Schauss explains, for example, that the average teenager in the United States consumes over 800 cans of soda a year, "soft" drinks that contain large amounts of phosphoric acid as a buffering agent.

In chronic delinquents whom he has studied, Schauss found that the average soda pop consumption was 1500 cans a year. "Veterinarians seem to know more than child psychologists," he remarks pointedly. "They have known for years that violent, uncontrollable rogue horses can sometimes have too much phosphorus and too little magnesium, and they give them magnesium salt to stop the violent behavior."

Various studies have linked malnutrition, hypoglycemia, deficits of vitamin B6, niacinamide, and ascorbic acid and other chemical imbalances in the body to hyperactivity and aggressive behavior. Research has also demonstrated the link between biochemical disturbances and such neurological and psychiatric disorders as Parkinson's disease, depression, schizophrenia, child autism, and the hyperkinetic syndrome.

The genes, too, have increasingly been implicated as a cause of violent juvenile behavior. Professor Mednick at USC has conducted studies of adopted children in Copenhagen, where the children had little or no contact with their natural parents after birth. Despite their upbringing by "normal" families, he found a higher than normal incidence of criminality in adopted children whose natural fathers had criminal records.

Some crimes are so bereft of logical explanation that "bad" genes seem to offer the only answer. In a fashionable Miami, Florida, neighborhood, in 1983, an adopted twelve-year-old boy who "had everything in the world" shot and killed his nine-year-old brother and his mother, saying he didn't want to be "bothered anymore." Both parents were young professionals: the father a management consultant, and the mother a realtor who was active in community affairs. They were described by all who knew the family as being caring and loving parents.

They had adopted both their sons as infants and despite the affection lavished on the twelve-year-old, he was always a troublemaker. "They gave him everything they could give him," recalled an uncle. "But he was just a chronic bad kid. Ever since he was a little boy, he would walk up, shake your hand,

and punch you in the belly. He was just becoming more and more incorrigible."

Despite the persuasiveness of the biological argument, most researchers have forsworn simple explanations about the workings of the juvenile mind. Instead they view the cause of youthful violence as the interaction between "nature" and "nurture"—the result of a continuous combination of influences, large and small, extreme and banal, psychological, biological, and genetic.

Dr. Otnow-Lewis is one of the leading proponents of the new eclecticism that unites biology and psychology. The violent young person, she says, is created by an "amalgam" of psychological stress, biological disorders, and "adverse social and intrafamilial conditions" that combine to "create the kind of serious, often violent, delinquent child feared by our society today." Researchers now speak more often about "vulnerabilities" and "predispositions" to suggest that there are a myriad of ways in which the worlds of nature and nurture interact in a particular child.

Evidence also exists that "outside" factors—including behavior itself—actually influence the biological and biochemical balance after birth. Levels of serotonin, for example, the chemical neurotransmitter in the brain that has been associated with aggression, are not "fixed" by genetic makeup. Studies have found that such controllable environmental factors as diet and social deprivation will affect the amounts of serotonin found in the body and have as much to do with the chemical imbalance as the genes.

In a Connecticut study, Dr. Otnow-Lewis found that the juvenile mind is largely a family mind. One would think that violent children are created by broken homes, but she learned that there were no major differences in the family structure of the Less and More Violent groups of children. Surprisingly, broken homes, divorces, one-parent families, stepfathers, live-in boyfriends were evenly divided among both groups. What did matter was the *quality* of that family environment, broken or otherwise. The amount of violence that took place in the home was the factor that made the difference.

In a later study, Otnow-Lewis discovered that many of the
violent children had watched viciousness in their own homes
that matched anything they could have seen on television. In
62 percent of the households of psychologically disturbed children who were homicidal, the fathers had been physically violent to the mothers, compared with only 13 percent of the
households of disturbed, but nonhomicidal, children. She and
her colleagues reported that 37 percent of the fathers of homicidal children had themselves been homicidal, as against 13
percent of the fathers of nonhomicidal children.

Among the former, two fathers were in jail for manslaughter,
one was wanted for murder, one had been deported from the
United States for stabbing a man, one had attempted to drown
his son, one threw his infant daughter against a crib, and one
was charged with assault after beating his wife so severely that
she was hospitalized for two weeks.

"The degree of violence witnessed by these children went
beyond mere fist fights," Otnow-Lewis has observed. "Several
children witnessed their fathers, stepfathers, or mothers' boyfriends slash their mothers with knives. They saw their siblings
being tortured with cigarette butts, chained to beds, and thrown
into walls. They saw their relatives—male and female—arm
themselves with guns, knives, and other sharp instruments and,
at times, use these weapons against each other. Some children
ran away from home at the approach of certain relatives, while
many reported defending their mothers with pipes and sticks
while their mothers were being attacked."

When these children were not watching their families batter
each other, they were experiencing it directly. Child abuse was
almost endemic in the more violent children's histories. A majority of the violent boys—some 75 percent—but only a third
of the less violent ones had been abused by their guardians.
"The degree of abuse to which they were subjected was often
extraordinary," Otnow-Lewis reported. "One parent broke her
son's legs with a broom; another broke a son's fingers and his
sister's arm; another chained and burned his son; and yet another threw his son downstairs, injuring his head, following
which the boy developed epilepsy."

Many violent fathers compound the damage, says Otnow-

Lewis, by marrying women with poor psychiatric histories. These often alcoholic, often criminal fathers gravitated toward "seriously disturbed women" who had been in psychiatric hospitals or drug and alcohol abuse treatment centers. If not themselves abusive, these women were usually incapable of controlling or deterring their husbands' violence. "A not uncommon family history of delinquents is that of a physically abusive father who after several years abandons the household, leaving the already battered children to the care of a distraught, emotionally disturbed, inadequate mother."

Violence among juveniles seems more understandable when one traces the pathology and abuse in their background. Whether carried mysteriously through the genes, or subtly through emotional starvation, or bluntly through the fist of a raging parent, violence is undoubtedly transmitted.

Still, it is a twisting, complicated path from a fragile, crying baby to a rapist and killer. The violent juvenile mind is a subtle and complex constellation of vulnerabilities. Though it is not yet fully understood, its virulence has destroyed our notions of childhood innocence and with it the sense that the young are meant to celebrate life, not destroy it.

Louie Hamlin and Jamie Savage changed that equation for the people of Vermont, perhaps for all time.

CHAPTER 21

The Injustice of Juvenile Justice

FOR YEARS, JAMIE SAVAGE and Louie Hamlin waltzed through life without having to account for their chronic thievery, lying, and violence. They learned that in the modern legal system antisocial acts of the young are seldom punished, that "justice" has no sting. As delinquents, their petty crimes were overlooked. But when they finally committed an act that horrified their fellow citizens, it was too late for meaningful rehabilitation. The question that Savage and Hamlin left all Americans to argue was whether anyone is served by our present system of juvenile justice.

Even when Louie Hamlin was finally arraigned in adult court for holding a knife to a girl's throat, his juvenile record was not considered in the proceedings. Now, if Jamie Savage commits another crime, he too will be a "first offender" in the eyes of the law. Even with the blood of Melissa Walbridge on his hands, Savage has never been a "criminal," only a "delinquent." After being detained less than three years for rape and murder, Jamie Savage has learned that society values the life of victims cheaply.

No one would claim that the life of a twelve-year-old girl has no value, yet Louie Hamlin and Jamie Savage are proto-typical examples of the "hell of good intentions" that now characterizes American juvenile justice. It is a code meant to prevent the violent criminality that Hamlin and Savage typify—a system intended to stop or rehabilitate them while they are still adolescents. Instead, throughout the United States, juvenile justice is burdened with failed ideals and faulty performance.

In most states, laws have sanitized the legal code as it applies to juveniles. No distinction is made between the types of un-lawful acts committed; there are no juries and no public records of the hearings. Juveniles found guilty of a criminal act are not criminals; they are "delinquents." They are "treated," not "pun-ished." They are sent to "foster homes" and wilderness "camps" and training and reform "schools," not to prisons.

The Vermont juvenile code, for example, is defined as a way of protecting the young offender. Its purpose is "to remove from children committing delinquent acts the taint of crimi-nality and the consequences of criminal behavior and to provide a program of treatment, training, and rehabilitation consistent with the protection of the public interest."

The process by which good intentions produce disastrous results was illustrated in an article entitled "Death of a Training School," by J. Thomas Mullen and Sidney Zirin, two admin-istrators in the New York State Division for Youth. In the early 1970s, New York State, responding to theories decrying im-prisonment for youth, started dismantling its twelve juvenile detention centers, euphemistically referred to as "training schools."

Some were closed immediately and their populations trans-ferred to foster homes, forest camps, and small urban and rural residential programs. With the removal of minor offenders such as truants and runaways, the remaining training schools became institutions solely for delinquents. The rules were then changed drastically to reflect new attitudes toward youthful crime. Cor-poral punishment was banned, and limits were placed on the administration of medication for control purposes. "Children's rights" standards were established and enforced. Ombudsman programs were instituted to hear the detainee's grievances.

After a few hours of schooling, the delinquents spent a typical day watching television, eating, and doing a few minimal chores around the grounds. Occasionally, trips were taken off campus to a nearby park where the boys were allowed to do whatever they chose. The most serious form of disciplinary action was to take away a boy's off-campus and home-visit privileges.

It all seemed civilized, enlightened, even reasonable. As Mullen and Zirin point out, "few would disagree with these changes." The problem was that in trying to make life better for the juvenile delinquents, the training schools relinquished their authority over their charges. "Because structure, order, and discipline were confused with abuse," they wrote, "the control function of the training schools . . . was diminished."

Despite the fact that these delinquents had been sent to the training schools *because* of their undisciplined behavior, absence of discipline became the reformed institutions' hallmark. The results were predictable: The juveniles tore the places apart. "The office and maintenance staff practically barricaded themselves in their offices and shops for fear of theft and assault, while the cottages were double-locked to prevent unauthorized entry as well as runaways," reported Zirin and Mullen.

What happened in the New York training schools is a microcosmic picture of American juvenile justice at large. At its center is a judicial system so preoccupied with protecting young offenders that it has left them prey to their own poor impulses. Meanwhile, it has forced the rest of society to barricade its doors against out-of-control adolescents.

Although called a judicial system, the patchwork quilt of juvenile laws in the United States resembles the adult justice system in name only. In fact, it is defined by its opposition to the adult court. Its central assumptions are that all children are innocent by definition, that delinquency is one part of the process of growing up, and that young people should not be punished for crimes—only rehabilitated.

Juvenile justice has been more a laboratory for the social

sciences than a court of law dispensing justice. Children, traditionally offered a reprieve from complete accountability for their actions, have become the perfect subjects upon which to experiment. Modern psychology has implicated early relationships with parents in the delinquent equation; sociologists have talked about such things as the locomotive of poverty, the pressures of a crime culture, and the deleterious effects of television.

Adult courts have partly incorporated these concepts in their willing accommodation of the insanity defense. But juvenile courts have digested them whole, as if all young offenders brought before the bar were insane. It is not so much that children can "do no wrong." It is, rather, that they can do neither right nor wrong. As Dr. Nurcombe said of Louie Hamlin, it is not so much that they are immoral, but amoral. It is not that they are irresponsible, but rather not responsible.

Sheldon and Eleanor Glueck stated the thesis of modern juvenile jurisprudence best in their work *Delinquents in the Making:* "Such an attitude and such an insight may be summed up simply in the recognition that in the eyes of science there are no 'good boys' or 'bad boys,' but only children who need less help in growing up and those who need more."

The modern juvenile system began when the Pennsylvania Supreme Court incorporated the doctrine of *parens patriae* into the American legal structure in 1838. The landmark case in Pennsylvania involved a young girl, Mary Ann Crouse, whose mother had committed her to the Philadelphia House of Refuge as "incorrigible" and whose father wanted her released. When Mr. Crouse, who had not been informed of his daughter's committal, petitioned the court to release his daughter because she had not been granted the benefit of a trial on account of her age, the Pennsylvania trustees vetoed his appeal.

In rejecting the Crouse appeal, the court concluded that the Sixth Amendment right to "a speedy and public trial by an impartial jury" did not apply to minors. Children did not have the same rights as adults, said the court. When the state intervened in their lives, it was not as an impartial custodian of law but as a substitute parent. "May not the natural parents, when unequal to the task of education, or unworthy of it," asked the judges, "be superseded by the *parens patriae* or common guardian of the community?"

The Crouse decision established a precedent for arbitrary juvenile justice that has been its hallmark until the present day. By exempting children from constitutional guarantees in court, the decision not only introduced an opportunity for the abuse of children into the legal system, it also confused theory and reality.

The judges justified the imposition of *parens patriae* by citing the good work of the Philadelphia House of Refuge, where Mary Ann Crouse was sent. "The House of Refuge is not a prison, but a school," they wrote, "where reformation and not punishment is the end." These lofty notions were the excuse for judicial intervention for years to come. In 1869 the New York Supreme Court, in the name of the "benevolent" parental authority of the state, upheld the right of the managers of the New York House of Refuge to hold a child on a charge of petty theft until he was twenty-one—a crime that carried only a six-month sentence for adults.

Such arbitrary authority could be excused only if it benefited the children. But in fact, as Professor Alexander Pisciotta at Kutztown State College in Pennsylvania has pointed out, the judges in the Crouse case were misinformed. They received their information about the "benevolent effect" of the Philadelphia House of Refuge from its board members, who, says Pisciotta, had lied.

He cites investigations of other reform schools in the latter part of the nineteenth century to show just how far the judicial establishment had been misled. Beatings, whippings with cat-o'-nine-tails and nineteen-inch leather straps, straitjackets, ice water torture, twelve-hour sessions in a "sweatbox," and hanging by the thumbs were some of the means of moral education employed by the managers of these "great charities."

These abuses—and those suffered by juveniles in adult prisons—resulted in the creation of juvenile reform schools. When the country's first juvenile court was established in Chicago in 1899, Jane Addams, the tireless reformer, saw it as the fruition of a wondrous ideal. "There was almost a change in mores when the juvenile court was established," she said. "The child was brought before the judge with no one to prosecute him and none to defend him—the judge and all concerned were merely trying to find out what could be done on his behalf. The element of conflict was absolutely eliminated and with it all notions of punishment as such with its curiously belated connotations."

The court's admirers were so hopeful about this new paternalism that some went so far as to predict the demise of juvenile crime. By 1909, ten states and the District of Columbia had authorized localities to establish juvenile courts. Twelve other states followed suit in the next three years, and by 1925, all but two states, Maine and Wyoming, had juvenile court laws. In 1945 Wyoming at last completed the roster.

Unfortunately, the promise of the new system was never fulfilled, or even approached. Instead of sinking, juvenile crime rates rocketed violently upward over the decades that followed. The state proved itself no better at parenting than true parents. Despite the fact that it was called treatment, youngsters were still sent to prison, often for crimes for which adults would not have been punished. They were given indeterminate sentences that would have been clearly unconstitutional in the adult system.

Not until the 1960s was any dent made in the thick walls of total autonomy behind which the juvenile judiciary operated. In two United States Supreme Court decisions—*Kent* v. *United States* in 1966 and *Gault* v. *United States* in 1967—the Court ruled that juveniles should be afforded certain constitutional rights in their hearings. These included a written notice of the charges, the right to a lawyer, and the privilege against self-incrimination.

But the Court did not change its basic thesis: Juveniles should be treated differently than adults. There was still no jury trial; the proceedings were still wrapped in secrecy; the judge would still be the sole arbiter of guilt or innocence. The enlightened despotism of juvenile court remained intact. In fact, the decisions compounded the problem by granting juveniles more rights without demanding more responsibility. It made of the state a more indulgent parent, leaving society more vulnerable to assault than ever before.

• • •

In less than a hundred years the pendulum of juvenile justice has swung totally about. While the old juvenile court, acting as the parent, doled out massive doses of arbitrary punishment for youths, the new court dispenses equally arbitrary leniency. In the juvenile court, children and society are still onlookers—either as unfortunate victims or as lucky criminals.

The modern juvenile system is meant to be both an agency of social welfare and an agent of justice, which is an impossible task. Such a dual role is entertained only because criminal justice and social welfare for children have been falsely considered to be the same thing. One of the most significant results of lumping all children, including young criminals, under a broad umbrella has been the creation of a large and bumbling bureaucracy.

Behind closed doors, family and juvenile courts across the country weigh every imaginable problem of childhood. The court is responsible for abused babies as well as abusive teenagers; truants and rapists; robbers and runaways. It must protect CHINS (Children In Need of Supervision) as well as delinquents, those youths who commit offenses that would be classified as crimes were they committed by adults. Even in the latter category the range of court responsibility is vast, from petty thievery to murder.

The result has been a monumentally inefficient and ineffective juvenile judicial system, a system that has itself become a prime suspect in the growth of juvenile violence. Poor record keeping, for example, is endemic throughout the nation's juvenile courts. A 1980 Rand Corporation study found that "juvenile records were often inadequate, unclear, incomplete, and difficult to assess." Youths charged with acts of delinquency are often handed probation papers before they even have a hearing. Such inefficiency inevitably filters through the system. Police, watching their arrests evaporate in dismissals, eventually lose their enthusiasm for capturing juveniles.

Even after cases of juvenile criminals are adjudicated, there are usually few facilities capable of either "treatment" or "rehabilitation." The private social agencies and foster homes that courts contract with are often under no obligation to keep the child. When tossed out, the child is either sent back home—often a euphemism for "back to the street"—or placed in an overcrowded detention center or, in some states, in an adult prison.

Even in rural Vermont, the juvenile system is incapable of coping. Burlington juvenile police officer Larry Soutiere has often found his hands tied by the workings of the juvenile justice system. Soutiere was once instructed by the Social and Rehabilitative Services Department not to report a crime if the juvenile was already under SRS supervision. "Therefore," Soutiere explained, "if a juvenile was picked up for another serious crime, we couldn't even pass the police report on to SRS or to the court. So when the juvenile was being considered for release from SRS, there was no way to show his criminal progressiveness. The result was that he simply stayed on the street."

Curbing the worst offenders early would do much to reduce serious juvenile crime, and probably reduce the incidence of adult crime. Numerous studies show that a relatively small number of delinquents commit most of the violent crimes. This same group "grows up" to join the ranks of chronic adult criminals. "It's about 7 or 8 percent of juvenile offenders who commit 70 or 80 percent of the violent crimes," according to Alfred Regnery of the U.S. Office of Juvenile Justice and Delinquency Prevention. Citing a study of 14,000 youngsters in Philadelphia conducted by Marvin Wolfgang of the University of Pennsylvania, Regnery reports that 7 percent of the group were repeat criminal offenders who had already been arrested five or more times.

The ability of teenagers to get away with less serious offenses contributes to the rise of violent crime as the youngster graduates from bicycle to car theft, from mugging to murder. "Very few people start off murdering somebody the first time they're violent," says Regnery. "They'll begin with a mugging and find out that it wasn't as bad as they thought it was going to be. And the next time a little bit more serious, and so on. For the violent recidivistic criminal it is an increasing thing. I suppose that each time they get away with it, it's more likely they'll do it again."

In the experience of Harvard professor James Q. Wilson, the whole system is a bureaucratic shambles. It is even unable, he says, to record the criminal progression of these repeat offenders. "I sometimes think that we are waging a largely symbolic crusade against crime. When I go to a large metropolitan area and ask to see the data that would show what happens to offenders when they move through the system— from juvenile court to family court to adult criminal court and into the correctional system—most cannot supply that information. If we tracked the state of the American economy or the money supply the way we track offenders in the criminal justice system, the people responsible for it would be impeached."

The greatest blame must go to the lawmakers and appeals judges who have given juvenile courts their paternalistic mandate. As New York University Law Professor Martin Guggenheim has charged, "Family court is a court that pretends to be helping even when it is harming. And that's what makes it our most dangerous institution."

"It was to be a civil court, not a criminal one," New York Family Court Judge Edward J. McLaughlin wrote in a letter to *The New York Times,* hoping to blunt the criticism leveled at the court. "The Legislature did not permit the court to punish the delinquent. Neither is the judge allowed to compel any institution to accept the delinquent for treatment." McLaughlin admitted that the leniency of the family court had exposed it to criticism as a "revolving door," and that much of it was valid. "But," he insisted, "correction must come from the legislature; it cannot come from the courts."

Not only is the system inefficient, say critics, but it hides behind a tradition of confidentiality that keeps its proceedings secret and closed to public scrutiny. Juvenile criminals are so protected from the outside world that, as Wendell Rawls, Jr., noted in *The New York Times,* records are kept "under a veil of secrecy in the juvenile justice system rivaled only by subjects of national security."

This veil of secrecy makes it almost impossible for adult court officials to know whether a person making his first appearance before them is, in fact, a first offender. He may well have a long record as a serious juvenile criminal, but that fact might not be revealed. The Rand Corporation study group asked a sample of prosecutors whether juvenile records were available to them. Sixty percent of the respondents said "never" or "rarely." Even if the records were available, the isolation of the juvenile system limits the use that anyone—whether prosecutor or public researcher—can make of them.

By hiding the child behind a judicial curtain, the court strengthens the delinquent's dangerous belief that crime has no relevant social context. This confidentiality addicts youngsters to a privilege that society will suddenly withdraw in a few years, when they come of age as "adult" offenders. Like so many other drugs made available to children today, an artificially lenient juvenile system provides not only short-term gratification but long-term addiction.

The combination of no trial, no publicity, no record, and no bottom line has, in the eyes of many critics, resulted in no justice. In Vermont, the large juvenile detention center, Weeks School, was closed and replaced by foster homes, a system adopted by several states. That move was greeted by police, among others, with criticism. Over the years the absence of the detention center was felt. "The hard-core juvenile delinquent placed in a group home or foster home and not wanting to be there," says Larry Soutiere, "has merely to disrupt the foster home or the group home and he will be returned to the street because of the lack of the bottom line."

Without the threat of being locked up, Soutiere believes, juvenile delinquents can hold the police and the courts hostage, prisoners of their own regulations. Moreover, deviant children—who avoid school, have unstructured home lives, no job, and no self-discipline—have time on their hands. They can wait while the bureaucracy sorts through its amorphous standards. And while they wait for punishment, they can—and do—commit more crimes.

"There have been a large number of juveniles who are in SRS custody and who are still on the streets committing crimes," complains Soutiere. "When I ask SRS what is being done, I am told that the juvenile has been through all available services and now there is no place to put him."

Even if treatment were theoretically possible, few juvenile systems—as in Vermont—have the resources to make it work. The delinquent is always in a process of "going through" the system. Rarely is he anywhere long enough to receive the treatment that the framers of the *parens patriae* doctrine intended.

The juvenile justice system is caught between a slavish attachment to the belief that children cannot be held responsible for their actions and the growing realization that acting on such a belief helps create juvenile criminals. The paradox seems to have paralyzed the entire system. Jackson Toby, director of the Institute for Criminological Research at Rutgers University, deplores the fact that in what he calls our no-fault juvenile justice system children can get away with such serious crimes as burglary, mugging, even murder. It is, he says, "because they are not considered to be responsible for their actions. But at some arbitrary age—it varies from state to state—youngsters are suddenly transformed into adults."

The present system is given little respect even among its youthful charges. "I went over to Maryland to pick up a student from our school who managed to get himself in a bit of difficulty while home on leave," recounts Richard Hall, chief psychologist at a Virginia school for seriously disturbed boys. "The police had a felony charge against him, but he informed me, 'Big deal. All they're going to do is take me to court and lecture me for a few minutes. Nothing's going to happen.' They hold our juvenile justice system in great contempt, and with good reason. How is a kid to understand that he can't break the law when he's been doing it for years and no real punishment has been meted out?"

The juvenile justice system is fundamentally arbitrary. It starts with a crudely fashioned line of demarcation by which a single calendar day can make the difference between going to a foster home for a couple of months or spending a lifetime in an adult jail.

But children do not, as the judicial system presumes, grow

up overnight. "These inconsistencies arise from the legislative failure to recognize that children are constantly maturing: they are not irresponsible children one day and responsible adults the next, except as a matter of law," argues Barry C. Feld, University of Minnesota Professor of Law. This "artificial distinction," he says, "has resulted in a disservice to public safety."

Society presently protects younger criminals and punishes older ones—a system that fails to meet the true problem. Ironically, the older a person is, the less likely the intervention will do him or society any good. Many studies show that chronic criminal offenders begin their career in crime at an early age, hone their skills through adolescence and into their twenties, then gradually reduce their criminal involvement. The bell curve of criminality, however, is not the same as that of the judicial system. Instead of nipping criminals in the bud, it operates mainly by chopping down old and tired trees.

"The greatest effect in crimes prevented would come from imprisoning younger, more active offenders, since individual offense rates appear to decline substantially with age," says another Rand Corporation study. Statistics in Vermont confirm this observation. In Burlington, Larry Soutiere discovered that of 121 juveniles aged ten through sixteen who had been delinquent for felonious acts, 78 already had two or more felonies on their records. Almost a quarter of them had been charged five or more times for various felonies. If these youngsters were adults, many would be liable for life imprisonment under the Vermont habitual offender law. "Yet these juveniles are placed back on the street," says Soutiere.

Sentiment throughout the country is finally moving toward reform of the system. New York State was among the first to pass a more stringent juvenile crime bill in 1978. It excluded all persons over sixteen years of age from family court jurisdiction and lowered to thirteen the age at which a juvenile could be prosecuted in adult court for such serious crimes as murder and rape.

The age limits vary widely, but by 1981 most states had devised some method for trying serious juvenile offenders over fifteen years of age in adult court. Vermont, as we have seen, has lowered the age to ten. The state of Washington has now completely revised its juvenile laws, perhaps the most comprehensive change in the nation. "They now treat juveniles much more like adults," explains Alfred Regnery. "There are many more due process protections. Records are not sealed. The basis of the whole statute is accountability on the part of the juvenile as opposed to rehabilitation. It is considered either the most advanced, or the most backward, juvenile law, depending on which way you want to look at it.

"A lot of people ask whether the juvenile system will survive," Regnery continues. "Some advocate its demolition, at least for kids over fourteen. I doubt if that's going to happen, but I think that increasingly with violence you are going to find more of them tried in the adult criminal court."

In California, juveniles are judged under a unique system that permits the court to treat them as children up to the age of eighteen. But unlike other states that must release the juvenile at eighteen, California can hold the young criminal in an institution until he is twenty-five, supposedly long enough to accomplish the court's goal of rehabilitation.

Some legislatures now require that a youth of a certain age who has committed a specific category of serious crime be automatically prosecuted in the adult system. But such a mandatory exclusion from the juvenile system is rare. Most legislatures prefer to maintain the power of *parens patriae* by leaving to the juvenile authorities the decision about whom to transfer to adult court.

The system is beginning to change, but there are many states still wedded to the philosophy that arbitrarily views youthful murderers as errant children. "There is pressure in the direction of change that is stronger than in the past," says John L. Hutzler of the National Center for Juvenile Justice. "But there are still quite a number of states where a juvenile judge has very broad discretion—can do almost anything with the case that he chooses."

Despite the call for change, most juvenile courts still conduct secret proceedings. "You would have a tough time pointing to ten states that have open proceedings in juvenile cases or who don't have some provision for confidentiality of record," adds Hutzler.

Some states are beginning to open up the juvenile system to public scrutiny. In 1980 the Oregon Supreme Court ruled that the juvenile proceedings against a thirteen-year-old girl accused of killing a four-year-old girl could not be closed to the public. And in 1981 a presidential task force recommended that conviction records of violent juvenile repeat offenders be computerized on a nationwide basis and made available to the public. (However, this has yet to be carried out.) The same year the Institute for Judicial Administration and the American Bar Association released the results of a ten-year study of juvenile crime and the juvenile justice system asking for radical change. Among the proposed revisions was a call to curb what Federal Judge Irving R. Kaufman, chairman of the project, called the virtually unlimited discretion of juvenile judges. Kaufman proposed making penalties for juveniles proportionate to their crimes.

Not surprisingly, resistance to change is coming from those who benefit most from the current system. "This is a field where judges, psychologists, and social workers all have their own concepts of what ought to be done," remarks Charles Schinitsky of the New York Legal Aid Society. "The juvenile judges have a very strong lobby," adds Judge Kaufman. "But you can't pick up a newspaper or turn on the television set without reading about juvenile crimes. The electorate itself realizes that something has to be done, that the juvenile justice system just isn't functioning right."

Jonathan Pincus, Yale University neurologist, believes that some juvenile criminals are being returned to society too soon. Speaking of fifteen-year-old murderers such as Jamie Savage, Pincus says: "I'd want to be very clearly assured that the kid wasn't going to do it again before I'd let him out in society. Which would mean that he would have to be under supervision—possibly in some sort of facility for juveniles—for a long, long time. And he would have to behave in that facility in a civilized way before I'd consider letting him out. At the reform school where we did one of our studies, even the kids who had done really terrible things were rarely kept there for more than three to six months."

Larry Soutiere is convinced the system must let delinquents know the value of staying crime-free. "The kid must realize exactly what is going to happen if he pushes the system too hard. He has to know that if he gets picked up committing a crime, he won't start at home but he'll start right at the prison or detention center or treatment center—whatever you want to call it. He's got to know that he'll be locked up and if he wants to come out, he has to earn his way out and show that he is willing to work with a group home, or willing to work in the community. That is simple logic."

It may seem simple, but contemporary attitudes toward juvenile crime have turned the subject into one of our greatest dilemmas. In the confusion, juvenile justice has been rendered ineffective, both as a crime preventive and as a vehicle for dispensing justice.

The dilemma—and the confusion—were amply demonstrated in June of 1984 when the United States Supreme Court upheld the practice of preventive detention of juveniles, a popular form of pre-trial imprisonment long considered unconstitutional in adult courts. And once more the rule of *parens patriae* in the administration of juvenile justice was affirmed.

The reaffirmation, however, was anything but unanimous; and the dissent was particularly pointed. Associate Justice Thurgood Marshall, one of three dissenters, found the decision to continue denying bail to juveniles "difficult to take seriously."

Perhaps, given the unseemly realities of modern juvenile crime, contemporary perceptions of "childhood" were changing.

But however more difficult it was to garner consensus on behalf of the traditional principles of juvenile justice—two lower courts had already ruled against preventive detention— they were nevertheless staunchly defended by Associate Justice William H. Rehnquist.

"Children, by definition," he wrote for the majority, "are not assumed to have the capacity to take care of themselves. They are assumed to be subject to the control of their parents, and if parental control falters, the state must play its part."

Thus, "by definition," juveniles would continue to be excluded from the rights—and responsibilities—of adulthood. And so a juvenile proceeding was "fundamentally different from an adult criminal trial," argued Rehnquist.

As the Pennsylvania Supreme Court had done in 1838, the U.S. Supreme Court in 1984 was engaging in wishing-well justice. Unanswered were questions about how a "child" could be magically transformed into an "adult"; how a birthday would give children the "capacity to take care of themselves"; how the state could legitimately and effectively act as surrogate parent; how incarceration without the right to bail could be compared with the practice of good parenting.

Martin Guggenheim, of the New York University Law School, attorney for the three juveniles who filed the original class-action suit against New York State's preventive detention statute, was one of many who criticized the premise upon which the Supreme Court based its decision. "Kids are being harmed under the guise of doing them good," he charged.

And Justice Marshall pointedly reminded his colleagues of the difference between "the guise" and the result. "The effect of the lack of procedural safeguards," he wrote, "is that the liberty of a juvenile arrested even for a petty crime is dependent upon the 'caprice' of a Family Court judge.

"Even the judges who strive conscientiously to apply the law have little choice but to assess juveniles' dangerousness on the basis of whatever standards they deem appropriate. The resultant variation in detention decisions gives rise to a level of inequality in the deprivation of a fundamental right too great to be countenanced under the Constitution."

Increasingly, the paradox of *parens patriae* as applied to juvenile criminals was showing itself. It was neither benevolence nor harshness which grated, but the "caprice" through which both benevolence and harshness flowed. And the result was anything but beneficial. "The net impact on the juveniles who come within its purview," as Justice Marshall concluded, "is overwhelmingly detrimental."

As our children embrace violence in increasing numbers, we do not know whether to punish them more or love them with greater intensity. It is probable that the answer encompasses both. Without compassion, we increase the hostility that breeds youthful crime. Without punishment, we seem to condone it.

By its inaction and inefficiency, the modern juvenile system has exacerbated the problem, dispensing uneven justice instead of communicating the rules by which society wishes to live. The young, with their ever-alert antennae, know what adults believe and act accordingly.

Society must take a stand by asserting the authority that is not only its right, but its obligation. Louie Hamlin and Jamie Savage are but two examples of our failure to do so. The results are not always as brutal as those that shocked the state of Vermont. But unless adults do something to safeguard the innocence of the young, while demanding greater responsibility from them, there will be more victims like Meghan O'Rourke and Melissa Walbridge.

Bestselling Thrillers —
action-packed for a great read